PENGUIN CANADA

HEART MATTERS

ADRIENNE CLARKSON became Canada's twenty-sixth Governor General in 1999 and served until September 2005. In her multi-faceted career as an accomplished broadcaster and distinguished public servant, she has received numerous prestigious awards and honorary degrees in Canada and abroad.

A Privy Councillor and Companion of the Order of Canada, she now lives in Toronto.

HEART MATTERS

ADRIENNE CLARKSON

a memoir

PENGUIN
CANADA

PENGUIN CANADA

Published by the Penguin Group

Penguin Group (Canada), 90 Eglinton Avenue East, Suite 700, Toronto, Ontario, Canada
M4P 2Y3 (a division of Pearson Canada Inc.)

Penguin Group (USA) Inc., 375 Hudson Street, New York, New York 10014, U.S.A.
Penguin Books Ltd, 80 Strand, London WC2R 0RL, England
Penguin Ireland, 25 St Stephen's Green, Dublin 2, Ireland (a division of Penguin Books Ltd)
Penguin Group (Australia), 250 Camberwell Road, Camberwell, Victoria 3124, Australia
(a division of Pearson Australia Group Pty Ltd)
Penguin Books India Pvt Ltd, 11 Community Centre, Panchsheel Park, New Delhi – 110 017, India
Penguin Group (NZ), 67 Apollo Drive, Rosedale, North Shore 0632, Auckland, New Zealand
(a division of Pearson New Zealand Ltd)
Penguin Books (South Africa) (Pty) Ltd, 24 Sturdee Avenue, Rosebank, Johannesburg 2196,
South Africa

Penguin Books Ltd, Registered Offices: 80 Strand, London WC2R 0RL, England

First published in a Viking Canada hardcover by Penguin Group (Canada),
a division of Pearson Canada Inc., 2006
Published in this edition, 2007

1 2 3 4 5 6 7 8 9 10 (WEB)

*Publisher's note: This book is a work of fiction. Names, characters, places and incidents
either are the product of the author's imagination or are used fictitiously, and any
resemblance to actual persons living or dead, events, or locales is entirely coincidental.*

Manufactured in Canada.

LIBRARY AND ARCHIVES CANADA CATALOGUING IN PUBLICATION

Clarkson, Adrienne, 1939–
Heart matters / Adrienne Clarkson.

ISBN 978-0-14-305669-0

1. Clarkson, Adrienne, 1939–. 2. Governors general—Canada—Biography.
I. Title.

FC636.C56A3 2007   971.07'2092   C2007-903372-5

ISBN-13: 978-0-14-305669-0
ISBN-10: 0-14-305669-7

Visit the Penguin Group (Canada) website at **www.penguin.ca**

Special and corporate bulk purchase rates available; please see
www.penguin.ca/corporatesales or call 1-800-810-3104, ext. 477 or 474

In honour of my parents

William Poy, 1907–2002
and
Ethel Poy, 1913–1988

and for
Kyra and Blaise and our Chloe

INTRODUCTION

I HAVE A TRICKY HEART. I believe now that the important thing in life is not knowing how many heartbeats you are going to live, but deciding how best to live the time in between those heartbeats.

Before my heart behaved like this, I used to think that I lived a perfectly normal life and that everybody wanted to put forth the same kind of effort I did. It had never occurred to me that it might not be physically possible to exert the force necessary to accomplish what you wanted to accomplish. In July of 2005, it was suddenly necessary for me to have a pacemaker inserted because my heart had stopped beating for seven seconds. It all happened so fast that it was only afterwards that I realized what it was all about.

The medical explanation was a bit daunting. "A pacemaker is inserted just under the skin and stitched into position in the chest wall. One wire is guided into the right atrium and the other into the right ventricle. The pacemaker will stimulate the heart when it is beating too slowly, but if the heart is alternating between fast and slow rates, drugs may also be used to slow down the fast heart rate ..." And so on. For a number of years I had been experiencing an irregular heartbeat, and I was told after my crisis that this had masked another problem, which was that of my heart not pumping well.

On that day when seven seconds separated my heartbeats, everybody around me was alarmed. But I did not feel any anxiety or fear. I wasn't in any pain; I felt that I could just close my eyes and drift away. Of course, I had long believed that we must live every day of our lives as though it were going to be our last. Yet, paradoxically, we must take a long-term view that we will continue to have a future.

Now, whenever I have my pacemaker reset to beat a certain number of times a minute, I think of the wires going down into the ventricle and the atrium and regulating the way in which the whole system works. Does a heart that works, pumps blood, keeps you alive, in any way reflect the metaphor of the heart?

The ancients all believed that emotions began in the heart and that personality traits lurked in other organs like the spleen and the liver. What I have discovered is that the consciousness of both the fragility and the mechanization of what keeps me alive has made me aware of my life in a totally different way. I know with certainty that the heart can break down mechanically, but there still exists within a force that tells us to go on living, to push with the beat, to live the life.

The journey I have travelled, the dream that was dreamt for me and in which I took my part, is one that I now regard with other perspectives. During my life in Canada, I have moved from a triplex at 277 Sussex Street, opposite the Canadian Mint, to One Sussex Drive, Rideau Hall. By an amazing coincidence, they are the same street. When I was a child I used to pass the gate of Rideau Hall riding in a streetcar with my family from our house to Rockcliffe Park on Sundays. It had, and still has, a brass plaque that says "Residence of the Governor General." It would never have occurred to the little Poy family to walk in and look around. It was special, with its black wrought-iron railings separated by impressive grey pillars. We knew we were to be kept out.

After my installation in the Senate Chamber on Parliament Hill on October 7, 1999, I was driven in the state landau to Rideau Hall, which was going to be my home for at least five years. I couldn't help but think, as I saw the grandiose entrance in carved stone, about the house at the other end of the street that had been my family's first Canadian home—a house with a coal furnace that terrified my mother and a backyard that became a Victory Garden with Swiss chard and tomatoes. As soon as it was in good shape, Mr. Robert, the landlord, evicted us to place members of his own family in it. Now I had moved up the street, which was called, grandly, an avenue.

I have come further than any streetcar could bring me, and I know that as I took my place in the Governor General's study and saw my name carved in the oak panelling, that is when my heart understood what it had been beating for all these years. The emotions and the energy that had brought me here were rooted not just in a chronology of a life lived but in the people and events that have seized my heart. They are the emotions and energy that have directed my whole life.

These beats have to measure a life that has meaning; everything must have meaning. And as Socrates said, "The unexamined life is not worth living." My physical heart, and the way it won't behave, makes me understand irregular events. That I ignore warnings at my own peril.

When I was younger, I used to ignore any symptoms whatsoever of fatigue. When I was working in television and travelling all over the world, I could go for weeks on end with only three or four hours' sleep a night. I don't think I ever thought that I could live any differently. You train yourself for the effort that you make in your life just as an athlete trains his muscles. I believe that there are athletes who, by setting their own standards to drive themselves, persuade their bodies to follow them and override the natural rules of their health. I have always felt that once I decided to do something I wanted to do, no amount of effort I asked of myself could be too much.

It was this determination that was the engine through my six years as Governor General. I travelled more than 900,000 kilometres to more than six thousand events, seeing tens of thousands of Canadians. I went to nearly four hundred communities, on state visits and at home, presiding over solemn ceremonies and welcoming foreign dignitaries.

What remains are the things that remind me that life has been examined, and that the memories of those I have loved, of the losses I have endured, are what has seized my heart forever. I remember a brilliant young filmmaker telling me that "the things you use to just get by come back to you as art—to help you to survive the endless stretching of your heart."

The pulse that failed me in July 2005 made me understand that I was making a journey where that heart mattered.

OUT OF THE FLAMES

WHEN THE PHOENIX SENSES THAT ITS END IS COMING, IT CONSTRUCTS A NEST WHOSE BRANCHES ARE DOUSED WITH FRAGRANT SAP, TURNS TOWARDS THE SUN AND IS CONSUMED BY FLAMES. AN EGG FORMS FROM THE ASHES OF HIS BONES AND MARROW. OUT OF IT RISES A NEW PHOENIX.

TOWARDS CANADA

I WAS BORN in a colonial outpost of the British empire, in Hong Kong, to a father who was part of the Chinese diaspora in Australia and a mother whose family had spent most of their lives in places like Dutch Guyana (now Surinam), Java (now Indonesia), and other outlying areas of the world like Peru and Jamaica. Being Chinese, coming out of that background, is ambiguous, and yet a sense of heightened identity, where every single detail matters, accompanies it.

Perhaps, then, my parents' attitude was that being Chinese was to be part of a huge, rattling, disparate world where individuals focused on economic success and swallowed hard to accept and manipulate colonial complexities. They had English names and Chinese ones: William Poy or Ng Ying Choi and Ethel Lam or Lam May Ngo. To the day she died my mother never said the word "Englishman" with anything less than contempt mixed with disdain. And yet my parents played their part in that whole colonial world: the Hong Kong Jockey Club where my father made his way up the social ladder with his dynamic riding, both flat race and steeplechase. He bought and rode his own horses and then, because he was really good, he was asked to ride his friends' horses. And that is how he became a "gentlemen jockey." The rules were for gentlemen, and gentlemen were the only ones who rode. That Jockey Club in Happy Valley was one of the few places where the lines between Chinese, Europeans, and Eurasians blurred.

My life until I was three was comfortable—our duplex on Broome Road had a rooftop garden, where the servants kept rabbits and chickens. On nights when it was too hot to sleep, my family took ferry rides to Kowloon. My brother, Neville, and I would be allowed to bring our own cushions to lie on the benches as we went back and forth or, later, when we occasionally drove up the Peak to try to get above the humidity. We employed at least five servants, including the chauffeur and cook, and my father was only a young businessman. But it was the kind of world where everybody, including the middle class, had servants. Until we came to Canada, my mother had never really been inside the kitchen. She used to tell me that the cook came to her bedroom every morning to discuss the day's menu. Learning how to cook was one of the traumatic events of my mother's early life in Canada. I remember smelling burning food and seeing her crying with a cast-iron frying pan in her hand.

There were some early 8-mm Bell and Howell films of Neville and me just before the war broke out—I was two and a half and he was six—on the roof of that house in Happy Valley near the racecourse. These films, which were later stolen in a burglary in Ottawa, are imprinted in my memory because we only got them back after the war. A neighbour had saved them when they were left behind by the Japanese soldiers who looted our house—who looted all the houses—after their victory on Christmas Day 1941. In the film, Neville pushes my head into different positions, perhaps practising a hands-on anatomy lesson to prepare for being the doctor he seemed ordained to become. He watches the camera carefully to make sure that I am not the only one in the lens. He gets annoyed at a potted palm and hits it with his arms, obviously shouting that he doesn't like that plant. Oblivious to everything but my own little blue starched dress, I pick up a bunny rabbit that has been dyed in splotches for Chinese New Year. My parents tell me those spots were red, and it is curious how I remember the black-and-white film with red splotches in it.

Apparently my father filmed us almost every day because having a film camera in 1940 was just the sort of thing an up-and-coming young family should have. We also had an Opel car, my go-getting father having somehow been involved in a distributing deal for this automobile in the thirties. All his life my father did deals, but I didn't realize that the reason we used Leica cameras and not Minolta was that my father was somehow involved in the distribution of the former and definitely not of the latter.

Whenever I asked my parents what they did before the war, besides go to the races, there would be a moment of glazed reflection. Then over my mother's vividly mobile face would come a flash of what could only be described as bliss, and she'd say: "We danced."

And dance they did, at least twice a week at various hotels in Hong Kong, including the beautiful Repulse Bay Hotel where they were dancing on December 11, probably to "Lambeth Walk" or "Lullaby of Broadway," when one of my father's friends rushed in to say the Japanese had broken into the New Territories. This invasion onto the mainland portion of Hong Kong was the sign that the war, which had been expected, had really begun. My mother and father rushed home because my father had to join his militia unit, the Royal Hong Kong Regiment, known as the Volunteers. He put on his uniform, mounted his BSA motorcycle and disappeared. We didn't know where my father was during the whole time of the bombardment of the city. We didn't see him or have contact with him again for the two weeks it took for the Japanese to defeat the Canadians and the British and declare their victory in Hong Kong.

The reality of the war began the morning of December 12, when my mother realized, as she looked out the bathroom window, that the large thing she thought resembled a giant frog in the garden was actually a Japanese soldier in camouflage. We quickly abandoned our house with a suitcase packed for each of us and went to my Po-Po's house. Po-Po is the Chinese name for grandmother—the mother of your mother, the Chinese language being very definite about specifics of relationships. We moved from place to place, sheltering from the bombardment of the city, hiding with friends or relatives, my mother fearing rape by Japanese soldiers. We were under siege, and my high-strung mother, who had never been in a kitchen, had to cope with two small children, who had always had a nurse each, with occasional help from my grandmother.

We had a beautiful borzoi called Snow White, whom my father had brought back from a business trip to Harbin, in northern China. My mother became very attached to her and even bathed her herself. She told me, in later life, that she thought Snow White had the same colour of hair as Jean Harlow. As the war continued, she anxiously and unsuccessfully tried to keep her clean and bright. Although we had dogs—collies, spaniels, and dachshunds—after we came to Canada, Snow White is the dog who can never be replaced. For years afterwards, my brother would do drawings of Snow White and my mother would again tell me the story of how she couldn't keep her clean, of how Snow White became greyer and greyer. Finally there were no leftovers of food to give her, so we let her out to scavenge in the streets.

The fighting was going on all around us, with bombings and battles on the mountain called the Peak. One day, Snow White returned from one of her outings with human entrails hanging from her mouth. My mother never ceased to tell this story to anyone she discussed pets with in our later life in Canada. Somehow that dog and its wartime needs symbolized the difference between our old life and this comfortable soft white country we had come to.

My father fought with the Volunteer Militia as a lance corporal. He never talked much afterwards about what he had done, except we knew he carried messages all over the place on his motorbike. He and his friend Willy were two of the few Chinese who were part of the Volunteers. They were under the command of the British and therefore saw the battle from that point of view. My father was brave but he never talked about that bravery. He told us that he was given the Military Medal, the highest award that can be presented to a non-commissioned officer, but he never boasted about it. We kept it in the house in a drawer. I have presented it and the commendation from George VI to the Canadian War Museum in Ottawa.

As dispatch riders, he and Willy knew how badly everything was going but they carried on. Once I asked my father, "Did you ever think what would happen to us if you had been killed?" He said, "Well, your mother would have looked after you, and you both have a lot of brains, so I suppose you would have been all right." Then, almost as an afterthought, "And you're good looking."

It's hard for me to imagine what it was like for my father to fight just a few kilometres away from where we were desperately finding shelter. While he was dispatched with messages in Morse code, we were hiding, occasionally meeting with one of my mother's brothers who had found another place for us to be safe. We had very little to eat, sometimes Jacob's Cream Crackers, some Nestlé's sweetened condensed milk, and a bit of Lyle's Golden Syrup—the colonial taste in a colonial war. I remember my mother being so upset that Canadians in Ottawa did not use Lyle's syrup.

Once, a bomb dropped close to our basement hideout. When we emerged, after the bombing had stopped, we saw a whole human being splattered against the wall like a bear skin. I have been told these things and I do not remember them. But what is memory? Is it what you feel? Is it what you've been told? Is it what you know deep inside your every tissue? Those memories were part of what we would talk about at nights as I was growing up in Ottawa. My parents didn't think that traumatic memories should be kept from their children, or from our close friends, the Marcottes and the Proulxes, French Canadians who lived nearby. They listened in our tiny living room or around the kitchen table as though we were telling ghost stories, fascinated and aghast.

An acquaintance of my parents—one of five concubines of one of the Jockey Club members—told my mother, in whispers, about being raped by Japanese who then pressed Japanese money into her hand. My mother always spoke freely of huddling in a basement when the Japanese came knocking on the door looking for women. My grandmother hid my mother and my aunt, covered with coats and blankets, behind a wardrobe in a closet. I was told not to say anything, or something unbelievably terrible (but not defined) would happen to us. Neville and I pretended to be playing with our grandmother. I can only imagine now the terror that my mother felt, her dread that suddenly she would be discovered and she would be dragged out. I think she never recovered from that fear, from that helplessness, from that horror of being an anonymous object of lust.

I've been told that as a child I talked all the time and was head-strong and impetuous. I never did what I was told. How I remained silent while five Japanese soldiers looked around the basement, seeing only an old woman and two small children sitting on the floor, is something that haunts me. Perhaps a certain unnatural penchant I have for silence, watchfulness, and immobility are rooted in that experience.

As the battle continued, hopes were raised as word passed from hiding place to hiding place that the *Prince of Wales*—the wonderful British ship—was coming to save us all. We awaited the *Prince of Wales* and the *Prince of Wales* never came. On Christmas Day 1941, Hong Kong was surrendered. My father, who had access to all the messages through Morse code, heard about the surrender and told his superior officer. He always remembered that the officer looked at him with something between pity and regret and said, "Poy, you and Willy had better get out of here because we're all going to be captured and put in a camp. But if they see you Chinese, they won't bother with camp, they'll just kill you." Released by their commanding officer, my father and Willy managed to get some Chinese clothing, folded up their uniforms and disappeared into the streets of Hong Kong.

The next day, the Japanese soldiers put the population's goods out on the streets for sale. My mother and her friends saw their silver, their curtains, their dining suites sold to the highest bidder. The Japanese used the fact that Hong Kong was an open city and that there was no protection for the civilian population as a way of keeping people in a state of terror.

We lived for six months under the Japanese occupation. It was humiliating, difficult, and frightening. According to the Japanese army, the concept of *bushido* meant that the conquered must suffer total humiliation. If they had been honourable, they would commit suicide rather than accept defeat. This was the basis of a profound misunderstanding between the Japanese and those that they conquered.

We did not have the kind of vast fortunes and property that enabled some Chinese families in Hong Kong to escape to their estates on mainland China. Not for us the beautiful fish ponds and rice fields of the Chinese interior, or the quantity of jade bracelets that were broken off women's arms and either sold or traded. To stay alive, my father occasionally was able to do a deal on watches or selling rice. But he knew we had to get out, and preferably to Australia, where his family—eight brothers and sisters and his mother and her new husband—still lived. But the war in the Pacific made that impossible.

So my father wrote to Canadian trade commissioners with whom he had worked and become friends. One of them, Ken Noble, had been best man at my parents' wedding, and a series of

characters like the Galloping Major and his wife, who sported the
name Sparkling, and Bert Butler had given a taste of a rather raffish
Canada to my by-no-means-unsophisticated parents. He also wrote
to Paul Sykes in India, with whom he had travelled to Manchukuo
when the Japanese occupied it in 1931 and the Canadian Trade
Commission in Hong Kong decided that business might be done
there. No one answered the letters. But one night in June there was
a loud knocking at the door. It was the Kenpeitai, the Japanese
equivalent of the Gestapo. My parents, terrified, opened the door
and, when asked who they were, identified themselves. The officer
in charge said, "You are on a list to be exchanged by the Red Cross.
Be down at Stanley dock with one suitcase for each member of
your family at dawn."

My parents had barely ten hours to decide whether they would
go. They would be taken to North America, where they knew no
one. There would just be the four of us. We would have only four
suitcases. They talked it through all night, and it was my grandmother who insisted that we go.

The conditions had been hideous in Hong Kong—there was
little food and many rumours that people had become cannibals. I
know that my parents were very worried from day to day about
where our food would come from. I, being two and a half, was
given the powdered milk that could be obtained on the black
market. Many people had fled to the mainland, and the city was like
a ghost town. We were desperate.

I consider that night to have been the moment in our family's
story that most created us. It was my parents' ability to take that
chance, to leap into that void, that gave us the second breath we
needed to live the rest of our lives.

THE NEXT MORNING, the four of us, plus my grandmother, who
came to say goodbye, went down to the Stanley dock, on the other

side of Hong Kong from where we were staying. A crowd of three hundred was there, each person with one suitcase. By now we knew that we were going to be exchanged, one for one, on neutral territory in Mozambique and put on another ship to go to North America. The Japanese vessel the *Asama Maru* had left Tokyo carrying Western diplomats, members of religious orders, and other flotsam; we joined them because our name, miraculously, had been put on a list of Canadians.

After the fall of Hong Kong and Singapore, everyone who was considered a diplomat or a non-British non-combatant became part of a one-for-one exchange of Allied nationals from the Japanese-occupied territories for Japanese nationals. Although it was an exchange between Japan and the Allies, only Canadians and Americans were included. The British were left in internment camps in places like Hong Kong. In a way, being stateless was a help to us. After all, we were Chinese, and although we were British subjects, we were not British.

On board ship were Canadian diplomats from the Canadian legation in Tokyo, among them Herbert Norman and D'Arcy McGreer, and also people like Joseph Alsop, the legendary American journalist, and the American diplomat Chip Bohlen—who were accompanied by the foreign correspondents from Associated Press, Reuters, and *The New York Times*. People who witnessed the boarding of the ship at Hong Kong say that most of the people were skin and bones. I know that my mother barely weighed 80 pounds, and my father, who was skinny to begin with and kept that way for riding, probably weighed about 110.

As we stood there on the dock, in what my mother always remembered as being unrelenting sun, we were lined up alphabetically. A Canadian official who was part of the group of five hundred that had come from Tokyo looked at us and then turned to one of his colleagues and said, "What are *these* people doing here? They're not white!" And just as in that moment when the Japanese were searching the basement, there was another pause in our narrative that would end in our lives being turned around. But the colleague said, "Well, they're on the list. Why don't we just leave them there? They're okay." It was a busy morning, and the man who had spotted us had other things to do, so he turned away. And by his turning away, we were destined for Canada, even though we were Chinese, even though we were Oriental, even though we were not wanted.

We spent the first night in the harbour, and the Japanese commander refused to let us use the big electric crosses that marked us out as non-combatants, protected by the Red Cross. He didn't want to alert American bombers.

When we pulled out of the port at Stanley, we didn't fully realize that there were nearly thirty thousand kilometres of travel at sea in front of us, three-quarters of the world's circumference. We would be touching four major continents, Asia, Africa, South America, and, finally, North America.

We were treated as virtual prisoners on the Japanese boat, because we were in the custody of the Japanese. There were precise orders to obey and bulletin boards everywhere. The signs outside bathrooms said: "Water will be available from 7:00 until 8:00 A.M.; and from 5:00 until 6:00 P.M." We were in steerage, and my father went to bunk with the men so that my mother, brother, and I could have a little more room, sharing with other women and their children. My father met and spent time with the Canadian diplomats Herbert Feaver, whose family I met in Ottawa when I became Governor General, and Matt Stewart and Herbert Norman. He also befriended some of the Maryknoll Fathers, an American missionary teaching order. They told him that a number of British and Canadian soldiers had taken refuge with them, and one day the Japanese soldiers arrived and ordered everyone to undress completely. They were marched down a clay road towards a gulley.

Their bishop started to give a general absolution because they were all preparing to die. Soldiers were sent ahead to the gulley and then returned wiping blood off their bayonets. My father's friends said that they never knew why they had survived. Survival came as accidentally as imprisonment had.

There were only two bathrooms for each deck of three hundred passengers, and my mother never told us how she managed to keep my brother and me clean. My mother said that the food was horrible. One day they thought they were getting oatmeal, but there was something wrong with it. Suddenly, one of the other women gasped: "Look at the dead worms!" Then my mother saw that our plates were filled with grubs, white and still. It was the last time my family ever ate oatmeal. Now, I love porridge and I make it frequently; I never think of the grubs.

When I think back on it—how we lived in that situation and why my parents later downplayed the degrading conditions—I realize that the trauma was so great it was numbing. Their every moment was focused on Neville and me, and also on what would happen to all of us when we got to the end of this incredible journey. The occupation and the time aboard the *Asama Maru* created an anxiety in my mother that never dissipated. As much as she tried to live a normal life again, and gave appearances of being normal, after that experience, she couldn't be.

Our trip took us first to Saigon and then to Singapore; more people boarded at each port. My parents remembered that each time we went to a Japanese-occupied port, the Japanese air force put on a show for us with their bombers and fighters roaring over the ship for several hours, flying low, circling the *Asama* several times before heading out to sea. The message was obvious: when you return to North America, tell them the Japanese are set to conquer everything.

When we crossed the thousands of kilometres of the Indian Ocean, it was monsoon time, and for two weeks we sailed through storms. Everybody on the ship was violently ill. My mother was extremely seasick, and Neville became quite ill. My father was sleeping on the deck with many of the other men, and occasionally we did too. The passengers were kind to each other, and my mother remembered an older European woman who rocked me while my mother looked after my brother. The portions of food on our plates, already scant, diminished; we ate scraps and rice. Even fish disappeared from the menu.

Although the circumstances and the discomfort were extreme, the ship became like a big family, complete with its little quarrels, none of them very serious. There were all kinds of children of different sizes, ages, and shades. Most of us, Chinese and white alike, had never been supervised by anybody other than amiable, indulgent Chinese servants, who were called amahs. Unlike the official on the dock, there was no feeling of racism on the boat, rather a sense of having escaped together. I do wish I could remember more of this; perhaps only my body remembers. But how could I have been on that remarkable journey with people thrown together and held virtually as hostages and recollect so little of it?

We were tugged into the harbour at Lourenço Marques, the capital of Mozambique, and immediately saw the Red Cross ship the *Gripsholm*, marked in the blue and gold of Sweden and carrying the huge painted warning "Diplomat Gripsholm Sverige." My father says that at that point we realized that within a day we would no longer be prisoners cut off from the rest of the world. The actual exchange was a very simple thing. We merely walked down the gangplank of one ship and up another. In 1990 I was dining with Cham Cham, a Thai friend, in Bangkok; during the conversation she mentioned that she had been exchanged by the Red Cross (Thailand was on the Japanese side) at Lourenço Marques. We had had the same experience, from opposite sides. We had been exchanged for each other and we were meeting fifty years later.

I've always been told about how good the food was on the *Gripsholm*, and at that first lunch I fell in love with Swedish rye crackers, which were dark and tasted like nothing else I had ever eaten. The stewards apparently dressed up in clean uniforms for us, and my parents remembered that there was ham and cheese, and bowls and bowls of fresh butter. I think my father pulled a few strings in order for us to have a cabin together. Luckily, as a family of four we were able to fit into one cabin; it was paradise compared to the *Asama*.

Decades later, when I was working for *the fifth estate* I returned to Lourenço Marques to do a story on the Frelimo rebels who had won their struggle against the Portuguese. I could hardly believe that I was really there, in the place that had spelled for us freedom at last. I'm sure most of the architecture had not changed in forty years—wide streets lined by palm trees and flowers, and Spanish-style homes with low flat roofs.

We went across from Lourenço Marques to Rio de Janeiro, and it was for this place that my parents reserved their pleasant memories. In Rio, the Red Cross had given us ten dollars each, and immediately we went shopping—an alligator handbag for my mother, alligator shoes for my father, a silk shirt for my brother, and a pure silk smocked pink dress for me.

Our shopping gave us a sense again of our elegance and well-being. I kept my little pink dress for many, many years, and even today I can see it in my mind's eye—pink silk with blue smocking and finely hemmed ruffles. Our shopping was so typical of us—we lived for the day, and somehow it assured us there would be a tomorrow. My father had heard that someone said that money was for throwing off the backs of trains, and he laughed as he used to repeat it. He never did anything just for money, although he liked having fun with it when he had it. My mother, on the other hand, saved at least ten percent of her household money and, by the time

Neville went to McGill to medical school, to our amazement she had saved enough to buy a triplex in the centre of Ottawa near the canal.

My mother was deeply impressed by the Statue of Christ on Sugarloaf Mountain, and the music and the fun there seemed to be in the whole city. My parents wanted to dance and took us with them to a nightclub. They learned to do the samba, as they were accomplished dancers. It would never have occurred to either of them to leave us in the care of somebody else. They wanted us to enjoy the experience just as much as they did. They used to tell me that we went to a samba club in Rio where three bands rotated so that there was never a moment off. In the fifties, when we all went to the Grill Room at the Château Laurier Hotel for special occasions, people clapped when they danced.

When we finally got to Jersey City in the United States, we had been travelling for more than two months; we had been sapped by the heat of the tropics; we enjoyed mild winter weather in Lourenço Marques and cold around the Cape of Good Hope. It was spring in Rio, and the equator off South America was just as hot as it had been at Singapore. Now it was summer again, August 1942.

My father told me later how anxious all the passengers were about being questioned at length by the FBI. This was part of the formal and official reception that awaited us in the United States of America.

Waiting for us to be processed were two very young Canadian Foreign Service officers—Ralph Collins and Arthur Menzies—who had been sent from Ottawa. It was Arthur Menzies who carried me off the boat. And it was extraordinary for him, and for me, when in 2001, nearly sixty years later, as Governor General I inducted him into the Order of Canada.

All the passengers, except several dozen who were shipped off to Ellis Island, were cleared before the night of the third day. The investigators wanted to know our stories and they put them together like jigsaw puzzles. Max Hill filed this story for the Associated Press:

> *New York Harbour, August 25—Thirteen Coast Guardsmen boarded the MS Gripsholm at 4:00 a.m. Tuesday and were welcomed by a small but happy group of people who have been up throughout the night for their first glimpse of the lights of New York Harbour.*

More than fifteen hundred men, women, and children were aboard the Swedish exchange liner, all from Japan or Japanese-occupied territory in the Far East. We had come from Tokyo and Yokohama, Hong Kong, Saigon, and Singapore. We were among the lucky, and we never looked back.

IN OUR LITTLE HOUSE on Sussex Street in Ottawa I used to hear my father typing quickly at night when I was in bed. He told me that he was writing a novel about his experiences in Hong Kong. This book, which he called "Bushido" (the Japanese warriors' code), is a fictionalized account of his war, and I have drawn a lot on it here. For about fifty years, the manuscript was missing. When I asked my father what might have happened to it, he said, "I think I put it into safekeeping at the Bank of Montreal." I was not living in Ottawa then and I simply tucked it away in my mind that the manuscript might be there, at the corner of Metcalfe and Sparks where our family always had its bank accounts.

In the fall of 2002, just after my father died, I went to the bank and asked for the manuscript. There it was, in its original brown manila envelope, typed on onionskin stationery. He recreates many vivid moments. When I read these words now, I realize that I lived through terrible deprivation, hunger, and terror. My grandson is three now, as I was then. How is something like that processed in the unconscious?

It was with the greatest good luck that my father was able to get to our apartment and prepare my mother for the fact that we would not be seeing many of our things again. He wrote of how he had secured a fake pass and was able to move around the city. He was also able to speak about ten words of Japanese because of his year in Manchukuo with Paul Sykes. My father's return to our home was an experience of degradation—all our books, pictures, photographs, silverware, and china were littered on the floor. A leg of the piano was missing and the top had been wrenched off and was lying on the floor, probably in readiness to be used as firewood. My father found some Japanese soldiers lolling about in our apartment. He found my mother's clothes—silk, woollen, cotton—torn beyond recognition, handbags with pieces cut out of them, and his own riding boots had been slit up the front with a knife. Because the toilet was not in working order, the entire apartment had been used as a lavatory and some of my mother's clothing had been used as bathroom tissue.

After we had left on the boat, my grandmother and my uncle went through our apartment and saved some things—my father's racing photographs and the bronzed booties that were my brother's and my first shoes. We have them to this day, but Neville's are more poignant, as one of the soles was ripped back by looters to see if it was a hiding place for money.

The way my father described the Hong Kong that he walked through—especially the section called Wanchai—is very vivid. People were selling all their goods in order to buy food. "Jap soldiers were elbowing their way among the crowd helping themselves to articles from the various stalls at will, to the grief of the owners. Cigarettes and peanuts were the chief items stolen, and the Japs were rewarding the entreaties of their victims to be paid with slaps across the face. Sometimes, they threw a few cents on the ground, accompanied by mocking laughter. They weren't stealing, according to them, they were paying their own prices." Some larger stalls had the earmarks of selling looted goods. Corpses were being moved off the main streets into out-of-the-way lanes, but a sickly smell of dead bodies still filled the air.

When he came to the address where he thought we would likely be, he saw what we had seen. "On the steps was a portion of a headless body, in the process of decomposition. Pieces of putrid flesh bespattered the walls and the lower half of the jaw was resting on a ledge near the balustrade—a stray shell had landed in time to catch its victim as he was about to leave the entrance." He was told that we had since moved to another house, and he describes his reunion with his family.

"My wife seemed to have aged considerably—her face pale and thin and her general appearance altered by the loose fitting and shabby black coat and pants of a servant. By her side were the three children"—my father the novelist here—"dressed in the manner of the poorest class. Each of them had a narrow strip of white cloth sewed to the front of their coat giving their names, their mother's maiden name and their grandmother's address in Kowloon. This was a precaution against their being lost in the rush or in case anything happened to their mother. They were happy to see me but they could not hide the fear in their eyes."

He then listened to my mother's story of our escape. "She had been prepared to remain in residence even as the Japanese were making their advance up the hills to the rear of our house, but that night the Japs had entered a house about a hundred metres down the street. They murdered twenty-seven people inside and had raped all the women except one. Early the next morning, she had made her escape to Happy Valley, taking only a tin of soda biscuits, a bundle of blankets, a few warm clothes for the children, and of all things, eight and a half pairs of silk stockings. She was worried about the activities of looters and visualized always the possibility of a hold-up during her flight. Her apprehensions were indeed justified because the looters were already attacking the house near her where the mass murders occurred.... As she had not been able to take any food with her, they ran short. And towards the last days before I arrived they had been living on two tiny meals of rice gruel and salt vegetables a day. I'm glad I wasn't with them at that time, because she told me how it made her heart ache to see the look of hunger on the children's faces and to see the ravenous manner in which they consumed their daily ration at lunchtime of three soda biscuits each."

My mother was hysterical and in tears. But she managed to give him an account of her ordeal just after he had left to join his unit, when Japanese soldiers paid a visit to our house and had looked around and departed. Shortly afterwards, screams came from an apartment two doors away. Two women were raped—one of them pregnant. My mother was with her mother and her sister-in-law, a bride of just a few weeks. They were trembling with fear listening to the screams in the night but they prayed incessantly and had placed implicit faith in the small gold crosses they and the children wore on chains around their necks, and the ivory-covered Bible that rested under her pillow. Even in their state of hysteria, my mother and her sister-in-law had to move the next day.

When my father found us, he decided that we all had to walk across the island to try to stay with friends who lived outside the downtown. My mother carried me on her back because I was refusing to walk, securing me with a four-stringed square of cloth usually used by servants for this purpose.

My father writes that he was more upset than anything by seeing my mother having to carry this weight, for during her whole lifetime she had probably never carried anything much heavier than a schoolbag. My brother was carrying a thermos flask almost as big as himself, slung across his shoulder. We had not eaten for about thirty-six hours, but we were promised that we would eat once we got to our destination.

Our whole family took the crowded route that led through Leighton Hill and along the tram tracks to Wanchai. All the time, mobile loudspeakers were blaring forth propaganda about the establishment of the New Order. Suddenly our progress was blocked. Sentries guarded the entrance into Queen's Road, and nobody was permitted to pass. Several thousand people around us were stopped— nobody seemed to know the reason and all we could do was wait.

After a while, my father went in search of food because we were complaining desperately about being hungry. He found a nearby restaurant; it was not open for business, but private black-market sales were being made on the side. They had some freshly roasted turkeys—part of their Christmas stock. My father parted company with the fifty-dollar bill that he had kept in the sole of his shoe and obtained two small turkeys and three bottles of lemonade. Our eyes apparently popped out when we saw this feast, and we sat ripping apart the turkey and eating it and drinking lemonade on the sidewalk while people walked around us.

The reason for the delay in our progress to the city had become apparent. The Japanese were putting on their victory parade. The population was made to line the streets, heads bowed in humiliation, while a long column of troops marched by led by a diminutive, wavy-moustached soldier mounted on a white horse. Some of the Japanese officers carried small white boxes on the front of their belts, probably the ashes of their fallen comrades. The column was endless—several thousand Japanese must have participated in the procession. Then the planes came over; bombers and fighters roared across in perfect formation barely above the rooftops. A few fighters appeared over the harbour at a fairly high level and performed stunts—a performance designed to awe the population. Afterwards, large bombers flew by showering leaflets in their wake.

The parade over, Neville and I, attached to my mother's waist by a rope, trudged wearily towards central Hong Kong. We arrived late in the afternoon, having taken about seven hours to complete a distance of nine kilometres. When we got to our friend's house, dirty and tired, we bathed immediately. We hadn't taken off our shoes, our clothes, or our stockings for more than a week. All we had been able to do was to have our faces sponged, on account of the shortage of water. We had been eating only twice a day, but that night my father told us that we would get a meal in the middle of the day too, and we all clapped with glee. That night, when we knelt for our prayers, he and my mother could not believe that we were all together again as a family. Even though the future looked very dark, they kept up their optimism for themselves as well as for us.

My father says that because we were together again, he had faith that we would get out of it. We asked him whether we would be sleeping here tomorrow night or be moving on, and when he reassured us that we would stay put, we said that we wanted to stay here for a hundred years. Suddenly, I turned to my mother and said: "Mummy, I want to cry." I was only three, and my parents always reminded me of this because it was unusual for a three-year-old to state that she wanted to cry. They always attributed it to what they considered my even-temperedness, as compared to my brother's "artistic" temperament.

I find it one of the most interesting anecdotes from my childhood. That simple announcement of what emotion was to follow tells me a great deal about the character that was even then formed—the determination, the caution, and a certain distance. Apparently, Neville and I did cry a little, but we were not hysterical. That night we all slept very badly as occasional shots rang out.

My father describes in his book the terror of the occupation—the unruliness of the occupying troops, the destroyed buildings, the streets filled with filth, rubbish, and broken-down cars and trucks.

Small-time racketeers established gaming houses all over the city. They did a roaring business in Chinese dominoes, fan-tan, and dice. Even on the sidewalks there were crap shoots. My mother saw some of her own belongings sold by a looter in the street. She could never accept that somebody could take your belongings and sell them right in front of you—your wedding china, your teak end tables, your Tientsin carpet.

If I think of myself now as having been stoical then, what am I to think about my father? After those years of hard work, he watched his success disappear almost overnight. But at least he had had the opportunity to help defend what he had worked for and believed in. Being a dispatch rider in that war was one of the most dangerous things you could be—riding around on a motorcycle in the midst of firing. There was no mission for which he would not volunteer.

When I was little in Ottawa in the late 1940s, it never occurred to me to think that there might be anybody who had never seen a dead body in a street, or a dead body plastered against a wall for that matter. These memories were all kept alive for me by my parents. The only thing they did not want to talk about was the conditions on the prison ship *Asama Maru*. But the hideous carnage and the humiliation of the loss of Hong Kong they kept alive by recounting the stories to all our new friends in Canada, who were always sympathetic. Canadians were intensely patriotic, and people were kind to us because of what we had been through in the war.

In 1943 my brother was chosen for a prominent role in a National Film Board production about children starving as a result of the war. We were the only Chinese in Ottawa who had escaped from the war, and people knew about us, so that was probably why he got the part. When I saw the film I thought he was actually starving, and became extremely upset. I could not bear to think of his not having enough to eat. Although I probably never remembered being hungry, it may be that my passion and obsession for food come from this early experience of near starvation. And the other memory I have is of being taken to see *Bambi* in the forties—I must have been about five and had to be carried out of the theatre in hysterics when Bambi's mother was killed. To this day, I have never been able to watch *Bambi*.

I admire my parents for the way they carried on despite their trauma. They took the wreckage of the first lives they had created together and tried to fit it into a completely new society. They never moaned about their losses; they seemed to have absorbed them and integrated them into the people they became. Only the stories remained. But that doesn't mean there wasn't bitterness: to the end of her days, my mother refused to go to a Japanese restaurant, and she indicated, with the slightest down-turning of her mouth, her displeasure at my owning a Japanese car.

When I was in university, my mother and I travelled to Europe together. She was deeply upset by Italian men smiling and saying "Sayonara" to us. Each time, she would walk up to them and say, "We are not Japanese, we are Chinese," and then turn away. Only with this brittle response could she keep at bay her memories of the bayonets, the bombs, the desecration of her beautiful little home, and her forced parting from her adored mother.

I once asked my father, after I'd heard the story of my mother and aunt hiding behind the closet when the Japanese broke in, whether it could be possible that my mother and her sister-in-law had been raped and had not said a word about it. My father looked at me and said very seriously: "If that had happened to your mother, she would have killed herself instantly." And I think he was right.

TRIP TO CHINA

I THINK MY PARENTS always expected to return to Hong Kong after the war. But then my father went back in 1946 and 1948 and was deeply frightened by the success of Mao Tse-tung. For my father, Communism was the most dreadful ideology that could exist; in fact, he never used any term but "Commies." During the Korean War, he would say, "The Commies are going to push the Americans right off that peninsula." His apprehension of them was more than a realistic dread. It was an absolutely irrational terror.

For me, then, China was almost a forbidden land when the Communists triumphed. It was clear to me by everything my parents said that we would never be able to go there; that door was closed. And it remained closed to me until 1979, when I returned to China at the request of John Macfarlane of *Weekend* magazine. Charles Taylor, one of the *Globe and Mail's* great China correspondents, and John Ralston Saul and I were invited by the Writers' Union of China, and it was understood that we would write about our trip.

Standing on the ferry boat crossing the river that separates the counties of Hoi Ping and Toisan, the ancestral home of my father, the water muddy and flat in the hot sun, my Chinese companion said to me, without turning his head in delicate deference to my emotions: "There is a Chinese poem that says that when one is returning to one's home for the first time, one does not know what one's true feelings are—apprehension or expectation."

I was returning to the village in southern China from which a man called Ng Wui Poi emigrated to Australia just before the turn of the century. He was my grandfather. And now I had come back to see the village he left more than eighty-five years before—the village my father visited for the first time in 1926. The clipped comment of my Chinese host captured my feelings exactly, and I marvelled again at how frequently during my few weeks in China my feelings had been so accurately gauged and understood. I felt it was amazing that I, who was not born in China and who does not speak Chinese, although I am Chinese, should feel these sentiments and this profound sense of attachment. As the ferry landed on the shores of Toisan, I reflected on all the stories my father told that had finally drawn me here. I had heard all my life about the villages of Toisan and their fortified towers and rich houses, all built on remittances sent from "Chinamen" slaving in distant lands on railways, in laundries, or in restaurant kitchens.

A visit to my father's village was the culminating point of my discovery, in a month, of what China was through travel, through conversations—all part of a physical and psychic journey home. Being part of a diaspora, I never felt I had the chance to understand the significance of where I came from, of what I had become. When I hear Jews say "Next year in Jerusalem," I feel a deep emotional understanding: for people of the diaspora, for the exiled, for whom *home* is an ambiguous word, "Jerusalem" is a metaphor for all, because it means a dream becomes reality in a future whose horizon recedes as we, who have sustained the loss, move on.

WE BEGAN OUR VISIT in Peking three years after the end of the Cultural Revolution and the fall of the Gang of Four, and were welcomed in the most extraordinarily gracious way. Peking then was a city of bicycles and few cars. There were millions of people, but somehow you felt that they gave you your own space, your own sense of being yourself. Whenever we wanted interpreters they magically appeared, but we were always able to walk and shop and eat by ourselves.

We met the minister of culture, who at the age of fifteen had walked fifteen hundred kilometres across China to join Mao in Yunnan. I tried to think of him working in a steel mill during that terror, while his wife was in solitary confinement. He looked at me with some ironic amusement during our meeting: "You are looking for roots in everyone, aren't you?" He told me that I was only the second person from Toisan he had ever met. The other was in Yunnan during the Long March with Mao.

We were accompanied by members of the Writers' Federation, and they were terrific company. They loved to discuss poetry, the meaning of revolution, and the history of China. The poet Bi Lao had been a secretary to Premier Chou En-lai and spoke wonderfully civilized English. At that time there was little contact between intellectuals of our two countries, and I understood quickly that this encounter was of enormous interest to the people who accompanied us, because I was Chinese and because I wanted to see my grandfather's village and find my mother's brother, whom my family had not seen since he left Hong Kong for Shanghai in 1932. My hosts said they would try to find him and seemed to accept the task of finding one person out of ten million in Shanghai with equanimity. It made me think that because the Chinese have never believed in the Almighty—the world simply has always been—they therefore have no sense of inferiority to the Divine. So, all things are possible.

I wondered at this China that I had been brought up to think of as not only remote but also dead. I realized that it was a kind of China that my parents had written off, because as Chinese who didn't live in China they were able to dismiss their past and any dreams about China. I think my parents both resented the kind of rebirth that Communism represented for China and they were determined that I should not grow up admiring it in any way. Whenever they heard of anyone in Hong Kong who had visited China and spoke favourably about the developments since 1949, they commented on it with derision or contempt. What persisted for my mother was myth and literature; for my father, who had barely two hundred words of Chinese, there was not even that. However, in both of them there was an enormous unspoken longing that I only realize now, so many decades after our releasing ourselves from China's thrall.

My family's mythology on my mother's side was filled with stories of my great-grandfather's concubines, and on my father's by his stepmother, his father's "village wife," who was an illiterate peasant with bound feet from the Pearl River Delta. Now I was seeing a China that was urban, in the throes of change.

When we arrived at the Shanghai airport, there was a banner on the airfield saying: "Countries Want Independence, Nations Want Liberation, and People Want Revolution. This Has Become an Irresistible Trend of History." Whatever revolution was, it had made a special aesthetic contribution to Shanghai. The girls there were prettier and better dressed than anywhere else in China. There was colour in the clothes and colour in their lipsticks. You could see how it had once been one of the great cities of the world—a blend of cosmopolitanism and Chinese energy.

It wasn't only cities that made their mark on me on that visit. We went to visit Hang Zhou, which is about two hundred kilometres southwest of Shanghai. My mother had visited Shanghai and Hang Zhou in 1933 on a brief visit from Hong Kong, and I had several pictures of her and her sisters there. We had a time-warp trip on a steam train with lace antimacassars on the headrests of our worn velour seats.

We took advantage of being accompanied by a poet on that train trip to ask him how a Chinese poem is actually put together. Mr. Bi lost himself in preparing examples for us and then eventually showed us the classical characters—five characters to each line, four lines to each stanza. Then he proudly showed us another poem, which he told us was his own commemoration of the death of Chou En-lai. Mr. Bi explained this poem, word for word, very slowly and with restrained but intense emotion. The poem ended with the statement that Chou was beautiful. We raised our eyebrows a little at this, but Mr. Bi stated emphatically that Chou *was* beautiful. Mr. Bi explained that the character of Chinese poetry could best be described as rather like the poetry of e. e. cummings. I told him that cummings was one of my favourite poets and quoted to him one of his poems I had by heart, about death and Buffalo Bill. Mr. Bi looked at me with his head tilted sideways and asked, "Tell me, in Canada are there many Chinese women as educated as you are?" I answered quickly and chauvinistically, "Oh, of course."

Earlier in the day, we had sat by the shore of the beautiful West Lake, which shimmered in the sunlight. I'm sure it was unchanged from the time my mother had seen it. She also must have glided on a long wooden boat out to the tiny islands that dotted the lake, the pavilion roofs on the shore glistening. Mr. Bi sighed and said quietly, "This is China." I said nothing. It was exactly like the images one has of China—the silhouettes of pagodas, the small mountains falling into the side of a lake, and the mist slowly rising to meet the sun. I could almost see the jade figures and amulets and the bronze mirrors and vases that my parents had collected placed in this setting. The lake was unlike anything else I have seen. There was a kind of purring quality to it, as though it were alive and yet eternal. We landed on an island, where we walked through azalea and peony gardens and past a pond holding the largest goldfish I had ever seen.

There are moments in your life when you can remember with almost alarming clarity the breathing of the people with you, the shimmering of the air as words are spoken. We sat under a tree beside a smaller pond, looking at how each rock and tree and plant was arranged carefully, while all around us the lake glistened and Mr. Bi fanned himself.

By the end of our train trip, John and I had translated Bi Lao's memorial poem to Chou En-lai. It was a statement of love and respect.

January 1976
My heart broken, I cannot cry,
Strong brow, wisdom in his eyes,
Ten thousand flowers—mute, serene:
Beautiful is Chou En-lai!

Earlier, in Peking, we had seen an exhibit of the clothing worn by Chou during the Long March and afterwards. No relics of a saint have ever been depicted more carefully, more reverently.

One night, we took a cruise of the Shanghai harbour with a well-known woman writer who had been a soldier in the 8th Group Army during the war with Japan and who, she told me, had been sworn into the Communist Party in a roadside ditch in 1944. As we hung over the rail watching junks weave between ocean liners, the Sleeping Beauty Overture hammered at us through the loudspeakers. She agreed with me that the liberation of women is based on economic independence, but she said very sternly: "You must never forget that marriage is natural and must come in time for all women." I asked if her husband was liberated, because I knew that he was a renowned film director, and she replied, "Yes, he does a bit of housework, sometimes the shopping," but of course they could never manage without their servant. I asked if having a servant was in line with revolutionary thinking. She looked a bit puzzled and then said, "But if we didn't have a servant, neither of us could work as well."

As *Swan Lake* replaced *Sleeping Beauty*, she put her face closer to mine and said, "You are Cantonese. Your eyes are typically Cantonese." I said to her, "You have the high, flat cheekbones of someone from Shanghai." It was a draw.

I saw my uncle in the lobby of the hotel from a distance, looking very much like the only photo of my grandfather I'd seen. My hosts at the Writers' Federation told me that they had found him even though there were six other people with the same name. He was thin, tall, and obviously did not smile easily. He shook my hand formally and introduced me to his wife, who I remember being told was his second, and to her son, a young man of twenty-four with a moustache who must have been well over six feet tall. I said awkwardly to my uncle, "Well, we've never met." And he said quickly, "No. I had never seen you, but I had heard all about you." He told me that he'd been living in the same house in Shanghai since he had arrived in 1932 from Hong Kong. I told him that in my only picture of him he was wearing spats and looked very smart in a white sharkskin suit, Hong Kong circa 1927. He nodded and said, relishing the words, "Yes, a sharkskin suit."

Now, he swept the lanes near his house and did a few odd jobs; he and his wife and son shared one large room in the house that was formerly occupied by my grandfather and other relatives. He said he'd spent the past twenty years trying to organize the sending of my grandfather's ashes to join my grandmother's in the cemetery in Hong Kong. Now he had done his duty, he informed me. I asked him how he sent the ashes, and he said he sent them through the mail by regular post. My cousin told me that he had been trained to be a carpenter and earned the equivalent of $30 a month. I asked if he had chosen to be a carpenter and he looked puzzled. My uncle interrupted and said the school chose him.

Talking to my uncle, I realized that he shared the same bitter yet passive acceptance that the maternal branch of my family emanated and that I had always found irritating or amusing, depending on my state of mind, an attitude of "everything is terrible but we must accept it all," stated in a tone of rage and impotence. Surprisingly, I found in myself the desire to tell my uncle to shut up and shape up. Instead I asked whether there was anything I could send him; he said that he would like me to subscribe him to *Popular Mechanics* and *National Geographic*. Just before we left, and after we had had our photo taken together in the laneway, he asked me if there was some way in which I could get him a TV. I looked past him at the dusty street, the respectable but dingy building, and muttered something non-committal. I then gave him the presents I had brought. "Goodbye now," he said to me, waving. "You have grown up very nicely." He had never mentioned my father and never asked about my mother, who was, after all, his sister.

My uncle and his two brothers were gentlemen about town when my father arrived in Hong Kong as a penniless nineteen-year-old from Australia via his ancestral village. I remember my father telling me that when he was a poor hotel clerk in Hong Kong my mother's brothers (undoubtedly in their elegant sharkskin suits) would barely speak to him. Now I had spoken to one of them for the first time in my life. I didn't ask if he remembered my father.

The China that I dreamed of was the China that I found in Guilin, which is about three hundred kilometres northwest of Guangzhou. It had sharp hills rising abruptly from the plain, a mist overhanging, bent trees silhouetted against the sky. The old city of Guilin was destroyed during the anti-Japanese war and during the withdrawal of the Kuomintang before Mao's victorious revolution-ary army. It's just a series of drab cement buildings, totally charm-less. But then we got on a boat to travel down the wide Li River. All around us rose the miraculous hills, shrouded in mist. I remember how I moved my deck chair far away from the Australian tourists so that I wouldn't have to talk with them. When I am travelling in a place that corresponds to one of my dreams of beauty, my illusions of home, I pamper my intolerance and give vent to my misanthropy. I'm happy by myself drinking Tsingtao beer. I think it's safe to say that I had no thoughts at that moment.

I reflected on the pieces of China that I knew from Canada—the food my mother preferred and learned to cook for us using ginger and fermented black beans and soy sauce. So much of China was—and still is—food to me. I remember as a child going to the Chinese-Canadian restaurant in small towns in Ontario and having plates of chicken soo guy followed by a chocolate sundae with a maraschino cherry on top. We were always told that these restaurant people were our relatives because they all came from the Pearl River Delta, the way my grandfather had. My mother, whose ancestors had come from Hakka, was reserved on these occasions and said very little. My father would bring out his entire—albeit limited—vocabulary of Toisan dialect. My mother would primly state that it was perhaps one of the sloppiest-sounding languages in the world.

One of our Cantonese hosts on our China trip, Miss Huang, had been a student in New York and she said she never liked to walk in Chinatown: she always felt that the lonely old men—not allowed to bring their wives to America because of immigration laws—stared at a Chinese woman with a kind of longing that she could not bear. I assured her that times had changed and that Chinese lived in North America with their families. Those lonely men I met in the restaurants and occasionally saw when I passed a laundry made me wonder what sustained them in living so totally alone and alien.

The next morning we made the four-and-a-half-hour drive to Toisan, our hosts excited as none of them had ever penetrated so far into southern China. They were intrigued also by the story of the overseas Chinese and the foreign currency that they brought into

China for a century. In Toisan there's a saying that the women don't need to work, no one cultivates the fields, and there is no one living in the big rich houses. The men returned from overseas when they had saved enough money to travel home, trips that would probably have occurred only every five or ten years. Toisan's buildings curiously reflect the country from which the owners sent the money; there is a strong California influence in some of the balconies and decoration.

As we sat down to lunch, someone came to our table to say that there were relatives waiting for me in the hotel lobby. I hadn't expected to see any more relatives, so one of our hosts went out to investigate. Apparently, the group in the lobby had visited my family in Hong Kong before the war, had seen my brother, who was then a year old, and knew that my father used to own and ride horses. I went out to the lobby and they embraced me, weeping. They were second cousins, the children of my father's first cousin, grandchildren of my grandfather's identical twin brother. They had been brought to Hong Kong by my village grandmother—the wife my grandfather left in the village when he emigrated to Australia. It was the custom to ensure that young men who were about to go overseas were married and had impregnated their wives before they undertook their long, solitary lives working abroad.

I remembered as I looked at my cousins and sat with them in the lobby that my mother had told me that these relatives used to come from the village and that she found it unbearable because they were always crying and clutching and speaking "that awful dialect." They had heard all kinds of garbled versions of our life in Canada, but the only fact they had straight was that my brother was a doctor. They were very proud of him. I could hardly believe I had so many relatives, because to me "family" meant the four of us, our little unit that had escaped.

The village of my paternal grandfather is called Fiftieth Market and is about twelve kilometres from Toisan City. In 1979, about four hundred people lived there. The buildings were one or two storeys and the village was built on a square plan with a surrounding wall. There were no stores, restaurants, or anything vaguely resembling civilization, either Chinese or Western. When we arrived, the ground was muddy because there had been a torrential downpour. We visited the site of my great-grandfather's carpentry shop, where he once made yokes for oxen and, of course, all the coffins for the village. When we got out of our car, it seemed the whole village swarmed us; it was suggested that we walk to the old village, half a kilometre away. As we set out along the road, John was pointed to with giggles by the children, because to most of them he was the first white man they had ever seen. What's more, he had freckles and red hair, and he even had red hair on his arms and legs—the perfect example of a "foreign devil."

The old village had two ponds to the right of it; my father had told me that my stepgrandmother, with her bound feet, used to hobble down from the house to get water. That day, a water buffalo was staked near the pond and some ducks were in a pen in one corner of it. We gathered more and more people as we took our walk. Luckily for me, my cousins were able to fend off all the questions and we were able to greet people. I was introduced as Ying Choi's daughter, my first identification with my father's Chinese life. Everyone in this village had the same surname as my family, which is Ng; it is the custom in all the villages that the residents have the same last name. Therefore I knew that I must be in some way related to every person here, and in the fields around the village, my ancestors had been buried for more than a thousand years.

When my grandfather emigrated to Australia in the late nineteenth century the officials asked him, in English, what his name was. He said, "Ng Wui Poi." Of course they took his first name, Poi, to be his last name, and so we were named Poy. But Poy is not a Chinese surname. And the middle name is given to all males of the same generation. When my brother, Neville, was born, his name was inscribed on the ancestral tablet in this village and his middle name was given as Wui, as my father's, Ying, was inscribed by his own generation; everyone in my father's generation has the middle name of Ying and everyone in my brother's generation has the middle name of Wui. No such naming occurs for girls; they were never considered important enough.

My village grandmother considered my father to be her son and my grandmother in Australia to be a concubine. I suppose that she thought she was very privileged—her husband was sending money from abroad and she knew he had sons by his other wife in Australia. My father told me that he and his brothers and sisters were unaware until they were almost in their teens that there was another wife in China. This story is so common to all people of overseas Chinese origin that it hardly needs to be recounted anymore. It just is.

While we sipped tea in a house with a beaten-mud floor, I met an old man who used to help my grandmother carry water from the well. He still lived across the alley. He told me they remembered my father, who had come to the village in 1926 and spent six months there; he spent his whole time trying to avoid marrying anyone. They asked me why he had not come back with me. Diplomatically, I said that he had sent me to return for him.

As I looked around, I got the impression that not much had changed since my grandfather left a hundred years previously, except that each house had one lighting source. There was electricity, but there was no furniture, and the houses were of identical plan, probably unchanged for the last thousand years. The village was simply a collection of buildings housing people who worked the land and received money from abroad. They gave me messages for my father on little slips of paper with their names written on them. My father could not read or write Chinese, and my mother would have to translate for him. I knew that if I told these people that he could not read their messages it would make no difference to them. We were all family.

It was while I was in China and after I had been to my village that I realized that the deep-rooted sense of Chinese identity was such that foreign encroachments or displacement to a foreign country mattered very little. When I told my hosts about my children and said that their father was not Chinese, they said, "But they are Chinese." They meant that the Chinese blood tie is so strong that nothing else matters. Bi Lao told me that if you have one drop of Chinese blood you are Chinese, and that is all there is to it. This sense of strength and identification and belonging is very different from the European idea of race, with all its hideous connotations of inferiority and superiority.

All my relatives knew that my father had married above his station into a very good Hong Kong family, renowned for its beautiful women. My cousins gossiped about this to my hosts and my hosts repeated it to me: he bettered himself in every way by marrying my mother. My hosts were interested in the story of how my father started to work at age eleven in a tiny grocery store in the middle of nowhere in Australia, but they were also intrigued that my mother had a classical Chinese education. They thought the contrast was humorous.

I learned at that meeting that two of my cousins were schoolteachers and had five children between them, all going into some form of higher education. They begged me to send pictures of myself and my parents to them when I returned to Canada. My distant cousin, who was a Chinese herbalist, appeared with his mother; she was dressed in black in the old-fashioned style of shortish trousers and a small buttoned-up blouse. She made a formal speech to me: she was happy to enjoy good health in old age, and it was a pleasure to her because now she had the opportunity to meet me while she was still presentable. She asked me to convey to my honourable parents her most respectful regards, that they could please send letters and come to her home on our next visit.

Back at our hotel the next morning, people who also said that they were cousins appeared in the lobby at six thirty. They had had a scribe write a letter to my father. We hugged each other and I waved their letter. They clutched at me as I got into the car and then knotted together on the steps waving goodbye. Looking back at them as they stood on the steps in their plastic shoes and torn undershirts, a mixture of compassion and pity and regret rose up in me—that I couldn't spend longer in the village, that I couldn't go to my grandfather's grave to sweep it ceremoniously with a broom as was the custom. There was a feeling of having been touched very deeply and then having to be torn away. There was an authenticity and an unchanged quality to the people in my village; it was too late for me to truly be part of it, but it was not too late for me to understand how I could regret it, to recognize with my heart what I could not change.

To have been in Toisan was to identify the place and the heartland of all the so-called Chinamen who kept their blood relationships intact even through years of being separated overseas. It kept the men who went abroad going even when they lived in the most appalling emotional and physical conditions—from the railway worker who often was namelessly sacrificed laying rails, to the laundry man in New Westminster, British Columbia, or the café owner in Estevan, Saskatchewan. Those little villages of the Pearl River Delta were etched on their hearts. Their names were kept on boards in the shrines of the village, as were my father's and my brother's. They sent money back and they would return perhaps three or maybe four times in their adult life, as my grandfather did, and see from time to time the woman they had married when they were young teenagers. Then they would die and their bones would be returned to their ancestors in the fields. Their sons would return to pay homage as filial duty, and that is what my father, who was born in Australia, did in 1926, when he travelled to his father's village in the Pearl River Delta, and what I tried to be part of for his sake.

MY FATHER

MY FAVOURITE PICTURE of my father is not the elegant one taken by Yousuf Karsh in 1948, barely six years after we had arrived in Canada. It always seemed so typical to me of our luck and my father's subconscious search for excellence that he should have decided to have his photo taken by an Ottawa photographer who would soon become so renowned. My father was starting his own business then—an export business to China—and he asked people where he should go. A number of his friends from the University of Ottawa, where he had done an M.A. at night school and had been given the credit of a B.A. because of his "world experience," told him that there was a rather good photographer named Karsh. I remember when we looked at the pictures for the first time my mother said, "That's not really you. You look like George Raft." And my father retorted, "A *Chinese* George Raft." The picture is elegantly posed and my father's remarkable hands are folded on his lap. He told me that when he was a small boy one of his aunts said that he had nails that were like filberts, and then we looked at them and agreed that they did look like filberts.

There is another picture of him, with my mother on their wedding day on the steps of St. John's Cathedral in Hong Kong. He looks very natty in his morning coat, and my mother, in her long white gown with a train, is leaning on his arm, carrying a bouquet of calla lilies. The photo is professionally tinted, as was the custom of the time. My parents epitomized the Hong Kong of 1934—a beautiful Chinese couple in European wedding clothes.

My favourite photograph of my father is the one that shows him being led into the winner's circle, mounted on Laughing Buddha, one of his own horses, in 1940. My father is smiling as only a winner can. He is being accompanied by his Chinese trainer and by my mother, in a floor-length Persian lamb coat, holding the reins that lead him to the winner's circle. She is plump because I have just been born. In the background you see the buildings of Happy Valley Race Course and the trainers wearing sandals and Chinese working clothes.

My father learned to ride bareback when he was growing up in a small village called Chiltern, in the back country of New South Wales, Australia. It was then a town of fewer than a hundred people, and his father ran a small grocery store that provided a subsistence-level life. He was the second of nine children, eight of whom survived childhood. My grandfather had arrived in Australia for the gold rush only to discover that it was over. This signified the kind of luck that he had throughout his life. There were hardly any Chinese in the area, but they knew of each other. My grandmother, who lived to be ninety-eight, was sixteen when she married my grandfather, and she always told my father and his brothers and sisters that she remembered her father being given ten gold dollars for her. She was the daughter of a Chinese man and an Irish woman who is listed on her birth certificate as Mary Jones. As soon as Mary Jones had had two children, one of whom was my grandmother, she disappeared, never to be heard from again.

In the great Australian novel about a colonial figure, *The Fortunes of Richard Mahoney*, Chinese gold diggers are alerted by an Irishwoman "clad in a skimpy green petticoat, with a scarlet shawl held about her shoulders, wisps of frowsy red hair standing out round her head ... spinning her arm like the vane of a windmill, and crying at the top of her voice: 'Joe, boys!—Joe, Joe, Joey!'

"Only the group of Chinamen washing tail-heaps remain unmoved. One of them, to whom the warning woman belonged, raises his head and calls a Chinese word at her; she obeys it instantly, vanishing into thin air."

When I read that page for the first time, I had an electrifying flash thinking that this could have been my great-grandmother. We often speculated about what kind of person she was, and we all agreed that somebody who would take up with a Chinaman in the backwoods of Australia would probably not be able to trace her ancestors to Celtic kings. But it seemed to add to the adventure of our lives to imagine her. In any case, it made us feel very matter-of-fact about who our ancestors really were.

As there weren't many Chinese to be married to in Australia in those days, a lot of Chinese married white Australians. Of my own grandfather's children, my father was the only one who was interested in China, the only one to marry a Chinese. My aunt Ruby married a Greek called Leo and ran a fish-and-chips café. And my uncles Roy, Lindsay, and Leslie all worked the racetrack, taking bets. As betting was the national mania in Australia, they did reasonably well for themselves. And I suppose that's what my father would have done had he stayed there. Instead, he went to look for the place he had come from, and when he had found it, as he did in the village, he left it. But at least he had found it.

Growing up in Chiltern, my father and his brother Les caught rabbits, rode bareback, and generally had an untrammelled rural life. It ended when my grandfather did not return from one of his infrequent trips to China, and my grandmother told the two boys that they would have to go out and work. My grandfather had died shortly after in China, having briefly lived again with his village wife. My father was then eleven. He was sent to Sydney, where he worked for an aunt and uncle who owned a vegetable store. He was forced to sleep in the basement, under the porch. He had been promised that he would be allowed to go to high school, but that turned out to be untrue. He told me that he used to cry himself to sleep thinking about how he could have done well if he'd had the chance to go to high school.

He didn't tell me this until I was already in university. I think he deliberately held himself back so that his children wouldn't think that they were going to school because of him. It didn't matter whether he said that to us or not; we knew we were doing something not just for ourselves but for that mysterious thing that I can only call a family spirit.

From then on my father never had any formal education, but when he went to Melbourne after he was sixteen, he took secretarial courses and could do both kinds of shorthand, Pitman and Gregg. He never forgot either of them; when I was going through some of his things after he died, I saw little notes he had written to himself in shorthand. He also learned to type 120 words a minute. He took part in activities in the Chinatown of the day, which he told me was an unhealthy part of town. People suffered from tuberculosis and lived in a grimness of exclusion and poverty while taking in laundry and working for restaurants. When we went to the Chinatown museum in Melbourne in 1989, my father found himself in a photo of a social club at the age of about seventeen. He is immaculately dressed in a suit and tie, and his shoes shine right through the photograph. Until that time I had no idea that he had lived and worked in Chinatown before going back to see his village in China. As soon as I saw this picture and he told me what Chinatown was like then, I realized why he never wanted us to take part in anything having to do with any Chinatown in Canada. He had moved beyond that and he was interested in it only insofar as he was old fashioned and felt that he had to be polite with what he called "the relatives." It seemed to me that the relatives were roughly half of Canton province, but that is the category into which he put them and he was always rigorously polite while making it very clear that we were not going to be part of that world.

My father went to elocution lessons, which he said cost him a half a week's salary once a month. This meant that he lost his Australian twang, which I suspect was his purpose. All his life he spoke English with an English accent. He, of course, had never learned any Chinese, because his mother didn't speak any. He had a longing to write in English and to do something that would help him to get ahead in the world. He told me when we went back to Australia together in 1989 that Australia had been a place he had to get out of because the racism was terrible. He knew that there would be barriers to advancing in life. What he didn't say was that his happy, affectionate brothers and sisters didn't have his ambition or his desire to be included in a larger society. They were happy to be part of the racing fraternity and to organize their social and business lives around the running of the Melbourne Cup. To this day, they are trainers of horses.

It's logical that my father's family should have gravitated towards what was basically a free world of small enterprise where nobody could tell them they didn't belong. They remained outsiders while happily enjoying the benefits of Australian life. My two uncles Lindsay and Roy fought in the Australian armed forces. I had a picture of my uncle Lindsay, who was severely wounded by shrapnel, in his dashing Australian hat with one side turned up, which I treasured for many years before ever meeting him. Uncle Roy, a prisoner of war for two and a half years, had nearly been left on the dock in Borneo when prisoners were evacuated. It wasn't until Uncle Roy said, "What about me?" in his broad Australian accent that they realized he was Australian, and they repatriated him too.

When my father was nineteen, he decided that he really had to see where he had come from. He had heard vague rumours that my grandfather had a village wife, and although his mother never spoke of this, he thought that he had better go and see the tablet that had his name engraved on it in his ancestral village. By this time his father had already died, and my father, as the second child and oldest son, also felt a little superstitious about doing his duty, and took off to see if there was anything where he had come from that could hold him.

The village wife, by now widowed for nearly ten years, welcomed him as her own son. She felt she had been one of the unlucky ones not to have been left with a son of her own, although she did have a daughter. To the Chinese, though, having a daughter did not count. It was my father who mattered to his stepmother. She had bound feet and she lived in a small stone house with her own pig and some ducks. It was 1926, and China was undergoing tremendous turmoil, though the reverberations barely touched this village. My father learned that his grandfather had been the local carpenter and coffin maker, and he stayed for six months while trying to figure out if there was a way he could make a living in China. If there was, it certainly wasn't what he wanted, and he left for Canton.

In Canton, he heard the Russian Communist Bakunin address a crowd, and he believed that if the Communists ever took China, it would be the end of civilization. Even though my father later studied political science at the University of Ottawa and earned his M.A. there, he never was a very astute analyst of political trends.

As he later told us, he saw no future for himself in China—but Hong Kong was different. He thought that since he spoke English so well, that was the place for him. He was right. In the late twenties, Hong Kong was a British colonial outpost with business interests ranging from the large, like Jardines, with all the money and power of the empire behind it, to the smallest herbalist shopkeeper. It was at the latter that my father found a job, grinding leaves and seeds. He took a second job as a night clerk in a hotel. But he told me that when he first arrived in Hong Kong and before he was able to get the full-time jobs, he was sometimes so hungry that he went for two days without food and drank from the taps in the street. That he never got dysentery was more a comment on his constitution than on the health standards in the colony.

Besides working at two regular jobs, he was able to learn to ride, realizing that the Happy Valley Race Course was basically a place for gentlemen jockeys—men who owned and rode their own horses and occasionally rode their friends' horses. The races were a great social event in Hong Kong, and the Chinese, who loved to bet, made it a lucrative centre of social activity. My father also realized that by riding, he could better himself socially. He would meet the kind of people who could help him get ahead in business. He would marry into a good family. In 1989 in Australia, all my uncles and aunts asked after my mother, who had never visited Australia to meet them. Uncle Roy said, "We know your mum was a real lady." Only once I had grown up did I realize how far my father had come. If we had continued to live in Hong Kong, and there had been no war, I would have been more aware of the differences in my parents' backgrounds because we would have been surrounded by people who would have reminded us of this. But when we landed in Canada, as though from another planet, there were no guideposts for me to understand that my father had married so much above him and that my mother never forgot it.

Also at this time, he had found a small job with the Canadian Trade Commission and its commissioner, Paul Sykes, who was roughly my father's age ("with such red hair!" said my mother). Japan had invaded Manchuria, and Canada decided that it would try to do some business with the newly named Manchukuo. My father asked the trade commissioner if he could accompany him as his office helper. Sykes agreed, and the two enterprising young men embarked on an adventure to a part of China that neither of them had ever seen.

My father was deeply impressed with the way the Japanese officers rode, and somehow he wangled his way into lessons at the Japanese officers' riding academy. There he perfected his technique and indulged his passion for riding. He learned not only to flat race but also to do steeplechase, which was his favourite. He loved the daring of the jumps, the excitement of coming up to the hurdle and realizing you could make it. I wish that I could have seen him race, just once.

What I haven't said yet is that my father was one of the handsomest men in Hong Kong. Even thirty years later, when I was with him in Hong Kong, people would offer comments like, "So you're handsome Billy Poy's daughter," or "I don't think I ever saw a handsomer man than your father." I simply took my father's looks for granted, although he certainly didn't. People talk a lot about beautiful women making their way up in the world; my father was a beautiful man who did the same. When *The Last Emperor* was playing at the cinema, we took my mother out of hospital where she was slowly dying of liver cancer and went to see it. When I looked at John Lone in that film I felt that I was looking at my father when he was young. When we returned to my mother's hospital room, both my mother and father agreed with me that he was handsomer than John Lone.

In his later years, we used to discuss how he had chosen my mother for a wife. He was very matter-of-fact about it and said that of the three remaining sisters who were not married, Auntie Julia was not pretty enough and Auntie Cecilia was a bit too young. My mother was the right age and she had a mother who was a warm and welcoming person and who was alert to the possibilities of marriage for her girls. I think my father wanted my grandmother to be his mother-in-law more than he wanted my mother to be his wife. He always attributed to his mother-in-law feelings that I'm sure were projections of his own: she cared more for my brother and me as grandchildren than anybody else (my father was devoted to us), and she always encouraged him to get ahead.

And get ahead he did in his small way—becoming a car salesman, and importing small goods from the United States and Japan such as cameras and radio equipment. His day job was at the Canadian Trade Commission, where he assisted a series of young men from Quebec and British Columbia and Saskatchewan who had been sent out in their twenties to try to encourage the sale of Neilson's chocolate bars, Canadian Raticide, and Chateau cheese to Hong Kong. Commissioners Ken Noble and Paul Sykes were, we were convinced, the ones who had put us on the list of Canadians to be repatriated, which got us out of Hong Kong.

These friends were in Ottawa during the war and they formed a little social circle once we arrived there. More importantly, they knew where we had come from and what we had lost. But there was one trade commissioner in Hong Kong whom my father regarded with a mixture of intense amusement and contempt. This man had been a major during the First World War and insisted on being addressed as such; his wife had discarded her first name somewhere along the way and wished to be called Sparkling. It was only when my mother got to Canada that she realized that this was not a common Canadian name. The major would come to the Trade Commission office inebriated. He once sat down on a bottle of ink, thereby causing severe damage to his backside and ruining a suit forever. He was incapable of writing two straight sentences, and my father did all the work and wrote all the correspondence. I think he did not begrudge it, although he thought it was a lamentable way for Canada to be represented. On the other hand, he was getting the best experience he could possibly have and he enjoyed it.

The way in which my parents lived in Hong Kong was typical for a young middle-class couple of the time. My brother was born within the first year of their marriage, and we had an apartment with an amah for him, a cook, and a driver for my father, plus someone who was vaguely related to one of those people who did all the cleaning. My mother would go to the market to shop—as she always told me in Ottawa after—not because she had to but because she wanted to get the freshest food and to make sure the cook wasn't cheating her.

When I came along there were two amahs and a motorcar. For six years before the war, my family lived a halcyon time, according to my parents. My father raced. He went to the racetrack every morning at five to exercise horses and to train and then he would go to his office at nine. My mother was surrounded by her sisters and cousins and her mother.

They had a gramophone and practised all the Western dances— the foxtrot, the tango, the waltz, the two-step. And they carried on dancing when we came to Canada. When we would occasionally go to the Grill Room of the Château Laurier in the late forties and fifties, my mother and father were the best dancers on the floor. I can still see them practising the tango in our tiny living room on Sussex Street and how swiftly my father could turn my mother and dip her. I was thrilled to watch them dance. As children, we were taught to ballroom dance as well. My father felt that I would never become a good female dancer because I always wanted to lead. He would look at me and say firmly: "If you're going to dance well, you're not going to lead." I never lost the habit and so I've never become a good dancer.

The self-contained, insular world we lived in then was not replicated in any way in Canada. Even though my parents were not rich, there had been a certain element of sophistication in their world. After all, Hong Kong was a British colony, and even though they

were not British, they could see the advantages of the stability and
order that the British had brought to Hong Kong. It was this that
made them feel that they were going to be comfortable in Canada,
that and being able to speak English well. They were raised colonial
people and they would remain colonial people, in Hong Kong or in
Canada.

My father, having come so far from his childhood, was in a way
adaptable to everything. The change was more difficult for my
mother, who perceived a lack of sophistication among Canadians
when she first came to Ottawa, a cold little white place with white
people. She and my father were determined that we would not be
part of either a physical or a mental Chinatown. My father had
spent his entire life escaping from that and he was not going to
have us slip back into it. He often derided the English of second-
generation Chinese Canadians who spoke with a Chinese accent.
He believed intensely that our English must be perfect and always
corrected us if we dropped a *g* as so many of our friends did.

My mother considered everyone in Chinatown to be on the
level of her amah or her cook. There would be no connection
between them. My parents' friendships with Canadians were ones
that they made directly and not through any intermediary of an
ethnic group. My mother responded warmly to the friendship of
the French-Canadian families who spontaneously helped us—the
Proulxs and the Marcottes—who taught her how to cook and shop
in a Canadian way.

Saturday nights at our house on Sussex Street, we would often
welcome friends from my father's office at the Department of Trade
and Commerce, where he was a clerk. I always remember his friend
Hoppy, who wore one shoe with a thick sole and used a cane, and
the various women, Viola, Madge, and Erma, who also worked with
him, all of whom would come over and sing while my mother
played the piano, and play Chinese checkers and gin rummy with us.

My parents thought the traditions of the British Empire carried on in the way people drank. My mother never drank and my father liked the occasional whiskey or beer. But they always had it on hand for their friends, who seemed to be able to get drunk on Saturday nights and still show up at work on Mondays. Whenever anybody left our house inebriated, my father would say, "Just remember that we are not like them and we're never going to be drunk." When I joined the hard-drinking television journalists of the sixties and seventies, I know they considered me a Miss Goody-Goody.

People had to be of the upper-middle class for my mother to regard them as any kind of companion for her children. I never thought twice about it and simply went along with what she believed. If there was ever any resistance to anyone I brought home, it would be because my parents did not think they were well brought up, or they didn't stand when a lady came in the room, or they chewed gum. On these kinds of things, my father particularly was unforgiving.

Once I asked him whether he or my mother had ever been concerned about my marrying somebody who was not Chinese. He looked startled and said, "No, it's perfectly natural that you would find your own level, and that wasn't going to be with any Chinese born in Canada." Of course when Chinese started to come in large numbers after 1960 it would have been a different situation. But my parents' attitude towards not staying in an enclosed group very much coloured my life.

It has only been in recent years that I have met and gotten to know people who grew up in Chinatowns across Canada. Because we usually share the common background of our ancestors coming from the Pearl River Delta, there is an instinctive bond, and now I feel that I do understand something of where they have come from, especially after my first visit to China. But the attitudes my father complained of in Chinatown—the xenophobia, the denigration of women and women's education—were frequently confirmed. I think I would be accurate in saying that I was probably one of very few Chinese girls of my age to be brought up in Canada to believe that she could be anything, and to be encouraged to get as much education as she wanted. This encouragement, this drive, this "the sky's the limit" conviction, defined my father. It emerged from his fierce longing, from his sleeping in a basement as a virtual slave, from his hard-won achievements.

My friends agree that my father was one of the funniest men they ever met. He used to say that life wasn't for taking seriously, just for doing seriously. He had wonderful ways of using little sayings that forever marked how he would view somebody. If he didn't like one of my boyfriends he would say, "He looks like the east end of a horse going west," or "He thinks that Rudy Vallee is a place between two hills." Nothing more needed to be said about their looks or their intelligence after those lines were used. And he loved dirty jokes. When he was in his nineties, I would always try to find a new joke or two that I could bring him, and his memory never failed for the old jokes.

He was always, and remained till the day he died, the nicest man. By his belief in me, this funny, quirky, bright, even-tempered man was the best kind of passport into the world, which is after all a world created by men. I was never apprehensive of men, nor was I ever worried that they would exploit me. My father never had, and I had that confidence like a wind at my back for all my life.

The day I became Governor General, I looked over and saw him sitting with my closest friends, and I had a flash of that eleven-year-old boy lying in bed in the basement of the grocery store in Melbourne. After the ceremony, he said to me, "I feel as though I'm living in a dream." I just smiled, but in my heart I said, "We've always been a part of your dream."

MY MOTHER

WHEN MY MOTHER was a little girl, she lived in a large house in Kowloon with her immediate family, her extended family, and servants. There were probably more than a hundred people under one roof. The servants presumably were housed in quarters either in the courtyard or just outside the house. My mother's family were Hakka, a part of the Chinese who went overseas but whose uniqueness lies in the fact that their women always refused to bind their feet. They came from the hills and were renowned as a formidable people. Certainly Hakka women were considered tough, and my mother said this with a good deal of pride.

Her father, George Lam, was born in Dutch Guyana, now Surinam, on a cocoa and coffee plantation owned by his parents. His father, according to the family legend, had been the son of a rich farmer and had taken the pigs from his village to market to sell them. On the way back he fell in with some gamblers, had a good time and lost all the money that he had gained from the pigs. He was so terrified of his father's wrath that he sold himself as an indentured servant and was sent off to South America. He ended up on a plantation run by my great-great-grandfather, who was a tough taskmaster and whose temper was legendary. My great-grandfather noticed that there was one daughter who seemed to dominate over the others. I'm told that she had dark red hair and a burnished complexion.

My father always teased my mother that we must have had Inca blood. To my father it made a lot of sense to think of all South Americans as being Inca rather than Spanish. Perhaps he had gotten this story from my grandmother. Perhaps he made it up. In any case, it always embarrassed my mother and she was furious every time he brought it up.

In time, the indentured servant worked off his debt and, as in a fairy tale, he married the heiress and the plantation became his. There was a lot of money to be made in those kinds of commodities then, and the family eventually sold and returned to live on their wealth in Hong Kong. It seems they had lost touch with their Hakka roots.

Every time Auntie Julia or my mother talked about their family, it was always in apocalyptic terms: towering rages, gambling debts, terrible drinking problems, too many concubines. My great-grandfather had thirteen concubines, and one of my great-aunts was born when wife number one was forty-eight and the baby slipped out into the toilet.

My mother was never nostalgic about her childhood; she was simply number fourteen grandchild. In a family of eight children, she did not get enough attention, and as her younger brother, eighteen months her junior, was very sick as a child, she was quickly made to grow up. And yet all the children adored their mother, my Po-Po. And to the day she died, she thought of her mother in the tenderest of terms. Everyone tells me that my Po-Po was a lovely person who put up with a lot, including her husband's probable crimes and bad temper. But what kept her going was her profound Christianity. All of my mother's family for several generations were nominally Anglican, but my grandmother fervently believed in God.

When my mother was a small child, they lived for several years in Indonesia, and it was there that my Po-Po had a vision. My grandfather had had a nasty disagreement with the Indonesian

woman who lived on the neighbouring property, and initially all
that happened was that the dogs, which were always German shep-
herds, were poisoned. Then my grandfather became ill for an
unknown reason. The Chinese herbalist told my grandmother that
a hex had been put on him by the woman next door through her
witchdoctor. My grandfather got sicker and sicker, and then my
grandmother became ill as well. One night she sat up with my
grandfather, fully expecting him to die, and as she sat with him,
holding his hand, she felt a light wind come into the room and she
saw Jesus Christ sitting at her dressing table. They looked at each
other in the mirror. She asked him if he was Jesus and he said to her,
in Chinese, "Yes, I am, Martha." That was her English name. "Do not
worry; your prayers have made everything all right." In the
morning, my grandfather's fever had disappeared and he recovered
within a couple of weeks.

When I was a child, I was told so often about this apparition of
Christ at the dressing table that I fully expected him to appear at my
mother's dressing table, purchased from Freiman's department store.
Unfortunately, he never did, but I was always prepared for him.

I don't know what kind of dreams my mother had for herself,
because we never talked about that. We never talked about anything
that would reflect on her loneliness, on her sense of not being
understood. When she was young, her beauty and her liveliness
covered this darkness within her, but as she grew older it emerged
more and more, leaving her virtually silent. Often the only reason
she joined in a conversation was to put up a good front. I saw her
making that effort and it hurt both of us.

One of the great advantages of having your parents live for a long
time is that you get to know them beyond your childish image of
them; I realized that my mother had been pretty miserable for most
of her life. I knew that even her children's love for her could not
assuage that pain. So we had to live our lives side by side with that

misery and accept the obsession she had for her children as the
deepest form of love that she could give.

I was with my mother the night she died, and we had just read
evensong together, which she liked to do and often broke into the
Chinese version in the middle of it. When we came to the Nunc
dimittis (Lord, now lettest thou thy servant depart in peace), the
most surreal smile came over her face. I knew that she would die. I
looked into her face knowing that there were still so many things
that we could have talked about now that I was really an adult, that
there were so many unspoken tracks of love. But there was an
underlying bed of corroded misunderstanding that we would only
solve in some kind of eternity.

MY MOTHER HAD an exquisite patterned-silk dressing gown with
a hand-rolled scalloped edging in which she had tried, when I was
eight years old, to commit suicide with an overdose of sleeping pills.
My father was away at the time, and I remember that there had been
raised voices the night before and my father standing at the door in
his black and white tweed overcoat saying that he had to go to
Montreal on business. These kinds of scenes were not unusual at our
house. In fact, the tenor of our family's life in private was the very
opposite of what it appeared to be in public. In front of other people,
we always behaved with a certain kind of exotic elegance. Many
people told us this, and I think we were proud of it, the way a small
amateur theatre group would be proud of coming second in the local
festival. I think we even believed that our clothing was part of our
presentation. We were playing the well-dressed, exquisitely groomed
people that we wished others to think we were. And perhaps by that
demonstration we were able to keep control of ourselves, a control
that could support us in other things that we were doing.

My mother and father fought a great deal, and I used to ask them
why they couldn't settle things between them. My mother would

look at me fiercely and say, "If he ever raised his hand to touch me, it would be all over!" But she never answered my question. In the event, the violence was verbal, and I learned to shut out the sounds of those voices, and only occasionally listened to them from a distance. This distance was like being on the prairies and seeing the landscape roll out like the sea in front of you, then suddenly a deep coulee would appear. Nothing really warned you about the coulee, but it was inevitable that you were going to come up against one— just like a break in the natural and emotional rolling that was our pattern. But, of course, what was natural was not what we were feeling most of the time. Most of the time we were seeing the earth break into the coulee and wondering how we could get to the other side and knowing that we would have to go down through it and up the other side.

My parents were united mostly by their love for their children. That was what I knew instinctively and that was the burden I carried. I have always believed that it was too much weight for a child to carry her parents' marriage on her shoulders. Perhaps I am wrong about that, and perhaps I gained a kind of responsibility to make sure that other people did not behave badly, which has stood me in good stead through my life. Perhaps what I have been doing during my life has been to try to get beyond the feeling that every-one's emotional equilibrium was all up to me.

For many years, I did not remember that my brother and I had discovered my mother at the end of her bed, nor did I remember that we decided between us to call our family doctor. My brother was eleven and I was eight, but we knew what the doctor's number was. After many decades, even though I had known in my heart that we had made this discovery, I still could not visualize it. That I now can doesn't mean that I actually remember it but rather that I wish there not to be a gap in any of my memories. I know that my reac-tion was different from my brother's: I did not feel enraged and abandoned or resentful of my father. Together with the loss of memory was the loss of feeling, and a new, deeply rooted distrust of my mother's abilities to cope with her own life, much less with mine.

This episode was never mentioned among us until my wedding day. Driving in a limousine on University Avenue in Toronto, my father asked me, out of the blue, "Did you know that your mother tried to commit suicide when you were little?" I stared out the window and did not look at him while I responded, "No." This was not true; I rarely lied to my father, because he didn't give me any reason to lie to him, but in this case, I simply felt that I had to say something.

Right after the crisis (and I do remember my father rushing home and having hushed discussions with people, including our doctor, in our kitchen), it was generally acknowledged that my mother had had a nervous breakdown. Years later, our family doctor would tell me, "Your parents are wonderful people, and your mother got better very quickly from her nervous breakdown." Because I had blotted it out of my mind so completely, I never really dwelt on it. All I know for sure is that she never saw a psychiatrist or had any kind of treatment for depression or anxiety. It was only thirty or forty years later when I realized that her wild upswings and down-swings of mood, her hysteria in conversations—often about the smallest things, like the colour of the tablecloth—were signs that she had been a depressive all her life.

She knew there was something wrong with her. She knew that she was not like other people, especially not like the jolly mums who came to my dance classes with their daughters. She was always a bit aloof, but as it went with her beautiful clothing (which she made herself) and her perfect makeup and hair, it was generally accepted because we were such a novelty as a family in Ottawa.

After this episode my mother became more withdrawn than

ever. She went about doing her cooking (Chinese meals at least five nights a week and what she called European food the rest of the time). She grimly used the pressure cooker to make Irish stew but announced that she really was not that interested in getting three square meals on the table a day. She became a better and better cook while denying that she had any interest in it whatsoever.

As far as I can remember, I continued going to school, and to piano and dance lessons, but one thing does stick in my mind: I can remember walking home one day from school down Bank Street and feeling a load of darkness fall on my head. I felt that I almost could not put one foot ahead of the other and I certainly couldn't think. I turned the corner before arriving at Calderone and Grieves, the fancy grocery store, and it was as though a light had gone out inside my head. I felt that I should cry, but I couldn't. I didn't know where the tears would come from, or, if they ever started, how they would ever stop.

My parents told me that we would be having a housekeeper from now on whose name was Mrs. McArthur, or Mrs. Mac for short. She was a wisp of a woman with carefully crimped white hair. She was so restrained in her manner that one could almost say that she didn't exist, but where she did exist she was quite competent and certainly kind. Her cooking, however, was truly terrible. Everything was watery and the stews were beige. I came to dread the thought that she would be cooking yet another meal for us in the pressure cooker—pulverized meat and gooey, tasteless gravy. I now realize that perhaps the doctor had suggested that there was too much stress on my mother domestically, and that's why we had to have Mrs. Mac.

My mother rested every afternoon and got up shortly after we arrived back from school. I think I imagined that she was physically not well, the way I tended to be, catching every childhood illness—red measles, German measles, chicken pox, mumps, and some mysterious flu that came and went for a year. My mother and I were both home a great deal for the next year because of our sharing a kind of sympathetic ill health.

And then one day, my father made an announcement. He told us that Mrs. Mac would be leaving and our Aunt Julia was going to be coming to Canada and would live with us for the next little while. As a child I felt so cut off from family abroad. My mother had seven brothers and sisters, and my grandfather, who lived in Shanghai, where he had taken refuge before the war, would occasionally— every second year—send me a beautifully written letter in perfect English. He spoke Dutch as well, and sent me a photograph in which he is wearing spats and smoking from a cigarette holder. He always asked after my studies and said he hoped that I would develop my mind and become somebody of note in Canada, where fate had thrown us.

My mother's memory of her father was extremely complex. I suppose he was the typical Chinese patriarch—stern, uncommunicative, and, ultimately, irresponsible. That kind of household— filled with concubines and rivalries about children and eldest sons—is almost medieval. The stories filled my childish imagination: how my real great-grandmother, who was number one wife, was betrayed by number four concubine. There never seemed to be anything really drastic like a murder or a disappearance, just constant discord and rivalry. When I took my then ninety-year-old father to see *Raise the Red Lantern*, which featured concubine rivalry, he quipped, "Well, that was happy home life in old China."

I initially thought my grandfather was irresponsible. My mother told me at least once a year that her earliest memory of her childhood was of being driven around the Peak in Hong Kong with her seven siblings. One of them, my uncle David, apparently pushed her out the door on the way up as they were grinding slowly in second gear. She sat by the side of the road waiting for them to come back for her. They didn't for several hours. When they got home and realized that she wasn't in the car, my grandfather retraced the trip and found her sitting by the roadside. That feeling that she had been abandoned and that no one cared for her or even noticed she was gone remained vivid for the rest of her life. This feeling of being unloved was something she managed to communicate to me emotionally more than almost anything else that she felt. The fact that she loved her children did not seem to make up for anything on her emotional register. She certainly felt that she was not loved by her husband. From the earliest age she would admonish me, "Marry the man who loves you; don't marry the man you love."

To my observant child's eye, we didn't know many couples who exhibited any love for each other. I didn't think any of their friends—Jean and Stewart, Ron and Iris—loved each other in the way that she was trying to indicate to me. Everything my mother said about emotions was tinged with unexpressed passion. Perhaps that is why she felt that she could take an overdose of pills, substituting a dramatic action for the absence of passion in her life.

Certainly she had all the sensitivities and sensibilities of an artist; she had a brilliant eye for colour and could create almost anything with her hands. She knitted marvellous sweaters and hats, gloves and socks for us without a pattern. She simply looked at a sweater in a magazine and made up her own instructions. It seems to me that was a paradigm for her own life. She made it up according to what she could see and used innate skills to get her through it.

When Auntie Julia, who was two years older than my mother, arrived, my life changed considerably. For the first time, I had what could be defined as normal motherly attention. I had somebody who would listen to what I said and who did not demand always that I simply do my best without complaining. It was new to me to talk to somebody who listened, blinked and said she thought that I was doing the best I could. Already, at that age, the seeds of pushing myself to do more than I could had been set, but I loved relaxing into that feeling that no matter what I did, I would still be loved. With my mother, I always felt that I was part of her obsession. She told us often about how much she had loved us when we were born and how worried she was about our health—I was born during a smallpox epidemic and therefore had a double vaccination on my thigh, which she was concerned about for aesthetic reasons. She was constantly afraid we were going to be sick or die. Whenever she read about a child having an accident or drowning (particularly drowning) in the newspaper, she said she didn't know how anyone could live if their child died. I did not know that later in my life, I would show her.

Everything with my mother was such high drama, such high stakes. Looking back on it now, I feel that I was engaged in some kind of heightened gambling situation where we played against each other with our emotions.

I always refused to take sides between my parents, even when at the height of one of their stormy disagreements in the car they would each shout back over the front seat: "Who do you agree with—me or your mother?" I would always say, "I don't agree with either of you." I would feel a kind of dull hard fist in my chest, but I knew that I had to maintain this stance at all cost. Mostly, I tried to blank out what they were saying to each other. Apart from asking me to be Solomon, they didn't ask me to intercede with each other.

When Auntie Julia was with us, none of this happened. She acted like a soothing blanket without saying very much. But she seemed to be the only person who could calm my mother down from escalating emotions.

She was soft-spoken, gentle, and yet wonderfully firm about her beliefs. She was a fervent Anglican. My mother's family had been Anglican for three generations, and she had a great-uncle who was an Anglican priest, so Auntie Julia had the background to comment on the sermon every Sunday to Reverend Burke, who gave extremely vigorous sermons, most of which I didn't understand, although I admired the energy and the conviction with which he delivered them. She invariably complimented him on his grasp of theology: "Mr. Burke, I liked the way you picked up on what the Gospel had to say today." I liked being with Auntie Julia and going to bed at night after kneeling and saying my prayers. She was such a calming influence and made me feel close to ordinary.

When the time for my dance recital came, she accompanied me to the rehearsal and to the recital itself. She insisted that I have a rest before the recital, and so I was given a small sandwich and a cup of cocoa and told that it would be good for me to lie down. This made me feel as though I were some kind of great star about to exert myself tremendously, when in fact I was only going to dance two numbers out of forty on the program. To this day, I don't know whether Auntie Julia actually approved of flamboyant dance recitals, but I knew that she would still support me because she loved me.

One of the most fascinating things about Auntie Julia, who was then a few years shy of forty, was that she was engaged to Eric. Eric was a family friend who had grown up, exotically, in New Zealand. His father had made a fortune with several grocery shops that he had run on the North Island, and that money Uncle Eric put into stamps. I believe he was one of the great stamp collectors in the Far East and that his collection was worth a fortune when he died. My parents gently made fun of the fact that Auntie Julia had the longest engagement in the world, and my mother, rather scornfully, said to me that she thought Auntie Julia would never get to the altar with "that man."

Auntie Julia had a photo of Uncle Eric on her bedside table, and he had all the allure of a caged gibbon. Once, she was writing him a letter, and I went into her room when she had gone to answer the telephone. The letter was lying there, and I read this wonderful phrase at the end: "Do not worry, my dearest, because we will float down the river of life together."

I mistakenly told the family that I had read this sentence, and the subsequent hilarity hurt Auntie Julia. For the first time, she looked at me with the deepest reproach, and tears welled in her eyes. She told me that she was sorry I had done such a thing—breaking her confidence, helping my parents make fun of her. Since I was already in trouble, I blurted: "But will you ever get married to him?" Auntie Julia turned away from me without a word and went into her room and closed the door quietly.

When my father told me that Auntie Julia was leaving us to go to Toronto to do her master's of social work, I was desolate. She was going to earn her keep by being a housemother at Moulton College, the private girls' school on Bloor Street. I wanted to go with her and thought that we would have a wonderful time with the other girls. She was the only one of my mother's sisters to go to university; I took her quietness and gentleness to be a result of education. I know that my father paid for Auntie Julia to go to the University of Toronto as a kind of reward for having come to spend a year with us. I knew she deserved it, but I was deeply unhappy. Who was I going to discuss the nuances of my friendships with? Who would answer my questions without an angry or sometimes even vitriolic response?

I never understood why my mother had these reactions and so I gave up asking her anything. Her answer was always something like, "Cut that girl off! Don't ever see Beverly again. She doesn't like you." I realized that this was not the kind of answer that was going to help me in life. And so I began to ignore any comments my mother would make about my friends or my relationships with them. Yet even though she seemed to dislike all of them, she still wanted to put on the best birthday party. She baked better cream puffs, three-layered cakes, and tea biscuits than anything at my friends' houses.

I think she was worried that I would not consider myself superior and therefore above discussing with other people our value to each other. I now realize that she was so isolated and so alone and that she had no way of dealing with what she felt or how she might feel about others. She always told me that everyone was jealous of me and taking advantage of me and, as a result, I have never been able to tell or care whether anyone was jealous of me or taking advantage of me.

I never really heard my mother's voice. I can, even to this day, drown it out with a kind of mental white noise so I can hear it but give it no value. I knew that my mother wanted me to cling to her, to follow her into her closet when there was a thunderstorm, to be sick when she was sick. I also knew that she didn't *really* want me to do these things, she only thought she did. I tried to outwit my mother, trying to figure out what it was she actually wanted, trying not to do it, and then trying to disguise that. It made for a complex emotional development.

Auntie Julia went off to the big city. She wrote me faithfully every week, and I wrote back to her. At the end of the year she got her degree and she went back to Hong Kong, and, amazingly, married Eric when she was forty-one. My mother muttered that, of course, Eric had planned all of this so that they would not have any children, as he wanted to be a baby all his life.

We continued to write to each other, Auntie Julia and I, for many years after she returned to Hong Kong. I think my mother did not write to her very frequently, but she did ask me, from time to time, how Auntie Julia was. She said to me more than once that she was the most deprived girl of her family, as her eldest sister, Beatrice, was the most beautiful young woman in Hong Kong and Auntie Julia was one of the smartest.

I ignored what she said; I thought that she was extremely beautiful and also very smart. That she hadn't gone to university didn't bother me because I knew that I would be going to university for her. I would make up for all the things that she had not had. And I knew that that is what she expected me to do.

Never once did my mother tell me that she loved me, and I never expected her to. I was not aware that other parents might say that to their children, but I also recognized her almost frightening focus on me as a form of love that I could neither reciprocate nor replicate.

My mother's obsession with our being well was actually a symptom of great unwellness. I realized that very early and struggled against it. She would let us go and visit friends just like any other mother and even stay overnight for pyjama parties. But she never wanted us to travel in our friends' parents' cars. Luckily, most people we knew didn't have cars until I was about ten, and so it didn't come up that often. I distinctly remember being allowed to go with our next-door neighbours to the dramatic falls at Hog's Back on the Rideau River when I was about nine. But it stood out in my mind as a rare occasion. Even though I seemed to have the same liberty as my girlfriends, I felt that I was circumscribed completely by a band of worry, anxiety, and anger. When my mother was worried she got angry. It made me deft at avoiding all subjects that might cause that anxiety and its angry side to emerge.

Many years later, when I was grown up and visiting Hong Kong, Auntie Julia asked me, "Is your mother still as angry as ever?" I realized that the anger my mother felt was totally unfocused; it was a stance that helped her to cope. It was not specifically aimed at me, but only at me as I represented different things in the world with which she couldn't cope. I knew that I wasn't alone in this and that most of the people she came in contact with made her feel that way. I suppose it would be fashionable now to say that she lacked self-esteem. She would have said that she esteemed herself, but that nobody else did.

My aunt and my mother showed me how different women could be. My mother never had a close female friend in her life; it wasn't because she had come to a new country and had been cut off from her roots. She simply did not have a friendly personality. She was extremely well brought up and was charming to the outside world, but she never had a friend to whom she could open her heart. She never regretted this nor mentioned it to me, but as I started to have close friends of my own I realized that she did not know what friendship meant.

All through her life, and particularly in her later years, she took part in women's church activities, which brought her into contact with a lot of women with whom she socialized. But there was some piece missing for her always, and I only learned about it well into my adulthood, when my father finally explained it.

It wasn't just that incident of being dropped out of the car and forgotten. There was something else that haunted all her feelings towards her family and therefore towards the outside world. When she was about fifteen, and all the eight children were still at home, her father did something dishonest in business, and rather than face the consequences in Hong Kong, he fled to Shanghai, leaving them all behind with virtually no resources. My Po-Po moved in with relatives, and when her eldest daughter, the most beautiful one, landed a doctor for a husband, my grandmother and the other girls moved in with them. Auntie Julia taught piano, and my mother felt that she was not able to continue in high school. The whole family— and perhaps my mother in particular—was never able to recover from the general calamity—the loss of face, the fall from society, the sudden impoverishment. The fact that my mother never mentioned this upheaval to me shows how deep and enduring the wound was.

This loss of status meant that my mother felt she could never trust anybody. Was her father some kind of criminal? Would people always point to her as she imagined they were doing when she was a child and say that she also was dishonest? Disgrace coloured my mother's life. My mother forever feared loss of status in the deepest and most primal way. She worried frantically about money. It was not that she worried about not having any; she worried about the very concept of what money represented. She found herself married to a happy-go-lucky gambler. And she came to a country where nobody knew how good her family was.

Having been alone with my mother the night she died, I can say that I felt that a resolution had happened between us, which helped me. My relationship with her was probably the most complex I will ever have in my life. Her perfectionism, her rage, her sense of the beautiful, her intense solitude were all things that I came to understand by the fact that she lived as long as she did. I think those of us who are over fifty when our parents die are very fortunate because we have been able to have a relationship with them that is like a plateau between the climbing towards them as a child and the continuation of the climb without them and their support.

The four months she spent at the hospital were filled with people coming to see her to say goodbye, and I believe that she was relieved to know that she was dying. The abandoned and unhappy person inside of her knew that death was the only escape.

My mother had always been hypercritical of me—the way I looked, the way I dressed—but she never expressed it verbally, never told me not to do something. I knew that she was happy with the person I had turned out to be, and although she never lived to see me become Governor General, which happened ten years later, I know that she does know. My friends used to go and visit her, particularly Anglican friends from her church at St. Paul's and also from my days at Trinity College. She said to one of them, "I think I'm going to die happy because my daughter became the kind of woman who goes out with people who have become archbishops." I only heard this recently, and it made me very happy that she could say that she was proud of me at all. She had always managed to make me feel that I was trying to achieve something that was never quite within my grasp. And I always wanted to succeed because failure was never an option.

GETTING READY

SHORTLY AFTER WE ARRIVED in Canada, it became clear to everyone that I should be going to school, although I was only three and a half. My mother had her hands full trying to learn to cook and keep house. Neville went to York Street Public School, and we could go together. He had already had one winter, which was one of the coldest winters on record and startled my mother into layering so much clothing on him that the principal sent him home with a note to say that he thought it was not necessary for him to wear two overcoats and two pairs of trousers.

In the meantime, my father had started to work at the Department of Trade and Commerce as a clerk in the Oils and Fats section, and he had quickly noticed that French was spoken as well as English. One day he asked me if I wanted to learn French. I answered yes with enthusiasm—although I had no idea what French was and no idea that I was speaking English. I was still speaking and understanding baby Cantonese quite well.

One day I was dressed up as though I was going to church or a birthday party, with my patent-leather shoes and little white socks that had pink edges when they turned over. My parents told me that I would be going to meet people at the convent of St. Joan of Arc, where I would learn French.

At the school, we were met by some soft-spoken nuns who had

beads and crosses hanging down the front of their robes. There was a big cross on the wall, too. I was entranced by all these crosses. Suddenly, we were getting ready to leave rather quickly. As we walked up the street I knew something was wrong. My parents told me that I would not be attending that school. And when I asked why, they said, "We have been told that you can't go there because you're not Catholic, and the French instruction here goes with being a Catholic."

I had no idea what being a Catholic was, except that several months before I had been a willing spectator at a funeral parlour around the corner. A neighbourhood boy of about my age had been run over by a truck and was lying in an open casket. From then on, I identified that open coffin with being Catholic. I had no idea what it meant in relation to the women in the black, white, and grey, or the black clicking crosses and the beautiful cross on the wall with the light hitting it, but my parents' disappointment was so palpable that I started to cry.

When we got home I was given a fuller explanation—which still didn't make any sense to me—about the French language being tied to the Catholic Church. I decided to have one of my tantrums and screamed around the kitchen about wanting to learn French and not caring about being Catholic. I didn't go so far, I'm told, as to say that I would become a Catholic, but I wanted all the rules to change so I could learn French.

My father sat down immediately and typed a letter to a friend he had made on the *Gripsholm*, Father Bill of the Maryknoll Fathers in the United States. Father Bill offered to write a letter to the Catholic school authorities in Ottawa, but said to my father, in his outspoken way, that the Church probably didn't want us non-Catholics around because they couldn't make us do what they wanted.

Later, my parents told me that if I could not learn French in Canada, I would go to Paris when I was grown up and had finished university. It was a promise that they never went back on; it was like a nightlight in the dark hallway that divided our country in those days. I suppose I convinced myself that I couldn't learn French in Canada because I aimed myself always at going to Paris. I never tried to persuade my parents to send me to Trois-Pistoles in Quebec, where many friends from high school and early university went for intensive courses. I felt I had to go to the source of French in order to be treated fairly and in order not to have to be a Catholic to do it.

One day—I must have been about four—my mother noticed that I could read the newspaper. I've come across a number of other people in my life who have told me that they didn't know a time when they couldn't read. I think it has to do with the way the brain is configured rather than with any kind of extraordinary intelligence. I knew somebody who could speak any language after hearing it for about an hour. He could take a train from Paris to Denmark and, in that time, learn a working vocabulary of Danish. No one could explain it, least of all him. I wonder how I would have been different had language not been such an imposing presence in my life. Would I have been able to understand sooner my love for and exhilaration about colours? Could I have become someone who expressed themselves only through the juxtapositions of forms and light? These are the questions I ask myself now, but when I was younger I simply took advantage of the fact that everyone considered me smarter than most people my age.

Because everyone had to begin school at kindergarten, I was packed off to York Street Public School in the middle of the school year. I remember my classroom so well, as well as the teacher, Miss Eardley. Her hairdo was identical to the hairdos of all my school-teachers, who rejoiced in their apparent virgin statehood, prim of lip with watchful eyes. Miss Eardley was gentle but seemed extremely firm.

Because I had started school midway through the year, I was not asked to participate in the class band. I sat on the sidelines the first day while the other children practised for a concert; they had little drums, tambourines, and something I had never seen before, a metal triangle that you hit with a rod to make magical sounds. I went home that day and it was the longing of my life to be able to play that triangle.

If Miss Eardley did not like what you did, you ended up sitting in the corner in a chair the shape of a black cat. This was called "pussycat corner time," and I dreaded doing something that would land me in that chair. Dread and longing; punishment and reward; the pussycat chair and the triangle. I never misbehaved to the extent of being put in the pussycat chair, and I never auditioned for the triangle. To me, the triangle has remained a symbol of something unreachable. Today, when I watch somebody in a symphony orchestra playing the triangle, I still feel that I could have played it, if only I had been asked.

I thought that I was having a good time in kindergarten but, at the same time, I didn't play with anyone and nobody sought me out. I was probably in a state of negative capability, to misuse Keats's phrase. My negative capability has made it possible for me to live through all sorts of things with a kind of suspension of feeling, and without truly understanding what it was I didn't like. This was the lesson I learned in kindergarten. But once I was in Grade 1, it was clear sailing right through public school. I had not had a chance at the triangle, so I moved on to other things.

I'M GLAD I GREW UP in Ottawa at the time when it was a city of fewer than a hundred thousand people, and when there were half a dozen public schools and four English high schools, and when everybody seemed to know everybody. What I remember best about the first day of school each September was that you lined up with your mother to register, and I always made a point of looking down the line of people about my age and picking out a couple of girls whom I thought I would like to be friends with that year. There were also girls I looked at whom I was sure I didn't want to be friends with. I can't recall on what I based my judgment. It certainly wasn't by the way they dressed, because we all dressed similarly, in utilitarian fashion, and we were mostly clean and neat. Nobody stood out for what they wore, but some people did stand out because their hair was copper red.

My mother was particularly upset by people with copper red hair because she thought it was terribly unnatural, together with freckles. The freckles I think she got used to, but the copper red hair, never. She told me that in Hong Kong there were two things she thought were particularly hideous about Europeans. The men had hair all over their arms and legs and chests; she had even once seen somebody, who was a riding friend of my father's, who had hair on his back! "Just like an ape!" she said with distaste. The other thing was red hair; it was enough to frighten small children. An old wives' tale held that if you saw something that repelled you while you were pregnant, it would be reflected in your unborn child. My mother told me calmly, and with great seriousness, that when she was pregnant she had averted her eyes from all things ugly and had made my father promise to tell her if he ever saw a red-headed person coming towards them. My father had a red-blond friend whom he rode with, and my mother avoided him assiduously during both her pregnancies.

As I went through public school, to three separate ones as we moved around Ottawa, I realized that we were all children together—we went to each other's birthday parties, we sent each other valentines on Valentine's Day. Mr. Steven, my Grade 6 teacher, appointed me the person who would write seven or eight to little Carl, who for some reason was not considered the friend of anyone.

As I was good at changing my handwriting, I did several from "Anonymous" or "Your Unknown Admirer" and therefore, I hope, made Carl happy. Mr. Steven was a gentle, soft-spoken man who had served in the air force. At Remembrance Day, together with all the other male teachers, most of whom had served in the armed forces, he always looked particularly sad.

A number of children in my Grade 7 and 8 class came from LeBreton Flats, an area where people worked in the small factories that surrounded them and which was considered such a blight that it was razed in the sixties. (The Canadian War Museum rises at the edge of where it used to be.) These kids were the ones who were examined once a month with ultraviolet rays to see if they had what we called cooties. Many of them also got ringworm and had to be humiliatingly wrapped in mustard cloth and come to school with this degrading mark of unhealthiness. The vestals of democratic education and public health always admonished us never to put our heads on the backs of movie theatre seats because we might get ringworm as well. To this day, even in the most luxurious of multiplexes, I can't bring myself to rest my head against the back of the seat for fear that I will end up wrapped in a mustard turban.

I had a horrible moment every day when half pints of milk were delivered to each classroom. Having to drink a half pint of milk at room temperature was ten times worse for me than being given cod liver oil the moment we came into class in the morning. It was my mother's proud boast to her new Canadian friends that I had not drunk milk since I was weaned at the age of two. She thought that the emphasis in Western societies on milk and cheese was revolting; the only exceptions for her were processed cheese slices and whipped cream.

Shortly after I became Governor General, somebody wrote to me to say that they could remember coming to one of my birthday parties. She said that my mother had been a stunningly beautiful creature in a silk dress and that she had followed her into the kitchen to watch her cutting the sandwiches. She told me that my mother was wearing a tiny silk handkerchief over her face like a robber's bandana and she explained to my friend that she had a bad cold and wanted to make sure that she did not infect anybody. Then she wheeled the mahogany tea trolley, which we had bought at Johnson's used furniture store, laden with egg salad sandwiches, asparagus rolls, salmon salad sandwiches, and radishes cut in rosettes, to the table where we were all waiting in our paper hats.

My mother would always make me a new dress in either taffeta or velvet for my birthday. One year my father returned from a New York business trip with two velvet dresses for me from DePinna's department store. They were beautiful, and he told me that they were the nicest ones that he could find. I knew my mother was unhappy about being upstaged, but all she said was, "Green looks so bad on her." I did not wear either dress to my birthday party. I wore the dress that my mother made with the eyelet insets at the elbows because—well, just because.

WHEN I GRADUATED from Kent Street Public School and moved on to Lisgar Collegiate, I went from one grey limestone building to another. Both of them were within walking distance of my home. Nowadays when I see the distance between Somerset Street and Elgin and Kent Street and Albert—twelve blocks I walked four times a day—I think of how life has changed for children. In the late forties, hardly any of our parents owned cars, and we all walked to and from school even when it was minus twenty-five. I still remember what it felt like to have my nose freeze to the scarf that was tied around my face and how my wrists got chapped from the wool mitts. My snowsuit was heavy and woollen. I longed to have a Red River coat with smart knitted leggings, but that was not to be. The navy blue with red piping should have appealed to my mother's considerable fashion sense, but she felt that I would catch pneumonia and die. An all-wool two-piece maroon snowsuit seemed to be my fate.

I ate at school perhaps twice a week, but my mother was convinced that I would be undernourished if I did that regularly, so I was always given the option of returning home for a hot meal— which is how I became hooked on the CBC Radio drama called *The Craigs*. From it, I learned what it was like to live on a family farm, as the noon-to-one programming was devoted to farming and farms, with ten minutes devoted to the Craigs. The day that the character Dick, the eldest son, died when the tractor rolled over him was a day of great mourning for me.

Next on the radio would be the prices of commodities, pork bellies particularly, "FOB the factory at 20 cents a pound." In all those years I never learned what FOB meant, but it seemed very mysterious and grown-up. At a quarter to one, I started my trudge back to school, no matter what the weather was like. Although my mother was obsessed with our health and our well-being, she had gotten used to the Canadian winter and did not think it was abnormal for us to trudge off to school in snow or sleet. As far as she was concerned, going to school was an enormous privilege. We were constantly reminded that if we had been in Hong Kong we would have had to pay, not only for school but for every schoolbook and all our uniforms.

At Kent Street School, Miss Jackson and Miss Dunlop had put a lot of emphasis on English grammar. We learned to parse sentences, and to this day the idea of the difference between a transitive verb and an intransitive one gives me a little shock of recognition. I learned to love language by taking it apart, analyzing it and putting it back together. We were seriously corrected on slips like "I" for "me," and we often had chanting sessions that went like this: "It is I. It is he. It is we. It is they. It is I. It is he. It is we. It is they." It was never said, but it was indicated to us that if we couldn't learn this, our whole education would be for nought and that only people who had no idea of the importance of language—the communications between human beings—would ignore this vitally important part of our education.

Later, I found delight in learning Latin because my foundation in English grammar had been so sound. I know it sounds peculiar, but learning about the things like the ablative absolute was part of an induction into a secret structure that kept the whole world in balance. I felt I was being given the key to it and I loved it.

But I also liked having fun and helping to run things. I was head girl in Grade 8, with undefined responsibilities but quite a lot of prestige. It was my duty to help newcomers find their way around the school. One of the shyest and most withdrawn of these new students was the daughter of a newly arrived Newfoundland member of Parliament, Newfoundland having just entered Confederation. This girl was as pale as a piece of paper, with a scattering of freckles and hair so curly it looked as though a comb could never go through it. I tried to be her friend, but we had nothing in common. I found her silence and wordlessness so pitiful that after Christmas I stopped dealing with her. She was the only daughter of any politician that I ever met when I was in public school, even though Kent Street School was steps away from Parliament Hill. I think in those days politicians generally didn't bring their families to Ottawa. And now when I think about the significance of her presence there, it probably meant that her family couldn't afford to have two places to live, so they had all come to Ottawa.

My Grade 8 class was divided into those of us who would go on to high school and those who wouldn't. The second group took extra classes called opportunity classes—which seemed to be training them to do more household work. In fact, when I was in Grade 10 I heard that three girls with whom I'd been in Grade 8 had already become mothers. This was so astonishing to me that I blotted it out of my mind. In any case, I knew my destiny was going to be different.

IN EVERY ORDER OF CANADA ceremony when I was Governor General, I always reminded the people who were being inducted that they, in turn, must remember those who had helped them to become what they were—a parent, a friend, or a teacher who has believed in them. As I watched a number of them struggling not to cry, I always thought of Mr. Mann and felt that I could almost see him, at the back of the turquoise ballroom with its gilt pillars, smiling and nodding his head.

Walter B. Mann was my high-school English teacher for three consecutive years, from the time I was fifteen. He loved literature and he always began class by reading a poem. He read with meaning and unselfconsciousness. He was never embarrassingly dramatic, nor did he simply sound like a dictating machine. To this day I can hear his reading of Browning's "My Last Duchess," with the little snarl at the end:

> She smiled, no doubt,
> Whene'er I passed her; but who passed without
> Much the same smile? This grew; I gave commands;
> Then all smiles stopped together. There she stands
> As if alive.

We were enthralled. Mr. Mann was very much a Browning and Tennyson person. The other poem in which he obviously found great joy was *Ulysses*, and as his voice rose and fell, all of life and its dreams were there: "To strive, to seek, to find and not to yield." He also taught us English composition, and the grammar lessons begun in Grades 7 and 8 continued strongly with him. By then, I was also taking Latin, so the structure of sentences and the way in which words could be put together in a frame became very real to me.

Mr. Mann was the perpetual candidate in Ottawa East for the CCF party that later became the NDP. He went through at least one campaign while I was in high school, although he certainly never mentioned it. I think he lost his deposit every time. We never discussed public affairs in his class, but everything that he believed in literature was obviously an outgrowth of his sensitivity to the needs of others and his fundamental sense of fairness and decency.

One day Mr. Mann spoke to me after class about entering the Rotary Club public speaking tournament. This was a well-known event at the time—all high schools competed for a cup through a series of speeches, with competitions that began in their own school. A student had to prepare a speech of up to ten minutes on any subject, and it had to be delivered without notes. This was followed by an impromptu, as it was called, in which one was given a slip of paper with a subject written on it and five minutes to prepare a speech. I was made to practise in front of the class about once every two or three weeks, and while it must have been hideously boring for them, I learned how to stand up in front of an audience and look at people. Mr. Mann told me that I must look out over the whole crowd and turn my head so that everybody felt involved in what I was saying. He also advised that it was best not to focus on just one or two people but to look just above the top of their heads in the back row. That way, everyone would think that you were looking at each of them.

After I placed second in the regional tournament, Mr. Mann and I sat in the Peacock Alley at the Château Laurier, where the event was held, and talked about it. He told me that I had done very well but he felt the judges had shown a definite bias towards the male student from another collegiate. He said, "I'm not saying you didn't win because you were a girl, but I think that if you had been a boy you would have won."

I knew what he meant, but I didn't feel resentful. Even then, I felt that that was the way it was, even though it was not the way it was going to be for me. Mr. Mann said that he thought I had been the better speaker in every possible way and that my opponent's proselytizing about Moral Rearmament was tasteless. "That group of people he's talking about," he said, "they're not interested in the creation of the kinds of democratic institutions that you and I are."

I think it was the only time he ever mentioned anything even vaguely alluding to the political. Rather, his messages about freedom, responsibility, and caring for other people came out in his analyses of poems like *Dover Beach*:

> the world, which seems
> To lie before us like a land of dreams,
> So various, so beautiful, so new,
> Hath really neither joy, nor love, nor light,
>
> Nor certitude, nor peace, nor help for pain;
> And we are here as on a darkling plain
> Swept with confused alarms of struggle and flight,
> Where ignorant armies clash by night.

The poetry of the nineteenth century spoke directly to him, and he was able to transmit that to his students. The honesty and the clarity of his life were communicated to us in every action and every poem he read with us. Many years later, when he was celebrating his eightieth birthday, I sent him a card with a tiny girl in a Victorian dress looking out towards the vast sea and simply wrote on the back of it: "This was what I was before I met you."

I hope that kids can still encounter teachers who have that true vocation, someone with deep commitment and the ability to reveal their character without self-indulgence.

Our great final battle as students before getting to university was the Grade 13 senior matriculation exams, which would determine our acceptance at our chosen universities. Besides just preparing us through the requisite plays and novels (very daringly for the Ontario authorities at the time, Hugh MacLennan's *Barometer Rising*), Mr. Mann suggested to me quietly that I might memorize all soliloquies and major exchanges in *Macbeth*, which was our designated Grade 13 play. He told me that if I did, I would have sufficient quotes to sprinkle throughout the exam and thereby convince the examiners that I knew what I was talking about. I asked him whether he thought I really would understand the play by memorizing it, and he said, "Yes, but you'll only know that after you've memorized it." His advice stood me in very good stead, and it is only very recently that those words from *Macbeth* have faded from my memory.

As an encouragement, Mr. Mann told me that *Macbeth* was Shakespeare's shortest play but a critically important one. When he introduced the play, he told us that it was not simply about somebody struggling ruthlessly for power but that it was about a man who gains the whole world and loses his soul. Interestingly enough, he was not very hard on Lady Macbeth. He read her parts to us in a blood-curdling manner but he never said anything about how ambitious she was or how much she pushed her husband around. I'll never forget his telling us that although some people thought Macbeth was a weak man, we were to judge him on his words and actions alone.

When I was in Grade 12, Mr. Mann told me about the Stratford Festival, which had just opened under a wonderful tent in southern Ontario. He shared clippings about the theatre and the plays that were going to be staged there. I started to dream about going to the festival: I wanted to sit in that big tent and hear James Mason, the English actor, portray Oedipus in *Oedipus Rex*.

I had a familiarity with that play already because I had been given a radio when I was eight or nine years old. I had told my parents that I wanted to listen to plays and music before going to bed. Going to bed was not a big occasion for tension in our household. I don't ever remember my parents saying, "It's time for bed." We simply went to bed when we felt tired. This is probably why I sleep so well to this day. On my little radio, I found the CBC *Stage* series, which played dramas for an hour on Sunday nights. On Monday mornings, I always regaled my parents with what I'd heard the night before.

One day I recounted to my mother the story of a man who as a child had been abandoned on a hillside to die, had been found and brought up by a shepherd, went to a city that was ruled by a king and killed the king and married the king's wife. I explained that he had been staked out on the hill because there had been a prophecy that he would kill his own father. And of course what happened was that his own father was actually the king, whom he later found and dispatched and then married his own mother! My mother thought that this was a great story, and I still remember the shivers I got listening to this story as it was dramatized for me.

Years later I realized that it was *Oedipus Rex* and that it is one of the central and greatest dramas in Western literature. I suppose I'm fortunate in that I was like a groundling at Epidaurus listening for the first time to this extraordinary tale and gasping with horror at the revelation and of being brought up short by the satisfyingly hideous ending of Oedipus blinding himself.

I talked to my parents about going to Stratford, but I knew it was not something that would interest them. Neither of them, as far as I knew, had ever been to live theatre since we had come to Canada. My mother liked only music, opera, and ballet; my father was benevolently indifferent, but thought it appropriate that I should be interested.

My father had a business friend in Toronto, and, miracle of miracles, I was invited by his wife, Mrs. Vanderploeg, to Toronto and to join her at Stratford for two days. This was one of the most exciting things that had happened to me yet. It was also pivotal in the rest of my life.

Margaret Vanderploeg was a lovely, intensely well-educated woman who was kindness itself. She and her husband lived in a big house on the Kingsway in Toronto, and I was put in the room of their daughter, who was at summer camp. In that room I found a pile of magazines called *The New Yorker*. I sat up that first night after dinner, reading until 4 A.M. The magazine featured wonderful cartoons but also had a tone of voice and viewpoint that introduced me to a life that was entirely different from my own, a life that I wanted to be part of. It was humorous and ironic; I loved the sense of detachment with which "Talk of the Town" told anecdotes of life in New York. It made me feel part of a larger world, to which my education could lead me. I would learn to be part of what this world signified.

The next day we drove to Stratford and saw two plays. The plays made a deep impression on me, and when the incense came up in *Oedipus* (it was played with masks and high shoes in the ancient tradition), I thought that I would expire with delight.

A whole world had been opened to me—the performance, the plays, the rich countryside near Stratford, the *New Yorker* cartoons, and then Toronto.

Mrs. Vanderploeg had gone to University College at the University of Toronto and she showed me the college buildings and where she had lived as an undergraduate. She also took me to look at Trinity College, because I had mentioned that Mr. Mann had gone there. The moment I stepped into the front hall of that stone place with its crazy towers, I realized that this was the place for me. We went across the street to St. Hilda's, which is where the women of Trinity lived, and I loved that instantly as well. I didn't know anything about architecture formally then, but I liked the double staircase and the openness of the hallway. And we were shown a little sitting room where gentlemen callers would wait for the girls they were dating.

Of course it wasn't just the neo-Gothic architecture that appealed to me. I suppose what I really liked about the whole place was its sense of structure. And as I was an Anglican and it was Anglican, I felt that we would fit each other and that I would learn a lot there.

When I announced to my parents that I intended to go to the University of Toronto, my mother had a fit. She raged around the house for two days, insisting that I must go to McGill, where my brother was studying medicine, and that nobody in the rest of the world had ever heard of the University of Toronto. She wanted to be able to say that both her children had gone to McGill. My father was more accepting. I was unswayed.

When I went back to school in the fall for my Grade 13 year, I told Mr. Mann that I had seen Trinity, and he smiled broadly and said, "I want you to go there because that is where I went and I loved it." I was now doubly satisfied: I had chosen a new path that would suit me, and I was also pleasing Mr. Mann.

When I graduated, I was the class valedictorian and was given a five-year subscription to *Reader's Digest*. I even managed to get a scholarship to the University of Toronto. I think going to Trinity College was one of the most critical decisions I ever made in my life. That I chose the advice of people who were outside my family, and had to struggle against my family's wishes, gave me a sense of independence and a confidence that I could form my own life, by making my own choices.

IT WAS TAKEN for granted in our family that both Neville and I were headed to university, he to become a doctor and I to do something else. It never occurred to us not to work to earn some money to contribute to our fees. Everyone worked in the summer to contribute to their education.

I never worked until I had graduated from high school and then spent the summer preparing for university. I had never worked at Christmastime at Birks Jewellers the way a lot of the girls did. I had never babysat, because my parents didn't want me to be responsible for other people's children. When I asked my mother once why I had not become a babysitter, she said she thought that I wouldn't be able to concentrate on it because whenever I started to read a book, I didn't hear or see anything else. She had read a news story about a teenage babysitter putting a baby in the oven by mistake, and this haunted her. She was probably right about my absent-mindedness, but babysitting might have helped me a little bit with being a mother later.

Nor did anyone ever babysit me. My parents never ever left us alone. There was no such thing as my mother dressed up to go out and kissing us goodnight before the lights were turned out, or the two of them standing there saying that they wouldn't be too late tonight. Until I was ten, they never left us alone; if they had to go somewhere they always took us with them. If they were invited for dinner, we went along, and, of course, if they had people for supper we were there too. Everything included us, and to a great extent I think I felt that our social life depended upon us: our vivacity, our attractiveness, and in Neville's case, his piano playing.

But as soon as I had finished my Grade 13 examinations, I got a job for the summer, through a friend at school, at A. J. Freiman's warehouse on York Street. (The Bay occupies the site of the store today.) The warehouse was an old factory building, and the main floor of it contained the cubicle of one Mr. Briggs, who was the theoretical manager of the department, which consisted of Mr. Ovide Prud'homme and Mlle Francine Couvrefeu.

And now me. Francine was Mr. Briggs's nominal secretary, although she couldn't type or take shorthand and was too shy to answer the telephone. She had one shoulder that was much larger than the other and a pair of very lively eyes. Her English was rudimentary, but she made an effort to speak it with me, although I preferred to work on my clumsy French. Mr. Prud'homme was in charge of a group of five repairmen for refrigerators, ovens, and other white machines, plus newfangled televisions. Television had come to Canada in 1952, just four years before, so a television set was still a mark of status and everybody was keen to get one and watch the two available channels.

I was welcomed with open arms by all of them, as I could answer the telephone, I could make my way a bit in French and certainly in English, and I was willing to test the small vacuum tubes that people who didn't want to pay for a house call brought in from their televisions to see if they needed a new one. I was also implacable towards the repairmen, who were being paid five dollars an hour for their attentions and who frequently goofed off to the men-only saloon on nearby Dalhousie Street. I was also the person who took all complaints.

I had a desk by the window and two telephones, one for incoming calls—the complaints—and the other for any other calls that I needed to make. At the age of seventeen, I felt all-powerful.

I loved the craziness of my work, and I loved going home at night and regaling my parents with stories of how I had gone to the door of the saloon, kicked it ajar with my foot and shouted, "Roly, A. J. Freiman's needs you!" They got quite used to me at the tavern, and as long as I stayed beyond the doorframe I was okay. I never wanted to test what it would be like if I went in and actually attempted to escort him out. He would grumble under his breath, undoubtedly something both unflattering about his job and sexist about me. Then he would lumber to the door and I would say to him, loudly enough for the people just around to hear, "You don't want to bring the name of A. J. Freiman into disrepute, do you, Roly? It all depends on you, you know. What will people think if the repairman doesn't turn up in time?" I can still smell his beery breath. I don't know how much the honour of Freiman's mattered to Roly; he never made any remarks about it. Once when Mr. Briggs asked me how I got Roly to return, I gave him my little speech, and he looked at me dumbfounded.

Whenever I brought one of them back in, Francine would clap, and the little aluminum tea set she had on her desk would practically jump up and down. Mr. Prud'homme, who had, I'm sure, a very adequate passive vocabulary, as he seemed to understand everything that was going on but only managed to speak about a hundred words in total all the time I ever knew him, smiled broadly and wrote out the slip that would send Roly out again.

Mr. Briggs had the air of a basset hound, and I learned later that he had been demoted from the main store to the warehouse because of "something." I never learned what that was, but when I told my father, he said, "Pinching someone's bum?" I thought it was more likely that he'd been put in a position where he had had to stop chewing gum. Gum was the enemy at Freiman's. The reason gum obsessed us was that Mr. Segal, the floor walker at the main store, boasted that he could spot a salesclerk chewing gum at thirty feet. We saw no reason to think that we wouldn't be fired on the spot if we were caught chewing gum, even at the warehouse, even on the street.

I was thrilled with my job and happy about my pay, which was $130 a month. I knew that the elevator operators, who were all francophones, were earning $98 a month, and although I realized that the disparity wasn't fair, it was certainly true that I had graduated from high school. Mr. Prud'homme told me how lucky I was that I had had an "education." He said this word to me almost every time he addressed me with an aspirated h in front of the e. He made it sound important and exotic.

Mr. Briggs told me once that he had seen me tap dancing with my brother at an Oddfellows event on Somerset Street when I was about ten years old. He said that he admired the talent I had "for step-dancing." I had never heard it referred to that way, and I didn't know then that the Canadian tradition in the countryside was indeed called step-dancing.

Dealing with the complaints made me very sure of my telephone techniques. If people started out by shouting and swearing, I would give them all the time to do that and then I would count to five after they had finished—which can seem a very long time when somebody has been shouting. Then I would say, "Well, Mr. Jones, I understand completely your feelings about this matter. And I assure you that A. J. Freiman's takes it very seriously indeed. In fact, we wouldn't want you, as our customer, to be so unhappy. We want our customers to be very happy indeed. I hope you understand that. Do you understand that? Your happiness is *our* concern."

If I got an affirmative to the question, I felt emboldened to continue with making things right. If the conversation went on at any length in French, I would pass the phone to either Mr. Prud'homme or Francine, and as their vocabulary in the one case and ability to speak to strangers in the other were limited, that would be the end of the call. However, I kept a ledger in which I noted all calls and all complaints: the refrigerator had been repaired but still made enough noise to drown out the radio, the washing machine washed but globs of soap remained in the bottom of it, the television had striped lines from time to time. This helped me to pre-empt some of the complaints. If someone began to say something was wrong with their washing machine, I would immediately ask, "Is there soap in the bottom of the machine after it's finished?" That I had somehow known the problem before they even had to say it seemed to make people feel so much better.

One day, Francine came in wearing the bright orange lipstick called Tangee. Normally she didn't wear any at all, because she lived at home with her aged parents and they didn't approve of makeup. Her mother was a member of the Church group Sodality at St. Patrick's, and Francine's father was always worried that she would become a bad woman. Lipstick was obviously the first stage down that road. But on this day, Francine announced to us all that she was engaged.

I will always remember how both Mr. Briggs and Mr. Prud'homme were so nice to Francine about her engagement, asking to see her ring with a minute sliver of something in it that, with some imagination, could be conceived of as a diamond. When I asked Francine how long she had known her fiancé, she said, "Fourteen years." I asked her why she thought they would get married now when they had waited so long. And she said, "Because it took me this long to make him promise." When I asked, "Promise what?" she said, "I want to get married but I have told him there is to be nothing physical." Mr. Briggs and Mr. Prud'homme had withdrawn quietly by this time, so I sat on the edge of her desk and said, "Really? Nothing?" And she shook her head so that her small black curls bounced and said, "He has agreed. Now we can get married." I took a big breath and asked her, "Don't you want to have children?" She looked at me with eyes wide, and the Tangee-tinted lips formed an O of horror. "I never want to have children! Do you know how many children are in my family?" I took a wild guess based on the families who lived in the countryside around McGregor Lake, where we had our cottage. "Sixteen?" She shook her head and said, "Twenty-one." She looked down at her hands. "And I am number twelve."

Occasionally, a couple of boys I knew from high school who would be going to McGill or Queen's (I seemed to be the only person going to U of T) would come by and we would take our lunch and sit in Major's Hill Park. Francine and Mr. Prud'homme would giggle and give each other telling looks. And when I returned from lunch they wanted the details of where we had sat, whether there was a tree over us, whether people had come by with dogs. They certainly participated vicariously in my life, as I did in theirs. Mr. Prud'homme had eight children and supported them on what he earned at the warehouse. His wife was a clerk at Caplan's department store, a little farther down Rideau Street. I don't know how they managed.

One day on the phone a man said, "Where's Briggs?" without any salutation, and when I indicated that he had not come back from lunch yet, he said, "This is Wildman. Tell him to call me." So I had at last met him, even if it was only on the telephone—Mr. Wildman, the general manager and the terror of the staff, who everyone said could actually go wild in front of you if he didn't like what you were doing or how you were doing it. Whenever he called after that (and Mr. Briggs took very long lunch hours), he'd ask me, "Are things tough enough for you?" And I would always reply, "When the going gets tough, the tough get going, Mr. Wildman." He would snort and hang up.

My days were always brightened when Mr. Wildman called and shouted for Mr. Briggs. I would practise my therapeutic techniques on him, saying things like, "Mr. Briggs told me that he would be back very shortly and I just know that the moment I hang up, Mr. Wildman, he'll walk in that door and he'll be calling you. Is there anything else I can do for you?" One day he said, "How long have you been working for us? Would you like to come over to the main building and do some other stuff here?" I said, "I really like it here at the warehouse, and anyway I'm going to leave at the end of August because I'm going to university." There was a long silence. "University, eh? Not good looking enough to get a husband?" And I said, "I don't know if that's the reason, but I'm certainly not getting married and I am going to university."

My parents would scream with laughter when I acted these conversations out for them over dinner. It may seem paradoxical, but even though they were so protective of their children and believed we should have the best of everything, they never worried about my going to doors of saloons and shouting for Roly or talking with Francine about her platonic marriage. I think they assumed, and quite rightly too, that by then I had made up my mind that my life would go in a completely different direction and that all of this was merely colour.

At the end of the summer, Freimans asked me if I would come back the following summer, and I said I would let them know. I really wanted to, because I enjoyed the job in a way that I had not expected to. The day I came to say goodbye to my colleagues, we all ate our sandwiches together around Mr. Briggs's desk, and he bought the Coca-Cola. They presented me with two packages of Joe Louis, which was considered the ultimate delicacy. Francine warned me, with mock admonishment, "Don't eat them all this week!" They asked me what university was going to be like, and I told them that I didn't know but I thought it was going to be really nice. I said I thought I would go dancing a lot and be able to spend time reading. Francine said, "I suppose you mean books." And I replied, "Yes." All three of them nodded, and it was as though they had spotted some zebra in their front yard—they recognized it but they didn't know what it was doing there.

Roly gave me a keychain with a small replica of a Kik-Cola bottle on it "because you're never going to drink anything else, are you?" Mr. Wildman called me one last time to see if I would like to have a permanent job with them instead of wasting my time going off to a city like Toronto. He said I could come and work at the main store and perhaps even be his secretary, if I would learn to type.

The next summer I took an examination as soon as I came home from university and was accepted by the Dominion Bureau of Statistics, as it was then known, to be a clerk at their offices at

Tunney's Pasture, in the west end of Ottawa. There followed three hideous and boring summers at the Bureau that were lightened only by some of the people who worked there, like Raymonde, who modelled herself on Kim Novak except that she rather overdid the pink-mauve rinse, and Mr. Bégin, who was just about to retire after having spent forty years pegging numbers for agricultural statistics. That is what I did, and I cleared an area of expertise for myself, which was the questionnaires demanding of farmers that they tell us how many acres they had under cultivation and how many in fallow.

The questionnaire was always sent out with a letter stating that no information would in any way be given to the Department of Revenue and was totally confidential. The replies I most enjoyed were the ones where the farmer scribbled across the top "None of your business" or "Over my dead body."

There was no air conditioning in the Tunney's Pasture building, so in the heat of the summer we always waited for the office nurse to come in to the large room where forty of us worked. She would look at the thermometer and if it was over ninety we were all released for the day, or even if it wasn't over ninety but someone fainted we were all sent home for the day. Raymonde of the pink platinum hair was an expert at fainting. Pale as the inside of an egg under any circumstances, she became almost negative white when she fainted. I always wondered if she had put wet blotters in her shoes the way we had been told at school you could do in order to faint and be sent home. Many a day we were very happy for Raymonde's fainting spell because then we were out by two instead of four.

I came to realize that this is what most people thought work was and how they spent their life doing it. I said to my mother—who had never worked and often wistfully said she wished she had so that at least she'd have her own paycheque to put in her own bank account—that I hoped she would never know the infinite boredom and the dulling sense of routine that comes over people in such a situation. Actually, I don't think she had any concept of it whatsoever and, no matter what I told her, I don't think she really believed me. I was earning more money than I had the last summer and would be able to pay my own tuition, which I was very proud of. Not that my parents would not have paid it, but I was happy to be able to contribute at least that amount to my education. Because my education was going to lead me beyond jobs like the ones I had had. My education was going to open every single door that presented itself.

WHEN I THINK of my four years doing an honours degree in English at Trinity College, I think of parties and of wallowing in books. I think of the close relationships I had with teachers like Arthur Barker, Milton Wilson, and Gordon Roper. They were committed to a deeply humanistic education embodied then by a remarkable honours program. Dismantled by the university after 1968 as being elitist, the honours program had a coherence, linking literature, language, philosophy, and history. Religious Knowledge was a prescribed course that was delightfully quirky—we studied the lesser Old Testament prophets like Amos, and the early Christian heresies—Pelagian, Aryan, and Monophysite. Maybe it wasn't relevant, but it was wonderfully bizarre.

But a good social life was also important to the girls of St. Hilda's College. In the first two years I had a fabulous roommate who conducted a series of flamboyant and dramatic love affairs. Meanwhile, I simply went out with almost everybody who asked me. There were a lot of places to go to—the Buttery, which was the coffee shop at Trinity, or for special occasions somebody might invite you to Diana Sweets on Bloor Street and you could have profiteroles, to me the ultimate in sophisticated desserts.

Our dances were fixed in the calendar, with a fall dance called the SJS, standing for Sophomores, Juniors, Seniors, to which we invited the men, and the big ball, which meant long dresses and white tie, called the Conversat, short for Conversazione. Your social life was in a total ruin if you didn't get an invitation to the Conversat. I went every year except one, when I was invited very early by somebody I didn't want to go with but whose feelings I didn't want to hurt, and so I said I was going to be going home that weekend for a family occasion. Subsequently, I was invited by two absolutely desirable persons and had to give the same excuse. You can't have everything in life, and I had a lot then, but I still remember it!

Most of all, Trinity deepened my attachment to the Anglican tradition. I joined the choir, which was a group of about fourteen people, none of whom had wonderful voices, but all of us together seemed to make quite nice music. On Wednesdays, we always sang evensong at 5 P.M., and singing a Tallis motet was a kind of participation in perfection, which our inspiring organist choirmaster, Mr. Sidgewick, said was our privilege, our chance to fill the space of the Gothic arches that were created for that very sound.

I discovered a different kind of liturgy, one still based on the Book of Common Prayer but somehow a little heightened in its sensibility. There was also a service at 10:30 at night called compline, a service that is part of the monastic life, to which I often went after studying in the library and before going back to St. Hilda's. I slowly came to realize that the tradition I had been brought up in was what was known as Low Anglicanism, and that Trinity was Medium to High. For really High, I went to discover St. Thomas's Huron Street and St. Mary Magdalene, where the great organist Healey Willan had been ensconced for decades and was still composing motets and masses for the choir there. For the first time, I saw the use and smelled the perfume of incense. I saw when people crossed themselves, and I realized that there was such a thing as personal confession being offered.

The church was a great part of our social life when I was growing up. Until she died, my mother was always a member of the women's auxiliary, participating in activities that brought her together socially with people whom she liked and respected, and with whom she shared basic values. Everybody was always very fond of her, as I was told many times after her death. But, as there was always something withheld in her, I'm sure that people who wanted to be friendlier felt as though they must keep their distance. I don't remember discussing any doctrinal questions with my mother—we never discussed the virgin birth or the resurrection. I suppose she felt that we would get enough through sermons and Sunday school, and that we were involved not intellectually but simply faithfully.

For our family, who had come as strangers to Canada, the church provided a solid and comforting base. It never occurred to me not to believe in God. I've always found that it's more likely that I don't believe I exist, but I've never believed that God didn't.

I used to say my prayers every night, kneeling by my bed, first with my mother or Auntie Julia and then by myself. I don't know when I stopped saying "Now I lay me down to sleep" and replaced it with "Our Father," but I know that from a very early age I used to pray that I might have an interesting life. I don't know where I got that idea. St. Theresa of Avila said, "More tears are shed over answered prayers than unanswered ones." I don't know about that, but I certainly found my prayer answered.

When I came to designing my coat of arms as Governor General, I took as a motto the phrase *Verum Solum Dicatur, Verum Solum Accipiatur*, which is from the collect for the Nativity of John the Baptist: "May only the truth be spoken, may only the truth be heard." I wanted to state, along with those words from the Book of Common Prayer, that I was an Anglican, and, to that end I had the cross and white disc taken from the badge granted to the Anglican Church of Canada in 1995 put around the necks of the tigers who are the supports of my arms. I wanted that Anglican motif to be complemented by the phoenix rising from the ashes, symbolizing my family rising from destruction and loss, and the supporters on the arms were tigers, which is my sign in Chinese astrology. In this way, the arms really represent the total person that I am, that I have become.

WHEN I WAS GOING to university, I had no idea what I would do next except that it could not be an ordinary job. All during my last year at St. Hilda's, my mother would send clippings from newspapers and magazines telling me about the responsible/independent/interesting life of a librarian. Whenever I went home for weekends, we never talked about what I would be doing next, and so I put off the whole thing by asking my father if I could just quickly go on to do an M.A. in literature. Like most immigrants, my parents thought very highly of education, and I knew I would be appealing to their greatest instincts about my being able to do better than they had when they were my age.

There were, and still are, generations of parents who wanted their children to succeed more than they had been able to do in their lives. Perhaps this is one of the energies of an immigrant population that had accepted sacrifices when they changed countries and knew that part of that sacrifice was their own dreams. The hope would lie in their children, their children's abilities, their children's wish to realize the emotional, spiritual, and intellectual energy that had been invested in them. In this way, I think those of us who are children of immigrants and who were the first in their families to go to university are children of unspoken promises and are obligated to succeed.

After getting my M.A., I finally went to France (more about that later) and when I returned, I continued with graduate work in English literature because I still didn't know what to do with the rest of my life. By then I had married my first husband, Stephen Clarkson, and had some freedom to make choices. So I drifted into doing more courses towards getting a Ph.D., because I loved reading so much, even though I knew that I was not suited to academic life. There was nothing wrong with my abilities to analyze literature, but I felt that I shouldn't do anything that somebody else could do just as well or better.

This judgment has guided all my decisions about my working life, from the moment I left graduate school, through my television career, my work for the Ontario government, as Governor General, and now, in the work I'm beginning as the founder of the Institute of Canadian Citizenship. I always ask myself, "Is this what I can do to contribute, to make a difference?" Of course you don't do it all alone, and I never have done anything in my life and my career that was totally and utterly dependent on me, except for writing. Otherwise, I have always worked in groups, sometimes small, sometimes large, but always with a nucleus of people interested in the same things that I was, heading towards the same goal, looking in the same direction.

The final blow to any academic aspirations I might have had came when I was lecturing in one of the first courses ever offered by Victoria College in comparative literature. On the surface this was an appealing course to teach, particularly as my last two years had been spent lecturing on Tennyson and Browning in the rather Romanesque terror of the Methodist chapel at Victoria College to at least two hundred third-year general B.A. students. I was scarcely two years older than they were, but I had some enthusiasm for the nineteenth century and I hoped that I could at least communicate that. What bothered me was that the students sat there like lumps. I never knew if I'd really gotten across what Tennyson was hoping to achieve in the *Idylls of the King* or what Browning was getting at in "A Toccata at Galuppi's." Whether the idea of Anglo-Saxon myth or the veiled Italianate longings for perfection were even transmittable to these late adolescents was something I didn't allow myself to think about too much.

So the opportunity the next year to teach a course aimed at science students headed for medicine, and which would include Beckett, Ibsen, and Günter Grass, filled me with a kind of delight. I was hopeful that I would be able to generate some enthusiasm for this course, and therefore perhaps settle my future.

Every week for an hour I lectured on one particular work in translation. When I look back on it I wonder how on earth I had the nerve to talk about *Waiting for Godot*, probably one of the greatest plays ever written, when I had absolutely no life experience to transmit. How naive and simplistic I was! But, on the other hand, I was trying to intellectually stimulate people who would someday be listening to people's hearts with stethoscopes and staring into their ears trying to make some assessment about their inflamed Eustachian tubes. One did not go to the University of Toronto and follow a literature, history, or philosophy course without emerging with a cultural mission.

The mission could be summed up in this way: if people were exposed to the best that was known and thought in the world, to paraphrase Matthew Arnold, then they would be better and more knowledgeable people. There is a kind of pathetic longing in this basically nonsensical thought that nevertheless impelled me for many years and, probably to a great extent, still does, even though, as George Steiner so forcefully points out in one of his trenchant essays, guards at Auschwitz put on Beethoven when they went home at night. Nobody ever said that just because you were wrong, you wouldn't still hang on to your beliefs. And my belief always was that if you were exposed to the good, the beautiful, and the true, you would inevitably become better, shine forth, and at least understand, if not tell, what the authentic was.

One day, I came into the lecture room and I felt a sudden and perverse reaction. I looked to the back row and picked out one student and said, "Mr. X, could you please tell me what Ibsen is writing about in *The Wild Duck*." I felt a kind of revulsion mixed with recognizable sadism (recognizable because I had experienced it from teachers of my own, especially in philosophy). I chose that particular student because he seemed to me likely to have read it and least likely to have volunteered any knowledge of it. He replied, "It's the story of a family that don't get on and there's one of them that really doesn't get on with the others and there's a little girl and they have this wild duck and when things get really bad one day they shoot the duck."

I turned and looked out the leaded-glass window at the bare branches of the maple trees on Queen's Park Circle. I decided then and there that I had to stop teaching, if not by running out of the room screaming at that very instant, at least as soon as I could decently leave. If I stayed, these reactions would ruin my own pleasure in the things that added grace and joy to my life.

Twenty years later, I ran into that same student: he'd become a United Church minister in Northern Ontario.

PARIS

MY FIRST SPRING IN PARIS—it was 1962 and I had just received my M.A. from the University of Toronto—was so luminous and beautiful that it used to make me breathless. I'd watched movies like *An American in Paris* and *Funny Face*, where Fred Astaire and Audrey Hepburn danced on lawns dotted with daisies at Chantilly and down the stone pavements on the banks of the Seine, but I was unprepared for the sheer physical beauty of the place. Chestnut trees, with their lanterns of blossoms, white and pink in the spring and golden-leaved in the fall, lined the streets. The city had a harmonious uniformity and tangible integrity; the buildings at that time rarely exceeded six storeys. When the appalling Montparnasse Tower was built in the seventies, it was a deliberate affront to centuries of city planning. Luckily, the later additions, such as the Paris Opera and the luminous pyramid at the Louvre, and the refurbishment of the Champs-Élysées have only added to the sophisticated urbanization that Baron Haussmann began in the 1870s. Yes, he did destroy nearly all the city's medieval buildings, but in return he constructed wide avenues of stone buildings, which make for elegant housing and are built in proportion to the width of the roads. The human scale of this wonderful city proves that it is possible to have grandeur, beauty, and opulence without gigantism.

I used to always carry a book called *Dictionnaire historique des rues de Paris*, by Hillairet, which told you what happened on those streets and in those buildings. I learned where Mme Récamier was visited by Chateaubriand, and where Balzac spent his last sou. It brought the streets, the history, the literature together for me in the city where everything had happened.

Still, the Paris of that time was hardly the City of Light. The buildings were dark, sometimes almost black, with grime. The great French writer André Malraux had become de Gaulle's minister of culture and was just beginning to apply a new law that required buildings to be cleaned regularly. So the Paris I saw at the beginning of de Gaulle's presidency was not a bright, shining place. Its streets were sombre, and the skies were dark in winter because Paris is so much farther north than Toronto. My first November in the city seemed all electrically lit; there simply didn't seem to be any sunlight after September.

I'd come to Paris to learn French, of course. But I longed for things Parisian, beyond the obvious attractions of food, wine, and fashion. To me, France was the remote, classical, dark place full of mystery, with the bright spots being what I could read and understand. And at that time, that was mostly limited to the standard works of French literature that I had read at university—Molière, Marivaux, Racine, Corneille—and a couple of French movies and a TV series that the CBC had imported and dubbed. One was a police drama called *Paris Precinct*, which starred Louis Jourdan and Claude Dauphin. It was about two cops working in a grubby, ill-lit, post-war Paris who rushed around in a squad car solving crimes—usually of passion—and whose humour and demeanour towards each other was adult, ironic, and worldly. It would take decades for American television to catch up.

But I wasn't going to France to watch TV: I was determined to be serious about how I learned French. I found what I thought would be the perfect course at the École supérieure pour le perfectionnement et la préparation des professeurs de la langue française à l'étranger, known as the ÉSPPFÉ. It was a course for people who lived in the little green spots—the former French colonies—on the globe; meanwhile, I had been brought up in one little and one large pink one. The pink Commonwealth stretched all over the world, and we had been taught, ever since I was a child, that the people who were lucky enough to be pink had democracy, a royal family, and a moral regard for decency and fairness, which nobody else of any other colour on the map possessed.

Now I was determined to enter the world of the green spots, which in the early sixties were still very much tied to France. Algeria had just declared its independence, destroying the long tradition and, perhaps, delusion that it was part of continental France, even though it was across the Mediterranean. I was to meet people in the next year who would say to me that the independence of Algeria was just as shocking as if Alsace-Lorraine had separated. There were people, not always right wing, who would explain that Algeria was a part of France, a part of the sacred Hexagon. This praise of the sacred Hexagon was something I never truly understood because, looking at a map of France, I could not make out six sides. Then I realized that the six sides were actually in the minds of the people looking at it, that their concept of France lay in their faith in where the boundaries were.

I lived at the Maison des étudiants canadiens and roomed with a nice woman from Rimouski. There were only a handful of anglophones, so we spoke French all the time. Hubert Reid, André Dufour, and Roch Carrier were all there at the same time. They later made their mark in law, government, and literature in Quebec, but none of us knew what the future held then. All of it was promise, and we were in Paris.

I was told that prospective students had to take an entry exam and we would be allowed to do so only if we came from a franco-

phone country. Luckily for me, Canada was considered a francophone country, so I got past the first hurdle. The next one was to
get myself admitted to the course, which meant a written exam
and only a short oral one. I was able to read and translate everything
that was put in front of me. For the oral exam, I sprinkled my tiny
sentences with references to Gide and Baudelaire and smiled
mechanically. I slipped through to the next stage, which was to read
into a microphone. One of my greatest moments of educational
triumph happened when the person who was listening to me
pronounce various words (I had not mastered the rolled French *r*
yet) came out from the booth and said, "Vous avez très bien fait
votre exercice, mademoiselle. Et vous n'avez plus la trace d'un
accent vietnamien."

I was thrilled to think that I didn't have a Vietnamese accent, and
that this in a way was what got me through the exam. I suppose the
French felt particularly benevolent towards the South Vietnamese,
who came to Paris at the time of General Diem and Madame Nhu;
they were the bulwarks against the Communists, who had wrought
the disastrous victory of Dien Bien Phu, thereby bringing down the
eastern part of the French empire and eventually causing the loss of
Algeria. I realized that I could perhaps get a bit of traction by being
Vietnamese in my classes, but these hopes were dashed when the
instructor went on to say, "Vous êtes très grande pour être vietnamienne, non?" I realized that I couldn't fake my way in that fashion.
(Many years later, when I was covering René Lévesque's visit to
Paris in the seventies, I rushed to the front of the press horde and
heard behind me a French journalist say, "Zut alors. Chaque fois que
j'essaie de prendre cette photo, il y a cette énorme vietnamienne qui
me bloque.")

Too big to be Vietnamese, I had to soldier on. The very first
morning of our first lecture on the rue des Bernardins, I walked into
an amphitheatre that held about 250 of my fellow students—people

who came from the likes of Madagascar, Laos, Cambodia, the Ivory Coast, and Senegal—lit by three single hundred-watt bulbs that hung down on wires. The professor came in, opened his lecture notes and told us that we were at the beginning of a great adventure, that we were exceptionally privileged to be at the centre of world civilization. France was the light of the West and the logical inheritor of Greek and Roman ideals; in Paris, all the great intellectuals' thoughts and ideas were processed. We would become part of this tradition, even though we came from small countries that could only aspire to the greatness of French civilization. However, we would be sent out with the flame of the French message to our unlit little green corners. In all my years of growing up in the pink spots (and I grew up in an imperial time when old loyalties were never questioned), no one had ever said to me that we, the English speakers, were the light of the West. In England, I have no doubt, it was simply assumed, but never openly stated, that everything English was superior. That pretty well sums up the rival British and French cultures—one with its disguised assumptions and the other with articulated declarations.

I had no difficulties learning how to speak French, but I did have a concern about the difference between *vous* and *tu*. As students, we all "tutoyed" each other and we were told always to "vouvoyer" our professors and almost everybody else, except our immediate families. It became quite a big moment when people you had known and perhaps were a little older than you, more remote, would say, "Tutoyons."

That ability to break through that first frontier, of beginning to have a kind of intimacy, still reverberates with me. I personally prefer always to "vouvoie" people, not from a sense of social superiority or from the idea of a power structure but because it seems to give breathing space between people. To me, these nuances in French make the language particularly intellectually challenging. I later learned to instantly "tutoie" Quebec camera crews and anyone from the same métier, because show business is show business and using *vous* would have seemed snobbish. Learning French helped me to understand distinctions of relationships between human beings, that language is not simply about the rudimentary elements of daily life but, particularly in speech, a delicate instrument denoting social and emotional context. I'm sorry we've lost *thou* and *thee* in English.

Canada's official bilingualism policy has meant that we all have access to the two languages. Unfortunately, one of the big problems is that some people feel that they are French speakers once they have completed a government language course. They never learn the proper cadences or sentence construction. They don't read the literature, which language is created to express; nor do children in French immersion programs. That's because they think that speaking a language is like transposing numbers for words. That is not what language is about. Language is about communicating the essence of civilization, and the French idea of civilization, as I learned so early, is very different from the Anglo-Saxon one.

The big barrier to my being able to really burst into the home stretch in French was the pronunciation of *r*. Our professors asserted that no English person could ever do the proper *r*, which was pronounced from the back of the palate and not from the front, like the Italian and the Spanish. In fact, one instructor told us that all native English speakers seemed to have eggshells for lips, as though they were frightened of breaking them. He demonstrated, with an alarming explosion of his epiglottal apparatus, the way in which French differed from our swallowed consonants. I despaired about this and used to walk around reading aloud signs with *r* in them, like "restaurant" and "cordonnier." Then one day, near the Louvre, I looked up and saw the rue du Louvre sign and suddenly, as I said "rue" out loud, I realized that I had mastered the *r*.

The reason I was able to learn French so quickly was that I had done a huge amount of reading through university. I had all the cultural coordinates, from Rabelais to Chateaubriand through Balzac and Victor Hugo. All I had to do was bring that passive vocabulary to the fore and I became quite a respectable French speaker.

AFTER LEARNING that Paris was the centre of civilization, it was quite wonderful, then, to stay on and learn how to live in Paris. By then, I had married Stephen Clarkson, who had finished his Rhodes scholarship at Oxford and was studying at Sciences Politiques, the celebrated nursery of political thought. In Paris in the early sixties, it was still possible to have a good time on a modest amount of money. You could go to a one-star restaurant and not feel that it was costing a month's salary.

One had to be equipped to shop properly. Packaging was almost unheard of. You had to buy egg holders at the droguerie (a cross between a hardware and a general store), which held two eggs, four eggs, or six eggs. Vegetables were wrapped up in newspapers, and you brought your own net bag to put everything in. Those net bags—ficelles—were the mark of somebody who was taking care of her household and her home. The stores were open from early morning until twelve thirty or one and then reopened at three thirty or four and stayed open till eight. Paris never seemed grim in November or December because the stores stayed open so late.

Where I first did my shopping, on the rue de Sèvres, I had a wonderful butcher who insisted on trimming each piece of meat of every scrap of membrane and as much of the fat as he thought would not add to the flavour. M. Dupré showed me how he tied his apron in a way that indicated that he was a master butcher, and he explained to me over the cutting of two hundred-gram steaks how the apprenticeship system worked for butchers. His wife handled the cash and stared out from a mask of orange foundation that sometimes settled into the corners of her nose. Mme Dupré probably wasn't much older than thirty, but her manner made it seem as if she had been around since the French Revolution, knitting along-side Mme Lafarge in the Place de la Concorde. There was some-thing eternal about people like the Duprés; I felt that they had had these conversations, every day, every hour, for years.

Often when I first went to the butcher's, I felt that I was holding everybody up by having these conversations. Then I realized that that was a large part of the value of shopping every day—the social contact. People shopped every single day, or even twice a day, not just because they didn't have a refrigerator but because that was what was expected. The commerçants considered you a regular customer even if you bought only a small amount each day.

Another of my favourites was the Maison de Fromage, at the corner of rue de Sèvres and the rue Vaneau. The store opened out onto the street, and white-jacketed women sold scoops of various thicknesses of fresh cream and carved off pieces of butter from a huge mountain, or "motte." These were sculpted to look like inverted bushel baskets, and it was hard not to imagine those women carving Rodin's *Kiss* out of that lovely material.

I learned about what quality was in those markets. Our best local vegetable store—we had two—sold three kinds of green beans, and the most expensive was twice the cost of the least expensive. But looking at them, you could immediately tell why. The ordinary, cheapest ones had smaller and bigger beans mixed together; the second category had beans all the same size but they were large; and the third—the finest—were thin, tender, and perfect. The French would pay premium prices for good food.

A friend told me that the French spent nearly a third of their income on food. And that did not mean in restaurants, because they mostly cooked and ate at home. (The exception was coffee: it was still treated as a great extravagance, and you went to cafés to drink it, if you had money.) The menus in a French home always intrigued me. In France, there were rules and customs. Breakfast was negligible—hot chocolate or coffee and a large piece of baguette. (Croissants were for special days or eating in cafés.) Lunch was your main, three-course meal. Soup was for dinnertime only, and the evening meal was always the lightest. Lots and lots of bread accompanied all the meals. There was then a law in France—I don't know if it still exists—that said each French person had the right to a certain quantity of bread every day. Therefore, bread was a subsidized commodity, to make sure that everyone had enough. The French never thought bread made you fat and, in fact, they were the thinnest people I had ever seen.

There was a distinct feeling in France that food was about ritual as well as nourishment. Making the really wonderful old dishes like coq au vin, or roasted veal stuffed with pistachios, or poule au pot (boiled chicken with leeks, carrots, and potatoes) was an unchangeable rite, one that not only comforted people but was an expression of the national character. Learning to make a hollandaise sauce or a beurre blanc required skill but also a recognition that a certain standard had to be met. All French people believed that nobody ate as well as they did and that no food ever produced in the world was better than their own. Of wine, of course, nothing needs to be said. They had virtually invented it.

Once a week, a farmers' market would be held in some nearby large avenue. Mine was on the Avenue de Breteuil, where the Eiffel Tower loomed over you. There, the excitement was great, because you didn't know what kind of cheese might turn up or what kind of new cooked creation. The tradition of the markets was part of the order of domestic society. They were not in competition with the stores; they were simply a part of the commercial life. They offered choice, variety, and a sense of freedom. Almost all the produce, both in the markets and in the shops, was local or came from the French colonies, places like Senegal, the Ivory Coast, or Cameroon. The latter was the source of the finest green beans. This, I'm sure, was what my professor's idea of the civilized influence of the French culture meant: perfect green beans growing in a field somewhere in West Africa, destined for the markets of Paris.

WHEN I WAS FIRST LEARNING French, one of the instructors suggested that, as foreigners, we should pick a French person we admired and mimic them; if you threw yourself into this character, you would be able to act and speak French more convincingly. A little while later, I did know such a person, Mme Antoinette Vincens de Bonstetten, after whom I would try to model myself, and who deeply affected my life.

She wasn't a professor or a great expert in anything; I didn't even search her out. She was a gift to me at a time when I needed a woman with a completely different background from mine. My mother raised feelings in me of admiration, apprehension, and longing; Antoinette was a polar opposite. Until I met Antoinette, I had not met a woman who gave me the sense of having known what it was to have experienced great loss and to accept it.

I had just been married, and my husband and I needed to find an apartment. I was given Antoinette's name by somebody who described her as a wonderful woman who had divided her flat off the rue de Sèvres into two in order to have someone living nearby who would help her to keep up her English. At that time, the rue de Sèvres was filled with boutiques selling religious objects— candles, crucifixes, holy water, and, of course, rosaries. There was even a shop specializing in nuns' underwear, discreetly telegraphed by small beige woollen vests. The street had a mysterious feeling; it made me remember when, as a child, I had been taken to see the boy in his coffin.

That first time coming up through the old streets, which probably had not changed since the Commune in 1870, towards a settled bourgeois district like the 7th Arrondissement, made me understand the levels of a city like Paris—the intellectual world of the 5th and the 6th gradually filtering into the solid middle-class of the 7th. In the early sixties, it was still possible to discern those subtleties in Paris. Nowadays, it has changed unrecognizably.

I turned down into the rue Rousselet, a narrow street, which on the right had a store in which a man was retinning the insides of copper pots. Farther on, a book binder with exquisite paisley-like paper (at this time most books in France were still published with the expectation that the buyers would have them bound for themselves). Across the street was a tiny hotel with the unambiguous name Hotel and a large key hanging outside. (Antoinette told me some weeks later, when I thought of reserving rooms for Canadian friends coming from London, that it was a maison de passe, where you could rent rooms only by the hour.) Along the left began a two-and-a-half-metre-high wall, with the tops of trees just visible, belonging to a hospital run by a religious order. On the right, across from this garden, was 19, rue Rousselet. I walked up the two flights of stairs and knocked on the door. It was opened by a woman who had a face of distinction and character. Her slight smile of irony was unlike any other greeting I had ever had from an older person. She stood there looking at me as I prepared to introduce myself and said: "J'ai toujours rêvé d'avoir une orientale dans mon appartement!" I had never been welcomed in such a way, before or since. To be the much-longed-for Oriental who was to share her apartment seemed to me both hilarious and touching.

I was shown the tiny apartment with the bathtub in the kitchen. At least there was a bathtub; many of my friends lived in apartments that shared one tap on the fifth floor with four or five other roomers. The minute living room and bedroom gave out on a small courtyard hung with vines in which birds gathered in the morning and at nightfall. Then Mme Vincens showed me into her sitting room, which overlooked the garden of the hospital where, she said with irony, "General de Gaulle had his prostate operated on last year." She always referred to him as General de Gaulle rather than the president, and I was to learn why later.

We chatted over tea for me and instant coffee for her. She had several round tables with huge plants on them taking in the southern sunlight. She announced to me that this was now the only garden she was left with since she had sold her house at St. Germain-en-Laye. I learned that she was Swiss and that her ancestors, the Bonstettens, had founded the Canton of Vaud on Lake Geneva. She had been brought up as a French-speaking Swiss but, of course, spoke German as well. For someone so unadorned—she wore a dark brown sweater set and a tweed skirt with sensible shoes—she exuded aristocracy. She was the absolute opposite of the bejewelled and painted viscountesses of the fashion magazines, and was more beautiful than any of them.

While the evening darkened I told her as much about my life as I knew at the age of twenty-four. She asked good questions and then she told me that she had lived in the thirties in what was now Vietnam, but then was Indochina, in Hanoi, and that she had travelled a good deal in Laos and Cambodia. She brought out one album (I was later to see many of these albums), and I was plunged instantly into the French colonial world of before the Second World War. She pointed out her husband, Jacques, a forceful-looking, handsome man with a black moustache. She said casually, "He was one of the youngest directors of the Bank of Indochina and he flew himself out to Hanoi in his own Piper Cub in 1932. It took him six weeks." There was a picture of her playing the cello in a trio. "It was what kept my interest in the arts alive," she explained.

She felt passionately about Indochina, but didn't subscribe to the usual French view that it had been something they had lost. She knew it well from her decade of living there, and did not regard it as part of a remote empire. For her, it was a place and a time she had loved and where she had found the only contentment she had known in her life.

Somehow she gave me the feeling that she knew things others did not, but that she wasn't anxious to be discovered. She was straightforward, a revelation of what an intelligent European woman was really like. She was never hesitant about discussing any subjects, including sex and politics. About politics, she informed me that she had so disliked the way in which de Gaulle had taken power in '58, taking advantage of the Algerian crisis, as she put it, that she always voted Communist.

She had married late. She told me that she had already been having an affair with Jacques Vincens, but knew she was not his only paramour. One day, as he was driving her back to her home, just as they went around the Rond-Point of the Champs-Élysées, he pulled a gold bracelet out of his vest pocket and gave it to her, saying, "I want you to have this. And I want you to know that there are several others to whom I've given one of these." She accepted that by accepting the bracelet. She admired him, as he was adventurous, brilliant, and, like her, a Protestant. He was from the Vendée, in the western region of France, known always as the place where the revolution had not been accepted and where counter-revolution happened.

Jacques Vincens went off to Indochina in his Piper Cub and, after about a year, he wrote to her proposing marriage. Antoinette thought it was because he had "le cafard des colonies"—a colonial funk. She considered it for some time, and decided that she would take that step because it meant a change of venue, a change of life, and a change of direction. They were married soon after she arrived and lived a life that now seems as remote as the Middle Ages. When they ate dinner on their patio in the large house the bank provided, the houseboys gave them big bags into which they stepped and which they tied around their waists to protect them from frogs or fruit bats that might want to land on them. Antoinette joined a group of amateur musicians, which gave her a different kind of life than her one as the wife of the director of the Bank of Indochina. She enjoyed it particularly because the group performed all over the colony, giving concerts in places like Hué and Phnom Penh and Vientane.

She mentioned casually to me, after I had lived with her for some time, that she had had an affair with the violinist in the group. Her husband never said a word about it, but once when they were returning from a trip, after the affair had been going on for some two or three years, she walked into the front hallway of their mansion and saw a huge silk banner and flowers going up the staircase. The banner read, "Welcome home." He then kissed her on the lips and on the brow and said, "I mean that. I *mean* welcome home." Only by this gesture was she ever made to feel that he knew about the affair, and that he did not feel that he had lost face.

When she became pregnant in her early forties for the first time, the couple decided that she had better return to France because of her age and because there were rumours of war. She sailed back to Paris and gave birth to her son before the war broke out in 1940 and France collapsed.

As soon as France surrendered, her husband rallied to de Gaulle and spent his war with the Free French, mostly in North Africa. When he finally returned to France and saw his son, who was six years old, he spent two days with them and then had a debilitating stroke and died at the age of fifty.

To Antoinette, this was simply one of those terrible things that always seemed to happen to her, things that had been predestined since her childhood. She was as old as the century, born in 1900, one of four children. When she was six, her mother ran away with another man. Because they were Protestants they were able to divorce, but she was never allowed to see her mother again. Her father kept her to be his companion, and her mother took the two boys to South America or somewhere. (Antoinette was always vague about this.) She grew up on her sizable family property, and was destined to manage the estate. She was sent to horticultural school in France. By that time she was only nineteen years old and finding it difficult to deal with a possessive father who expected her to look after him until his death.

One day, after our exchange language lessons—that was one of the conditions of living with her—she told me about falling in love with her second cousin and how she felt magically and totally transformed. Even her father approved, because her fiancé was willing to help on the family property. It was forty years later that she was telling me about him (she never spoke his name), and her eyes were filled with tears and her hands were balled into fists. The Spanish flu epidemic hit in 1918, and he died within two days of their engagement party. "I thought that my life was over and I was convinced that I would never know happiness again."

Perhaps this is what I had seen in her eyes that very first time when the door opened. Beyond the immediate eagle-like observation was a certain detachment, which I had interpreted as irony but which I now realize was a desperate need not to feel too much. I asked her if she thought her heart was broken, and she smiled slightly and said, "Of course."

She realized that she could not continue in the same way, living with her father and minding the garden. Through friends, she was introduced through correspondence to the great German poet Rainer Maria Rilke. He was dying in a sanatorium in Switzerland and was told about this young woman who was close to suicidal but who loved gardens. A wonderful compassion rose in him for her, and he developed the beautiful conceit that he was creating a garden and he needed her help with the details. They exchanged letters for over a year until he died. They never met.

Antoinette went to the beautiful rolltop desk that she kept in her bedroom and brought out a number of drawings that Rilke had sent to her. It was magical to look at the poet's own handwriting and his formal address to her, "Chère Mademoiselle." He wrote beautiful French (as a young man, he had been the sculptor Rodin's assistant) and he was obviously deeply touched by her story and by her attachment to flowers and plants. I asked her if she had copies of her own letters back to him. She looked at me with consternation and said, "I burned them when they were sent back to me after his death." I practically screamed, "Why?" She said simply, "He was the great writer. I am not. I would have been putting too much of myself into it if my side existed. He was the one who was important, not I." (Nearly fifty years later, a group of her friends finally prevailed upon her to publish these letters, which are called *Lettres autour d'un jardin* and which show the delicacy and empathy of a great German poet towards a young heartbroken woman.)

The prevailing idea that she had, that she was not important, was not from a lack of self-esteem but rather was a desire to efface herself, to take out of existence her personality and any effect she had on others, and therefore, I think, to make pain no longer exist.

It was the first time in my life that I realized that you could take yourself out of pain by systematically refusing to participate, or by leaving yourself out. This was different from denial of yourself because you were actually saying, as Antoinette did, that you existed but you didn't want anybody to know it. People have different ways of dealing with pain, and hers was the one that made the deepest impression on me. What Antoinette was doing was withdrawing herself while still staying alive. The irony is that by being so original she was bound to stay alive in the memories of the five or six people whose lives she deeply touched.

After I had been living there for a couple of months, she edged towards the topic of Canada. Nobody in France ever asked about

Canada, because for them, Canada wasn't very important; it was just a place where people spoke French with a funny accent. I told Antoinette about our family moving to the country during the war, and because of her intense interest in all things oriental, I was able to give her quite a colourful account of my family's life and mine. Casually, she asked, "Do you know artists in Canada?" I said, "Yes, I do. I like art quite a lot, so I follow it, and we have some wonderful artists in Canada." She hesitated and then she said, "We had someone who called himself a Canadian artist living here on the main floor." It was now an accountant's office and looked straight out onto the street. It was also very small, maybe eighteen square metres, with a kitchen tucked in a corner behind a folding screen. She said, "He died here about three years ago. They say he was quite famous in Canada." I said, "Oh, yes?" not hoping for very much because I knew three-quarters of the people who went to Paris thought they were artists. She said, "Yes, his name was Paul-Émile Borduas." I could not believe my ears. I explained that Borduas was considered one of our greatest artists and was responsible for *Le Refus global*—a manifesto for Quebec artists that changed the direction of Canadian painting. She said, "Do you like his work, then?" I replied, "Yes, very, very much." And she said, "Well, I have two paintings of his and I will hang one in your sitting room." And so it came about that I, as a student in Paris, lived in a room with the work of Paul-Émile Borduas.

I loved the painting, which had the typical two black squares on it and then white pushing up into it with a bit of red, and I felt that he and I were communing. I had come far from home in order to learn new things. Borduas had come far from home because there was so much to change in his society and he had to give himself time and distance to continue to be the artist that he was meant to be. Later, Antoinette showed me some of his watercolours, which he had given her for Christmas or her birthday. When I had my first child, Antoinette gave me one of them for her, and my daughter bears the second name of Antoinette.

Once a week we would spend the evening together and take turns reading, me in French and she in English. She really didn't speak it very well but she said that she would like to be able to speak it better because she had once had an English governess for five years and somehow her English had disappeared. She also wanted to know it better so that she could understand English movies. She, in turn, would correct my accent and my cadences. I read to her the memoirs of the Prince de Ligne and some Benjamin Constant, both of whom were connected in a familial way to the Bonstetten family. Antoinette was endlessly at work on research on the Prince de Ligne's social circle, which included Madame de Staël. She read to me, at my suggestion, Hemingway's short stories, and we went through *Winner Take All, In Our Time,* and *The Sun Also Rises.* Afterwards, we would have a cup of tisane and discuss, usually in French, the merits of what we had just read to each other.

When I think of conversation held by civilized people about topics of eternal importance, I think of those evenings in the room filled with bergenia plants, with a tiny coal fire going and our accented voices taking turns in telling each other stories.

Antoinette stayed in my life for the next thirty years; whenever I went to Paris I would visit her and tell her my problems, and also some of my successes. She would say, with typical deprecation, "You can't have all the success you're having without being halted at some corner or other." Or, "That doesn't seem to me to be a logical way of proceeding, but perhaps you can do that in Canada." Once I took her a fur-lined raincoat, and although we were not in the habit of giving each other gifts, I know that it pleased her because it really was warm. I knew that she lived on the pension of a man who had died working for a bank in 1945. She had seen her son become an artist with fine ideas but no success. And she had never had any grandchildren.

   The tranquility of Antoinette's room and the containment of her life are something I think about a great deal when I am particularly harassed or busy. I think of that quiet street in the heart of Paris, across from the walled garden hospital where de Gaulle had his prostate operation, and the religious order who ran the hospital would ring the bells for services three or four times a day. I think of the outside wall of the apartment on which there was illegible graffiti, and the window, which Paul-Émile Borduas used to look out, covered with a grille. I think of walking into the carriageway and buzzing the door open with a buzzer and climbing the wooden stairs covered with a worn red carpet. I think of ringing her doorbell, having the door open, and hearing those magical words: "I always dreamed of having an Oriental in my apartment."

SOMETHING HAPPENED

IN THE 1950S, all women assumed that they would get married or their life would be a failure, or that they would become a teacher. All teachers at that time were unmarried, and to me that's what signalled your decision about your life—either you married or you went to teach for forty years. Occasionally at our high school, we heard rumours that one of our teachers had had a fiancé who died in the war, and that enveloped her in an aura of romantic tragedy, which was so dramatic to us as thirteen-year-olds.

I grew up at a time when everybody assumed they would be married (or be a teacher) and they were simply looking around to see who, or what, that person would be. In my case, my search was complicated by the fact that I developed a condition known as endometriosis, which is a growth of the endometrial lining around the reproductive organs. I was twenty-two when this happened and had to be operated on, having one ovary removed completely and half of the other. I was told in no uncertain terms by the great surgeon who operated on me, and who saved my life because of my hemorrhaging after the operation, that I should get married as soon as possible and try to have children, otherwise I would be infertile.

It has to be remembered that this was some time before the widespread use of hormones, which would later help with conditions like this. Although it seems ludicrous now, I felt my time was running out. My mother was not particularly helpful, because all she wanted me to do was get married to almost anybody so that she would have grandchildren.

There were a lot of nice young men at university, and all of them had in common the fact that they had interesting families, were reasonably good looking and wanted to do fascinating things in the world—like join the foreign service, become engineers in developing countries, or study in France. Now, when I look back on it, I realize that a certain psychic desperation must have driven me to feel that if I didn't have children, I would somehow not be fulfilling my destiny. That seems odd, given that I was brought up to believe that everything I did was to affirm my individuality and to make sure that I had a role in a world that was not defined by biology. If you are not a genius, and I am certainly not one, it is difficult to escape all the constraints of your time.

I married Stephen Clarkson, whom I met at Trinity in the early sixties. He was brilliant, went to Oxford on a Rhodes scholarship, and he also wanted the French language to be a part of his life. (I do not intend to describe my first marriage, because I have an aversion to a narrative that would of necessity be one-sided.) We were unable to have children for nearly six years. My life was a whirl of biopsies, salpingograms with dye, the usual temperature taking. We felt that this was worthwhile because we did want to have children. Two years after we married, I started working in television, on *Take Thirty*, and was immediately successful at it. Life was fulfilling me in one way by the joy I had working and learning and moving far, far from the academic world.

We had promised ourselves that, if we could not conceive by the end of five years, we would adopt a child. We were on our way to doing that through a private adoption, which was much more common in those days and more informal than adoption is today.

We had five more months to wait for that baby. Three months before it was born, I discovered I was pregnant.

We wrestled with the question of whether we should go ahead and adopt the child as well as have our own. My mother wanted us to do both because, she said, an old Chinese proverb said that when you adopt a child it is the flower pot, and then your own child is the plant that grows within it—the two are inseparable. As it turned out, we did not adopt, and Kyra was born in 1969. I managed to incorporate her into my work on *Take Thirty*, as we had a weekly report on pregnancy, birth, child feeding, and so on. It was a rare blending of public and private life, and I was very happy when we were doing it.

When Kyra was a year old, I became pregnant again. The day I felt venetian blinds come across my eyes, leaving little strips of light, I knew something must be wrong. I was about four months pregnant and had recently gotten over three months of morning sickness, during which I lost twelve pounds. Although we were surprised by the second pregnancy so soon, I was not apprehensive in any way because the first one had gone so well. Kyra was born with the speed of lightning, so that I had no need of an epidural. Naturally, I thought this second one would go well, until I couldn't keep any food down, and then the little venetian blinds started. We were staying out in the country with friends, and I worried that I was about to become blind or had a detached retina.

When I returned to the city on the Monday, I realized something was dreadfully wrong when the doctor looked very grave. He said, "You are having a toxic pregnancy and your blood pressure is going through the roof. I don't know what's wrong, but this happens sometimes." I asked him if he thought that I would miscarry, but he said he didn't think so. He said, "There are reasons, of course, why some pregnancies aren't carried to term, but I don't think this is going to happen to you."

I've always wondered whether he meant I could have had an abortion, even though I was already in my sixteenth week. In any event, it never occurred to me to ask for one. Perhaps I was remembering that when my mother was expecting me she was very, very ill, and her uncle the gynecologist—my great-uncle Arthur, who was the great European-trained doctor—advised her that it would be wisest if I were removed so that she would not become sicker or develop fluid in her lungs. My parents, being young, both agreed to that, but then my beloved Po-Po intervened and said that that was absolutely not to happen. I was always grateful for that and, if you believe in prenatal apprehensions, I probably knew at some level that I could have been done away with before I had even begun. And that feeling has very much coloured my life and my position as a woman. The late sixties saw women agitating for the right to control their own bodies, which I endorsed enthusiastically. It seemed to me that every woman should have the choice of what she was going to do when she became pregnant, and nobody, certainly not the state, should tell her what she should do. But after this pregnancy, I realized that my views had focused. I came to feel, and still do, that I would never be able to have an abortion but that I do not want to tell other people whether or not they should. I feel this is a matter of conscience and a matter of being able to live with yourself and with the decisions that you have made.

During my second pregnancy, I was still working on *Take Thirty* and taking a day off at a time. The executive producer was extremely unsympathetic, like most male bosses of the time, and he never indicated in any way sympathy with my condition. I think he would have preferred me to have stayed home, as his own wife had with their three children. (She had never worked except early on in their marriage when they were both struggling to survive.) He had qualities, but sympathy for women was not one of them. He was later notorious for his response when one of the women on the show asked for a raise. He looked at her startled and said: "You seem to be well dressed and well taken care of. I'm sure your husband must earn enough money to take care of the two of you, plus what you earn." This was in the days before you could have called somebody before a tribunal for such things.

I did not quit work. I simply dealt with the splitting headaches and the flushing in my face with makeup and great concentration. I was afraid to take any pain killers because of the pregnancy and also because I disliked taking pills of any kind. Finally I was told that I would have to go to the hospital for about a week. The executive producer made me feel that I had let everybody down, and I was overcome with the feeling (remember, this was 1971) that I really shouldn't be holding down such a great job and trying to have children as well.

By this time, I was at the end of my fifth month, and I was told that I was losing so much protein in my urine that I could suffer kidney failure. I was told sternly that I would remain in hospital until I gave birth, which would probably be prematurely. So I was looking at least another six weeks, if not eight, in the hospital. Every day, religiously, before the doctor came I took a ketone test with my own dipsticks, and every day, unhappily, I was in a state of ketosis, still losing protein.

I wasn't depressed when I was in hospital with this complication. It's interesting to me now that I never thought at the time, "Maybe I'm going to have kidney failure and actually lose my kidneys." I felt that somehow things would work out, but I didn't know exactly how. One day, my doctors sent me for an x-ray so they could explore why there was so much movement and some contractions. Afterwards they stood at the end of my bed and looked gravely at me. "You're going to have twins," they said.

This was a total surprise to all concerned. They said they had not seen this in an earlier x-ray because one twin was lying over the other. I hardly had time to call my parents and husband about this before I went into labour and gave birth to Blaise, who weighed just over three pounds, and Chloe, who weighed less than two. They were rushed over to the Sick Children's Hospital and put in incubators, and I did not get to see them until the next day. I think that Chloe was one of the smallest in the premature ward in those years.

All this drama was kept within the family, and all the viewers of *Take Thirty* knew was that I had given birth to twins. Even to this day, thirty-odd years later, I meet people in the street who say, "We had twins when you did!" and I still feel a sharp flash of pain because of what later happened to Chloe. Immediately after the twins were born, I ran a high temperature. Not only had I had a toxic pregnancy but I now had, the doctor informed me in an amused way, the disease that killed most women before 1900—puerperal fever. Luckily, with antibiotics, this was cured, but the source of it was found not by the doctors but by a marvellous young nurses' aide, Miss Fulford, who said to me, "I think there's something in there that's causing you still to have the fever and I wouldn't be surprised if it was a bit of placenta." I asked her what she thought we should do about it and she said, "Do you mind if I just give your stomach a big massage?" I said, "Of course not, let's go ahead and see what happens." She massaged my lower abdomen vigorously and, lo and behold, a piece of placenta popped out. She slid it into a bowl, and when the doctor came for his call about five minutes later, she presented him with it, and he looked, I do have to say to his credit, extremely chagrined. After that, I recovered quite well and was able to go over to Sick Children's Hospital every day and then to return home with Blaise and await Chloe's arrival.

The children stayed in Sick Children's Hospital until they reached five pounds. In Blaise's case, that took about six weeks, with my going every day to spend time there and feed her. She came home and settled in calmly.

As Chloe approached five pounds, we were excited at the prospect of her being able to come home. The pediatricians warned us that there was a serious possibility of blindness or of developmental problems. I don't think I thought very much about that and was quite prepared for anything. I was just glad that she was alive.

The day that Chloe came home was a wonderful one, and we had two cribs in one room plus another baby of twenty-two months in another room. An excellent nanny had come to help. I was still feeling quite tired, and every afternoon I had a nap. That Saturday, I had done something in the morning—gone for a meeting, I believe, of Jean Vanier's branch of l'Arche at their new house in Richmond Hill. When I returned home I felt exhausted, so I lay down right away. Suddenly the nanny was at the door of my bedroom saying, "Something's happened to Chloe, you must come." I hurried to the bedroom and picked Chloe up, but she was already cool. I don't know what exactly happened then, but I think the fire department came, and the ambulance, and the next thing I knew I was by myself in the waiting room of Sick Children's Hospital. A young doctor, who probably was a pediatric resident, sat down beside me, shaking uncontrollably. She was probably younger than Blaise is now, and what she had to tell me was that Chloe was dead. I remember that I felt absolutely frozen in denial. I had a thought, looking at this sweet chubby girl beside me, whose hands were shaking, that it must be horrible for her to sit with somebody and tell them their child has died.

Chloe's funeral was at St. Thomas's Church. The rector was Edgar Bull, who had been chaplain when Stephen and I were undergraduates at Trinity. It was a great solace to have him perform that ceremony. Religion and religious beliefs are not only about ceremony and ritual, but in any traumatic event the timeless order that ritual represents can be very comforting. It is the time when we actually feel the touch of the sacred, and there is great comfort in hearing the words that for centuries have helped relieve the pain in so many people.

When the worst thing you think can happen to you happens, you realize that in a way it has indemnified you against everything. Our society never brings you up to believe that you could lose a child; yet within my circle of friends at the time, two other women had lost infants, one by drowning before he was two and the other very similarly to mine at the age of less than a year. All our lives prepare us for gain, for increment, for increase. We're so ill equipped to actually suffer loss.

In all the centuries before the mid-twentieth, people were used to having many children and losing three-quarters of them before adulthood. We so quickly adapted in the Western world to expect each child to grow to adulthood. However, the religious ritual cannot protect you; it can only make you accept. Accept with a kind of instinct that is either spiritual or intellectual, or a combination of both. I believe that there is nothing that happens to you that you do not accept. This acceptance is, to me, the mark of living the true life. It is the way in which people manage to continue even if they would say to others that they have never accepted what has happened to them. I believe that the fact that they can go on living means that they accept it.

Soon after Chloe's death, I felt as if I'd been wrapped in a kind of cellophane. It was like being contained in something and yet not touched by it. I was wholly visible and yet not part of the sentient world. I had help from many sources—the love of friends and family, the generosity of colleagues, the sympathy of the wider circle of my social contacts. The one exception to that was an occasion that I've never forgotten, even though I do like to blot out unpleasant experiences.

About three months after Chloe's death, I went to a literary party for the launch of a friend's book, where a woman writer, a generation ahead of me, said, "I can see that you're still feeling badly about your baby." I nodded automatically, and my instinct was to walk away without continuing the conversation, but she persisted: "You know, other people wouldn't tell you this but I will. I'm really glad this happened to you because it will make you more human and maybe take some of the polish off you." My feelings towards her remain determinedly neutral because I don't want to admit how much she had hurt me. I think she simply took an opportunity to be cruel to someone she didn't like. To be attacked with such downright meanness and, yes, hatred was astonishing to me then and it remains astonishing to this day.

As Leonard Cohen writes, "There is a crack in everything; that's how the light gets in." What I have learned about suffering in my life is that everyone suffers in their own way, and even if they do not show it, there is a sense in which they take responsibility for it. Different people do this in different ways. And I have done it in mine. I also know that if you cannot be spared suffering, you can be given the strength to bear it.

I always wonder what Chloe would have been like: she was not an identical twin, therefore she would have been different from her sister. How different? Since Kyra became an architect and Blaise became a doctor, would Chloe have become a lawyer? My daughters have seemed to prefer structured professions as opposed to my totally unstructured life. So perhaps the answer would be yes. Her memory lives on in the second name of my first grandchild, and that is an affirmation of her life. Having children makes you aware of your mortality; having grandchildren gives you a sense of immortality.

They say that losing a child puts an enormous stress on a marriage, and I am willing to believe it, as this was my experience. Every person mourns a loss in a different way, and it is difficult to make that adjustment of feeling, even between a couple who have managed to make other adjustments to their life. This was not the only reason for which my first marriage came apart, but I certainly think that this was one of the situations that ended up highlighting other problems.

All I can say is that I was not prepared for this kind of breakup and that I consider it to be my greatest failure. I don't blame anyone, nor do I really blame myself. It just happened. All I know is that the misunderstandings and bad feelings that happened around the divorce carried on for many years. It alienated me from my children, which was exceedingly painful and something I still feel I did not deserve.

I had the legal right to access, but the children were separated emotionally from me. I did not want to interfere with them and damage them in any way, and so I did not go to court. I decided to draw back because I did not want to hurt them.

Most peculiarly, their birthdays came and went and nobody who was a friend to me ever saw them, including their godparents and, particularly hurtfully, their own grandparents. My parents were of enormous strength and restraint during this time, and never expressed the pain they felt. My father was extremely helpful in his folksy but shrewd way, saying, "People can't hurt other people without getting hurt in the end. No matter what happens, things even out. What goes round, comes round. People who hurt other people have to live with their consciences and they never get what they want in the end."

I look back on that period of estrangement and do not know where I got the strength to deal with it. I knew I had the right to see them, but they wouldn't see me. I was rejected, I was a victim, and I suffered. Then one day, when they were independent and adult, they came back to me. They sought out their grandfather first and then me. I am so sorry for the many things that we didn't share in the years that we were estranged—the birthdays, the summer holidays, the decisions about boyfriends—and yet it was their good sense and their intrinsic sense of survival that made it possible for them to come out right in the end.

Now my life is full with my daughters, my remarkable sons-in-law, and my four grandchildren. My daughters are extraordinary people with wonderful professions and great husbands. Of the grandchildren, I will say nothing more than that they are perfect.

Many friends have said to me that they didn't know how I could continue to live my life with this terrible pain. I found within myself resources to deal with phenomenal pain. I masked the pain in public. The tight group of friends, parents, and godparents protected me with their love and concern. And always, I was helped in this by my understanding that others had suffered much more than I had and that they had recovered without ever giving up hope. My own pain made me mindful of other people's sufferings, and makes me have empathy with them. In order to understand what pain is, you must never hope that others feel the same; your only way of coping with it is to say that you recognize it in yourself and therefore you understand when it happens to another.

I realized I had to do what Yeats urges in one of his most wonderful poems: "Go down to where all the ladders start / In the foul rag-and-bone shop of the heart." Because I think one of the ways to keep yourself alive is to say, "I will survive even if nothing ever happens." But something did happen, and for that I am grateful. The love between us, my daughters and I, never actually disappeared, and has returned, radiantly, now.

Those who supported me through those years of estrangement are now as happy as I am, and none of us can really believe that it has worked out as beautifully as it has.

Sun Tzu, the greatest military strategist of all time, said that the greatest victory is the one you win without fighting. I believe that to have been true in my own case. I have a personal life with John Ralston Saul that has lasted for more than thirty years, and all the other rewards of a family now. That is my victory.

RIDING TIGERS

HE WHO RIDES A TIGER CANNOT DISMOUNT.

Chinese proverb

My father (far right) with his mother and three siblings in 1913 in Australia. Five more children would come in the next seven years. *(All family photos courtesy of the author)*

Ethel and Julia Lam, my mother and Auntie Julia, in 1932 in Hong Kong.

My parents' wedding in 1934 at St. John's Anglican Cathedral in Hong Kong.

This photo says it all. My father with his elegant, tailored jodhpurs, my mother with her puffed sleeves. It is 1934, and they are at the Happy Valley Racecourse with Auntie Julia.

My father entering the winner's circle at Happy Valley on his own
horse, Laughing Buddha, led by one of his trainers and
by my mother, who is plumper after my birth in 1939.

My brother, Neville,
and me with our parents
two years before the war.
My mother told me she
loved her purple suede
shoes and my pink
organdy dress.

In our backyard at 277 Sussex Street, Neville and I enjoying
dolls with our French-Canadian neighbours from Lower Town.
We had been in Canada for two years.

Auntie Julia and me in
1948 in the backyard of
190 Somerset West, where
we lived after 1947, before
she went to Toronto.

My father's portrait
in 1948 by Yousuf Karsh.
He is forty-one in this picture.
(Courtesy of the Karsh estate)

My mother and
me in 1953 at
our cottage on
McGregor Lake,
Quebec. The
chartreuse cottage
with the salmon
trim is behind the
trees in the upper
right-hand corner.

Take 30 with Madame Benoit in 1970. Besides the great chef herself, there is Ed Reid, tentatively grasping chicken with tongs, and Paul Soles, quietly anticipating the delicious delight to come. *(CBC)*

John and I having fun at the seaside, in 1977, within a year of our first meeting. *(Charles Gurley)*

The first program of *the fifth estate* in September 1976. Entitled
"Death at 100 Below," it was memorable for many reasons. At Rae Point
in the Arctic, from left to right, Robert Crone, the cameraman; a technical
assistant; me; Gerry McAuliffe, the brilliant investigative journalist
who dug up the story; and Gordon Stewart, the producer.
(CBC)

The Shah of Iran in the Sa'ad Abad palace in Teheran, 1976. I am
the shiny black head in the right foreground, and the Empress
Farah Diba is portrayed behind the Shah. Note the bodyguards.
(CBC)

In 1975, Vic Sarin and I in Egypt. He was one of the camera assistants in Studio Six when I first auditioned; he became one of the greatest cinematographers Canada has ever produced. *(CBC)*

With René Lévesque in 1979. We had known each other since he came to host *The Public Eye* on the CBC English Network in 1966. He remains one of the greatest communicators in Canadian history. *(Canadian Press)*

1979. The building in my village in China where they keep the tablets with the names of all male children. I am surrounded by relatives.

TAKE THIRTY

IT IS ONE OF MY CHARACTERISTICS to refuse to reveal when I am dissatisfied with what I am doing. I attribute this to the fact that I was never allowed to act on any dissatisfaction when I was growing up. Enthusiasm, energy, and stoicism were the rules of the day, and even now it is hard for me not to put forward that face to the world at all times.

I had been studying for a Ph.D. and teaching literature at Victoria College at the University of Toronto and had become dissatisfied. Reluctantly, I was admitting it to myself. One day I ran into an old acquaintance from Trinity who told me she was a script assistant at the CBC. She was working on a daily program called *Take Thirty*, which I had occasionally seen and which was hosted by Anna Cameron and Paul Soles. I had thought it a very enjoyable show. It went on at 3:30 P.M. on the entire English network and was enlightening, fun, and intelligent. My friend said, "We've been looking for somebody to do book reviews on a weekly basis. Maybe you would like to audition?" I asked what that would involve. "Well," she said, "you read a few books and then you come in and talk to the camera about them for about six or seven minutes." I thought that would be interesting. Anything would, at that point, have been more interesting than teaching.

So I was given an appointment for the next week and I prepared my book review, which I think included the latest Saul Bellow, probably *Herzog*, and the *I Hate to Cook Book*, which was a big hit with young women, teaching them how to make beautiful crab casseroles using a can of tomato soup mixed with a can of mushroom soup and laid on a bed of frozen spinach with crab stirred in somewhere in between. You were told to let something broil for the time it took for you to hang over the sink, smoking a cigarette.

I was told that I would be made up and that I would simply go into the studio and talk directly to the camera. And so I went down to Studio 6, which was in the parking lot behind the huge Studio 7 where ballets and dramas were produced, between Jarvis Street and Mutual Street. I was made up with very thick pancake makeup and a lot of mascara and eye shadow. I looked as though someone had painted a replica of my face on top of my own. I had my notes with me but I had memorized everything, and I thought of what Mr. Mann would have said to me as I went in to do my audition. He would have said, "You'll be all right. You just go in there and do it." I walked into Studio 6 to the table where I was to put my notes and where I was going to be able to lean my elbows. The near-total darkness was dramatically broken by a few overhead spotlights.

Television cameras still had cables at that time, so each camera had not only a cameraman but a cableman, who would carry the cables as the cameras moved to get different shots. Each camera had what was called a turret on it with four lenses. But when I walked in there I didn't know any of that. I sat down and in that darkness I felt warm and at home. I loved it from the first moment.

The studio director explained that I was to speak for seven minutes and that when there were thirty seconds to go, he would make a cross sign with his arms, and when there were ten seconds to go, he would start counting down on all his fingers and I was to be finished by exactly then. I remember how excited I was at the idea of doing something that was going to be timed so perfectly. That to me was a real challenge and it was how I came to realize that you can actually say two coherent sentences in ten seconds. This ability always to be able to "come out in time," as they call it, gave me a delicious feeling of control, of assurance.

David Major, with whom I would work for ten years, then told me, "When the red light goes on, that camera is on you. There's one on top of each camera. And when I make a signal to you between the cameras, you will turn towards the camera that has the red light on." That was the total extent of my technical TV training.

I remember that I started out with the middle camera, which was Camera 2, and when I was swung over to Camera 3, which was on my right, I felt a tremendous sense of self-possession. What I didn't know then was that up in the control room they were able to see all three images of me and that the director was able to call a shot while looking at two others. But what I did know was that while I was speaking to Camera 3, I could feel Cameras 1 and 2 changing the position of their lenses and moving silently, or crabbing as it was called. I instinctively understood that they were going to get a different-size shot of me. I've always been able to feel cameras when I've been on television. I have to admit that when electric zooms came in, much of the fun disappeared. You as the person in front of the camera no longer got a chance to feel with the director what kind of shot he was after.

I finished my audition, and the director came down from the control room with my friend, the script assistant, and said, "That was very nice and we'll be calling you if we would like you to come back." I didn't really expect to go back—I did not dream then that the red light signalled the beginning of a career in which I would variously appear in, write, and produce more than two thousand television programs—but I knew something had happened to me because I had felt so at home in that studio and chatting with those cameramen and the cable pullers (all of whom went on to become distinguished directors and cinematographers).

I went home and waited for the phone call, which came the next day. I was asked if I would like to come in regularly to contribute a book review—any books of my choosing. So I went off to read *The New York Review of Books* and some other magazines with book reviews in them. For my next review, I picked a book by Mario Praz on decoration. I felt that there should be variety in what I reviewed, and that this book would give me an opportunity to be satirical and yet educational. As the show aired in the middle of the afternoon, I assumed (and quite rightly too) that the women of the audience wanted something different and something that would connect them to a larger world without making them feel that theirs was small. I always believed that if we were reviewing only novels, that would make them suspect that that was all they could read. All of us at *Take Thirty* wanted our audience to be encouraged.

It seems to me now that I felt a great rapport with those women because I realized that many of them were stuck in the way I had always worried that I might become stuck—with small children, no help, and a lot of ideas. It was 1965; Betty Friedan had written *The Feminine Mystique* only two years before. Female consciousness was stirring and waiting to be encouraged and exhorted.

I negotiated my contract with a formidable character named Eric Koch, who was witty and amusing. The first thing he said to me, with his wide, impish smile, was, "We have picked you up from the gutter and we can throw you back down there whenever we want. We will give you $42.50 for every review you do here. Of course, you will have to join the union because the CBC is a closed shop. A part of your pay will go towards your union dues and pension, and you will perform every three weeks."

I remember I almost burst out laughing, but I decided to play it straight, and I said, "I hope that if you throw me out you can throw me out a door before I fall into a gutter—perhaps a back alley." He nodded and smiled and that was that. I don't think that kind of exchange could happen anymore, because people don't have that kind of humour when they deal with each other, and because such a joke would probably be considered some kind of trespass against human rights. In fact, Eric meant that I was going to succeed, and his joke was absurd. Underlying that exchange, though, was a morbid truth: television is a cruel business, and it has never been known to treat people well.

And so I went on regularly for the next couple of months and sat around the makeup room each time with Paul and Anna, and we became friends. One day Anna took me aside outside the ladies' washroom and said, "I'm going to be leaving and I think you should try for my job. I think you'd be really good and interesting. Are you going to do it?" This was so startling to me that I said, "Yes, of course." This is another one of my major characteristics and flaws: I always say yes to things and sometimes, but not always, regret it.

So then it was known that, after four brief, brilliant appearances as a book reviewer, I was going to be considered to replace Anna as co-host, and the director said to me, "Perhaps if you're going to be one of the contenders for this job, you should do an interview. Would you like to do an interview?" And I said, "I would love to. Whenever you want."

The upshot was that, two days later, I interviewed Francis Robinson of the Metropolitan Opera. He was not particularly forthcoming, but I had boned up a great deal by reading an account of the Metropolitan Opera broadcasts, and opera was a great passion of mine. I realized two minutes into the interview that he had cut himself while he was shaving and therefore was being particularly recalcitrant because he was embarrassed about how he looked. Unfortunately I had not noticed it in time so that we could have placed him where the Band-Aid would not have shown. I think I lurched my way through the interview all right, and I stuck to the five minutes allotted.

When the formal announcement came that Anna was retiring, one of the last big cattle calls of the CBC followed. There were at least thirty of us, including several variety producers' girlfriends and assorted ladies with long legs and mascara and the false eyelashes they wore all the time. We were filed in one by one to interview a gentleman from the Royal Ontario Museum about the textile collection there. This was something we were to do completely "cold"—that is, without doing any research. This poor man looked desperately unhappy and uncomfortable by the time I got to him, having been put through I think at least seventeen of these interviews.

As a student at university I had gone to the Royal Ontario Museum many times to see the clothing and the costume exhibits, because embroidery fascinated me. I found the cut of men's waistcoats particularly gorgeous. I always wondered why men today looked so dowdy, when two hundred years previously they were wearing these beautiful silk waistcoats, practically to their knees, embroidered in exquisite pale colours and wearing linen that *looked* like linen around their necks and on their shirts. Anyway, the interview went quite well, and the interview subject, who had been like the Dormouse at the Mad Hatter's Tea Party, came to a little while we were talking.

Again I was told, "Don't call us, we'll call you." I went off to Paris for the summer, and about two weeks after I arrived there, I received a call saying that I had the job.

You can see from my account of this that I had absolutely no professional experience. All I had was a wonderful education and a great deal of curiosity. That is why I think I was able to make my career in television. I already knew a lot of things through books and I wanted to learn about the other things. It was as simple as that.

Now the question that's most important is: How did I know I could be good at it? There's no answer to that except that I felt I could probably be better than anyone else that I saw. It's hard to say this without sounding as though I speak from a certain amount of demented arrogance. But I think if you find work that is truly the expression of a certain aspect of yourself, you will feel comfortable and on top of things. I always felt that way about television, no matter what show I was doing—*Take Thirty, the fifth estate, Adrienne Clarkson Presents*. I always felt that I could master the material and give it a point of view that would make it interesting, illuminating even.

At *Take Thirty*, we realized how much people longed for knowledge in Canada. It was the beginning of my understanding that this country is filled with people who, no matter where they live, want to be a part of the whole, want to be connected to each other, to know about each other. As Governor General I saw this over and over again. To me, this is what a true egalitarian society is all about. It was something that was perfectly well understood when our society was less consumed with acquiring things, with earning money being the criterion for everything.

The Canada I came to know in the mid-sixties was not that. It was still a part of a world that had known the sacrifice of the Second World War, the uncertainty of the Korean War, and the delicacy of the balance between getting ahead and being part of a good society. I knew people in high school whose fathers had ridden the rails during the Depression and I had friends who remembered eating porridge for breakfast and dinner. Those are the kind of people I first related to when I was doing national television.

I also realized that my audience was smart, what my father called "quick on the uptake." They wanted to communicate to the person that they saw every day. The letters I received from women were extraordinary. I learned about all the small towns because that was where the CBC and only the CBC went in those days. Maple Creek, Alberta, Chetwynd, B.C., George River, Quebec—all these places were real to me because people who lived in them sat down and wrote letters, not only longhand but frequently well typed. At *Take Thirty* we were all given the strength to push the envelope with our subject matter because we knew the intelligence and the understanding of our audience. I have never underestimated the intelligence of Canadian people ever since receiving those letters through the ten years that I worked at *Take Thirty*.

Those years I spent doing a daily program were so much fun, and I was learning new things all the time. Our supervisor of daytime programming, Dodi Robb, was an imaginative programmer who loved us in an expansive way, which made us do our best. She made us all laugh; most of my producers and my co-hosts, Paul Soles, and, later, Ed Reid, were warm, funny, and bright. We knew we were producing one of the best programs on television, even if it got short shrift because it was on in the daytime. It was lucky for us, and for me personally, to have that time slot, because it meant that we lacked pretension; we didn't think we were the absolute final word on anything. We wanted to present different points of view, and take a lot of time to do it. We did series like *Men and Marriage* and *The Single Woman* and devoted a whole week of programs to each of these subjects. Leonard Cohen sang for the first time publicly on *Take Thirty* in 1966, and I interviewed him, asking him archly why he had taken to pop music. He replied, "The time is over, Adrienne, when poets sit on marble stairs in long black capes." We've been friends ever since.

Our highlight was the weekly visit of Madame Benoit, who came from Montreal and gave a cooking lesson, showing us how to make everything from puff pastry to macaroni and cheese. Her warm personality exuded friendliness, and she made everyone feel that they too could approach good food without any fancy equipment or the best stove in the Western world. She was disarming and warm and had what everybody loved, which was a wonderful Québécois accent.

She sent a message to those people all over Canada who had no knowledge of French Canada that this kind of friendly, civilized person existed and wished to speak to them and help them in their daily lives with something as vital as food. She always masked the fact that she had a university degree in food chemistry, but she had gone on from those basics to become one of the best cooks in Canada.

The crew, of course, always loved Madame Benoit days because they got to eat up everything that she cooked. She wrote several cookbooks while we were working together and I still use them to this day. She was an extremely acute and sharp businesswoman and had many contracts with food producers and with publishing companies, which she managed with an air of insouciance. One of the great treats, of course, was to go to her house in Montreal and enjoy a meal cooked by her in the company of Barney, her devastatingly handsome second husband. They had met during the Second World War when he was an officer and she had gone over to help make the cuisine a little bit better for the armed forces. None of us ever tired of hearing about this romantic love at first sight: Madame Benoit had gazed across the room and seen a man who looked like a Bronzino portrait. Madame Benoit knew her art as well as she knew her kitchen. She already had a husband, and Barney was ten years younger than she was, but every barrier was overcome. Paul and I loved hearing this story over the years.

Starting this way in television meant that I have never been cynical about the audience or felt detached from them. I feel this attachment because I was able to do thousands of television programs in the ten years in which I did a program every day, five days a week. I never could distrust the viewer who cared to watch and then to write. For every person who wrote, I was told, there were thirty who would like to write but didn't. I've always felt grateful for the attention of the people who are the audience. They're not there just to look at you; they're there to be part of what you want to convey to them.

All of this helped me when I became Governor General because I was going out among people and hoping very much that they would understand that I wanted to know what *they* thought and that they could tell me anything that was on their minds. In the same way as on *Take Thirty*, where I never asked anything of the audience, I never asked anything of the tens of thousands of Canadians whom I met while I was Governor General. I just felt that my presence would give them the opportunity to say what they had to say or to open up their lives a little bit.

Nothing can match the magnetic connection between human beings who are face to face. This was the logical outcome of everything I developed when I was at *Take Thirty*. We didn't have the budget or the time to go out that often to different parts of the country (I later did that with *the fifth estate*), but all my memories of *Take Thirty* came back to me when I was travelling around the country as Governor General, going to eighty or ninety communities a year. People want to make a connection to you, otherwise why would they bring their mentally challenged child to stand in line for a half-hour in order to shake your hand at a levee at the high-school gym in Iqaluit? They want to know that you can look at them and that they are proud of who they are and they want you to see their lives as they are. That is the true privilege.

There is a lot of skepticism on the part of the printed press about the relationship of television to its audience. From my experience, television activates people in a way that goes beyond words to an understanding that is more complete. I would much rather see people explaining themselves for two minutes on television than read what a print reporter says they said. I want to be able to judge how that person looked as they said that they hadn't found the body of their wife until two days after they got home from a trip.

I worked for more than thirty years at the CBC, and I was never without a major program because I always believed that that was how I was going to make a difference. I had the opportunity to make innovative programs. Sometimes, I had to fight for a good time slot, for budget, for the desirable staff. Looking at the structure of the place, it was continually discouraging to see that president after president had no broadcasting experience. Perhaps because I had grown up with complex family dynamics, I was particularly well prepared to work in a dysfunctional organization that seemed to specialize in benevolent neglect and bewildering manipulation. In the forty years that I have known it, the CBC has always been the same—perhaps that is reassuring—lurching along with the threat of imminent annihilation, and always creating programs anyway, because CBC people always come through in the end. Good programs do get to air, and new ideas find nurture somewhere.

WHEN I BEGAN my regular job at *Take Thirty*, we were housed at one end of the top floor of the Radio Building, which had started life as a girls' school. It had three staircases exactly like the staircases at Kent Street Public School. As I was going up the stairs the first day, a man was hanging over the top balustrade looking down at me. He radiated civility and humour. I didn't know it then, but it turned out that he was Peter Campbell, the head of Current Affairs, and therefore, in a way, the person for whom I would be indirectly working.

I had forgotten my gloves that day, and as I arrived at the top of the stairs this man took my hand and said, "Che gelida manina, signorina!" I knew instantly that I would always be able to be connected to this place where I was welcomed on my first day of work by an elegant bachelor saying the first words that Rodolfo sings to Mimi in *La Bohème*. I knew that it didn't matter what subjects we would be dealing with, whether I would be talking about agriculture or social problems or the Metropolitan Opera— everything could be seen through this screen of civilization. An operatic line being said to me as a first greeting, I thought, was a perfect harbinger of all the good things to come.

THE FIFTH ESTATE

ONE OF THOSE GOOD THINGS was meeting John Ralston Saul, in 1976, the year we started *the fifth estate*. The first time I saw him was at my front doorstep after I had been on my own for about three years. My best friend delivered him to me without realizing exactly what she was doing, but he is the greatest gift she has ever given me. She had already sent me the manuscript of his first novel and she thought she'd bring along the author to meet me too. He was then working in Calgary for Maurice Strong, starting Petro-Canada, the national oil company, and was visiting my friends for a weekend because he had known them in France.

People often ask, "When did you really know that this person was meant for you?" I can say that for me, it was two weeks after meeting him, when my phone rang and he introduced himself again to me. He asked me if I had had a chance to read the manuscript, which was about to be published in Canada, England, and France. I was working crazy hours at *the fifth estate*, with very little time to read. "I'm sorry," I told him, "I just haven't gotten around to it, but I'm looking forward to it." Then came the disarming words: "That's all right. It was only an excuse to call you." As far as I'm concerned, the rest is history.

We found that we had much in common. We shared, immediately, the feeling that we had both been outsiders—me for the obvious reasons, and him because he had been to thirteen different schools while moving around the country with his army family. There was something about our mothers: his mother was an army officer's daughter, an English war bride who, like my mother, had been displaced from her class and background. They brought a different perspective to the Canadian life they had had to absorb.

We liked pears, poached with a bit of pepper on them. We both disliked anything having to do with small spherical objects being hit, batted, or aimed: tennis, golf, volleyball, basketball, baseball.

We had each lived for some time in France (John spent the better part of seven years between the ages of twenty and thirty there) and learned French and had a background in its literature and theatre. France continues to be a big link between us. We have a whole other world of friends from our days there—an almost parallel world to our lives in Canada. Conversation has always been fun with John, once he got over his initial disappointment that I did not speak Mandarin.

We both crave a certain kind of solitude, which we have created for ourselves in the beautiful area of Georgian Bay where we have our cottage. It is a world in which we are off the grid and have only six electric light bulbs run by a solar panel, no hot water, and a composting outhouse. We share completely the view that you should be intensely urban or give yourself over to the wilderness. Anything in between does not appeal to us.

As to what else makes us compatible, that is nobody's business but our own.

John has been an unfailing and strong support for me, in both my personal tribulations and in my work as Governor General. I can honestly say that I don't think I could have done the kind of work I did without him—without his courage, his high intelligence, his enthusiasm, and his dynamic energy. He sacrificed writing time and many of his own personal goals to be with me for ninety percent of my work; he withdrew himself for six years from being a contender for all literary awards in order not to be in a conflict of interest. Yet he managed to write two books. It is the marketplace that has appreciated and continued to support him.

When he decided to make writing his full-time career, after the success of *The Birds of Prey*, I was delighted to think that he could live an uncompromised intellectual life, independent and free. It's wonderful to live with somebody whose only source of anguish is whether he has expressed his ideas clearly enough and whether he can explain them to others. To be with somebody who is always thinking about what really matters in the world is a great privilege, and I recognize this.

Our life together began at a hectic, frantic time for me—the creation of CBC's most important public affairs program, *the fifth estate*, which was a blur of research, travel, and intense writing to ominous, unavoidable deadlines. And it didn't seem to let up. Over the years I interviewed politicians and criminals and ordinary people all over the world. I was on the spot when the Soviets invaded Afghanistan in 1979, examined kickbacks in a number of provincial liquor boards, and met dictators on several continents. Our criteria for *fifth estate* stories were, and remain: where is the public good being betrayed, and how can we change that?

In my television career I covered politicians very closely, and then, when I became Governor General, I saw them in a different way. It's as though I looked through different lenses. In the 1960s and '70s, the world was changing rapidly. In 1976, I interviewed the Shah of Iran, who was trying to use his big oil dollars to thrust his country towards modernization; this was the first major attempt to use oil supplies to challenge the hegemony of the West. In 1977, I went to Haiti to interview Baby Doc Duvalier, the son of Papa Doc, who had tyrannized Haiti for decades. Baby Doc did the interview with his loaded pistol lying between us on his desk. The hideous poverty and suffering of the Haitian people seemed totally remote to this man, who looked like a cream puff in his wedding-cake palace modelled on the White House.

I am fortunate that I was given these perspectives early as a journalist because they helped me to understand the background of everything that I was confronted with when I became Governor General. My trip to China in 1979, at the time of the thirtieth anniversary of the founding of the People's Republic of China, prepared me to talk with the president of China in one of the last state visits I received during my mandate. It is one thing to cover an event or a person as a journalist and quite another to receive him or her on behalf of your country and with a certain amount of self-interest. I'm glad that one experience came before the other!

I am proud that I was part of a show that pulled no punches and is still on the air after thirty years. Our executive producer, Glenn Sarty, had been my executive producer at *Take Thirty* and at *Adrienne at Large*, which ran for one season before it became a part of *the fifth estate*. Ron Haggart, who came with a brilliant reputation as a print journalist, was senior producer, and it was understood that, besides smoking about five packs of cigarettes a day, he would be in charge of the quality of investigative journalism that we were dedicated to.

The very first program, "Death on Ice," was a fascinating lesson in trying to find information years after some troubling event had happened: it was about the crash of a Panarctic Oil airplane in the Arctic and the subsequent inquest into the deaths of nearly thirty people who were being flown from a drilling site in the North. The show landed us in a suit for libel, and after nearly two years of examination for discoveries and a trial, we lost the case. However, we did not have to pay any damages, and that was for us vindication enough. I learned a lot about libel, which has stood me in good stead in public life.

I had already fallen in love with the North in 1973, when I joined the Committee for an Independent Canada with people like Walter Gordon and Peter Newman. Our trip to the North was a revelation to me of how different we are as a country. So two weeks in Yellowknife in 1977 during the libel trial was time I actually enjoyed. When the Berger Commission began a few years later, I returned to hear deliberations about whether an oil and gas pipeline would destroy the Aboriginal way of life, disturb the patterns of migration of caribou, and bring a boom-and-bust development. Georges Erasmus was a brilliant Aboriginal leader, and I'll always remember the passion, determination, and intelligence with which he argued against building the pipeline. Twenty-five years later, I was happy as Governor General to be part of a reunion of the people who had reported on and worked for the Berger Commission, including Thomas Berger himself. The inquiry was a terrific means of educating Canadians about the North, and also about how decisions get made regarding our natural resources. Thomas Berger changed the way Canadians perceived the North. He gave me the rationale for what my heart already knew—that the North is the reality of Canada.

The most important story of my first season with *the fifth estate* was a trip to Iran to interview the shah. We knew that he had millions and millions of petrodollars to spend on arms. We wanted to get a look at all of those Bell helicopters he was buying, whose numbers indicated a military purpose. He was an imperious figure, and several years before, he had had a celebration of two thousand years of Persian history, to which our Governor General, Roland Michener, and his wife had been invited. All the heads of state and royalty were put up in dramatic tents at Persepolis, and this splendid display was meant to overshadow the fact that the Shah's father had seized power as a simple sergeant in the 1920s. We had been led to believe by all our research that the Shah had gained enormous self-confidence with his money from oil, but on the ground in Tehran we sensed a chaotic atmosphere: the profiteers were there, the halls of the Hilton were crammed with foreigners, and there was a great deal of unfocused excitement. Tehran was booming, full of people attempting to get oil contracts, not only with the Iranians but also with each other. In the hotel's dining rooms and coffee shops, men were straining across tables to whisper to each other. I met crazy people and CIA agents; often they were crazy and CIA in one person.

After we'd been in the city for about a day we were summoned to the Sa'ad Abad Palace to interview the Shah. I was very anxious to meet him, as there had been a lot of press in the past year about the secret police of Iran, SAVAK, using torture. I wanted to ask the Shah about the development of his country, the role of secret police, and his hopes for the future.

When we arrived at the palace, we were met by security men and taken into a large drawing room decorated in deep blue and gold. With one huge Persian carpet, it was in a style I would describe as anxiously imperial. There were guards at each corner. When I stood to meet the Shah, I realized that we were about the same height; I noticed right away that there was a strange grey cast to his skin and he was perspiring heavily.

He was exquisitely polite, and had probably done as much homework on us as we had done on him. In preparing for an interview like that, you try to speak to absolutely everyone and read everything you can get your hands on, even if only one tenth of the material shows up in the final broadcast. We had even talked to people who had been with him at the Swiss finishing school Le Rosey forty years earlier.

We sat down and the interview began. We had a discussion about the development of his country and his hopes for educating his people and for providing them with health care. I told him that we would be travelling to a number of cities in Iran, including Isphahan, Shiraz, and Qum, the holy city. He nodded non-committally, so I went further and asked him if we would be able to film the airfield at Isphahan, which we knew from our reports was filled with hundreds of Bell helicopters. He said, "It shall be done."

At that point, I went in for the heart of the interview and asked him if there were secret police in Iran. A cloud passed over his face. "Why do you ask me this?" I said, "Because newspapers like *The Sunday Times* of London have reported that SAVAK, your secret police, have used torture on your citizens." He said, "*The Sunday Times* of London is garbage." I replied, "In my country, *The Sunday Times* of London is not considered to be garbage. It is considered to be an excellent newspaper." And he snapped back, "When I say it is garbage, it is garbage." He did not look agitated, he simply looked extremely displeased. I asked him: "Is there torture in Iran?" He took a deep breath and, holding himself rigid, said, "We don't have to have torture in Iran. Our methods for finding information are just as sophisticated as yours in the West." I felt that the interview had accomplished a number of things—not only had we gotten the content and the questions right but viewers would be able to see the look on his face and the contempt with which he dealt with my questions. It was a message in itself.

By the end of the interview, he had regained his charm and shook my hand with a smile. I had the feeling that he still felt in control and that this strange intervention by a television reporter from Canada, of all places, was not something that worried him. And indeed, as we followed him around the country and filmed him in various cities as he arrived in his airplane, I sensed that he noticed us, but benignly.

There was much talk at the time in the foreign press about how the Shah was yanking his people into the modern age using all that money. But when you saw people throwing themselves to the ground in front of him as he walked along a carpet between his airplane and his car, you realized that there was really quite a lot of modernizing to come.

Two years later, the Shah, after having been ousted by the religious fundamentalist Ayatollah Khomeini, and refused hospitality in various Muslim countries, was dead. I was always grateful for seeing Iran before the Islamic revolution and the destruction that inevitably comes with a revolution. When people talked later about how women were forced to wear the chador under Khomeini, it was made to seem as though everyone had been modernized and in Western dress until the religious revolution. But one of the most memorable sights we saw in Tehran was while driving down a street past a tiny girl on the sidewalk, and as we looked at her, she drew her chador over her head and face. I remember thinking that if you were about four years old and doing that already, your chances of being modernized were remote.

That first year at *the fifth estate* brought a number of challenging assignments. Brian McKenna and I were the first to probe cost overruns at the 1976 Olympics in Montreal. We saw dozens of cranes working on the construction of the buildings on a cost-plus basis. Budgets weren't being surpassed; there just weren't any budgets. We knew that money was being thrown at the project and that the people of Montreal would be paying for it for decades. The show not only won us an ACTRA Award but also prompted an investigation headed by Mr. Justice Albert Malouf. A story like the Olympics scandal had all the necessary ingredients—the mismanagement of money, charismatic and sometimes careless main characters, and the background of a wonderful city in a country not used to corruption on that scale.

Following a story could put us in danger. Judy Jackson and I went to Guatemala in 1980 to investigate the civil unrest there and track down the Canadian widow of a prominent politician who had been assassinated. When we arrived in Guatemala City, the capital was almost empty of tourists, and people seemed to be fearfully awaiting what might happen next. In order to get interviews with people in hiding, we went to parking lots where we were picked up by other cars, taken to a safe house, and then driven by car to yet another place where we were able to be met by our own vehicle. I interviewed a quiet, confident Irish priest who was obviously a believer in liberation theology and who struck me as one of the bravest people I had ever met. He told me he would kill himself if he were caught by the other side. When I asked him how he, as a Catholic, could do such a thing, he answered that, for him, suicide was a lesser evil than betraying his friends under torture.

When Judy and I got back to the almost empty hotel, we were exhausted, and so we went down to have a sauna. It was only after fifteen minutes of chatting and sweating that we realized somebody could have come down and locked the door and we could be cooked to death. We beat a retreat.

When I was in Northern Ireland doing a program on the IRA, we were in Belfast, and we were filming from the car with a long lens. Suddenly, the car was surrounded by British soldiers with their guns cocked. It is the only time I have known that taste of metal in my mouth, the real taste of fear.

Not all the stories we did were intense political dramas. We were frequently after the quirky and unexpected. Once, in 1976, we went out West to look into a story about a biker gang in Calgary that had been the subject of one television reporter's crusade; he believed the bikers were being persecuted by the Calgary police. The gang members had just been cleared of arson charges after two years of litigation. What is interesting about the story now is that the reporter was a man named Ralph Klein. Four years later, he ran for mayor. And then … Whenever I met Mr. Klein in later years, I would always remind him of how we had first met, but I got the distinct feeling that he'd much rather not be reminded.

Before she became prime minister, we followed a campaigning Margaret Thatcher to the Gestettner factory on the outskirts of London. She was determined to be charming, and could run in stiletto heels better than anyone I have seen. We had a series of interviews throughout the day, but she seemed to be much more interested in knowing how my career had gone because her own daughter, Carol, was about to enter the world of television. She was straightforward and she was absolutely convinced that Canadian labour legislation was more "sophisticated" than Britain's. This was the woman who later, as prime minister for more than a decade, insisted, "There is no such thing as society."

Often when you're going to do a perfectly banal interview with a retired politician you expect to contribute to a bit of history. You do not expect to witness any revelation of the person, as politicians rarely reveal their true selves in modern times. When the power game is over, they try to disguise themselves, either as false populists or as bluff victims of circumstance. I expected the same from former British prime minister Harold Wilson in 1978. He had come to receive an honorary degree from the University of Toronto, and we had asked politely for an interview, which he granted as the only one that he would do while he was here. Perhaps he thought that we had all lived under the rocks of the Precambrian Shield in the last few years because he was totally unprepared for my question about the Rhodesian situation and whether he was aware that Britain had violated sanctions against Rhodesia during his term in office. His eyes popped out and his voice shook with fury as he told me that he would not answer this question, and, as I persisted, he rose to his feet and said: "This interview will never be shown. Do you know who Lord Goodman is? He is my lawyer. And this interview will never be shown." And he stomped out. The producer and I were astonished that he would have lost his cool to this extent, but we believed that it was a perfectly legitimate item to broadcast to the Canadian public. We had some disagreement from the senior producer, who felt that it was inappropriate. However, we persisted and the item aired. It caused a little sensation in Canada and a huge one in Great Britain, where it was replayed on the BBC. I think it was the only one of the programs I've done that the BBC picked up which garnered as much notice and approval.

We also tried to do items that focused on general, social problems, and for this I found that my history with *Take Thirty* was valuable. We did programs on women in abusive relationships and people with schizophrenia, which in the late seventies was only beginning to be recognized as a largely chemical problem. We also ran the occasional lighter piece. One of the most seductive and beautifully produced items was called "Love $tory," produced by Alan Burke, and it was a look at Harlequin romances and the huge success they had among women. It was estimated at that time that the average Harlequin reader bought between a dozen and twenty of these romance novels a year. The books followed a formula: tall, dark stranger, initially not sympathetic, meets spirited young woman and eventually all obstacles are overcome and they live happily ever after. It's essentially a retelling of Jane Austen's *Pride and Prejudice* and seemed to have worked for a long time.

The author that I interviewed used the initials R. L. In the middle of the interview she closed her eyes and began a Harlequin romance: "When she first met him in the hallway of the Royal Ontario Museum, Adrienne thought that Julian was extremely good looking but arrogant. They made their way towards the dinosaur gallery and at that point she noticed that the light came into his eyes in a fascinating way …" The author composed almost half a chapter with her eyes closed in front of me, and I was told that this later did appear as the beginning of one of her novels.

We didn't often cover religious subjects, but when we did, they were frequently surprising. Brother André, whose heart is kept in the Oratory of St. Joseph on the mountain in Montreal, was being considered for beatification and sainthood. In 1978 we went to Rome to look at how his dossier was progressing and found ourselves interviewing a fascinating character known as the devil's advocate who, at that time, was a Yugoslavian priest. He had about thirty dossiers, and his job was to be the prosecution in the trials that determined whether the candidates deserved canonization. Father Mitri's job was to find flaws in the character and life of the candidate and bring them to the fore in what resembled a courtroom situation. Father Mitri had a book of miracles allegedly performed by Brother André, and each one of them was being checked out carefully. If someone said that they had been cured of cancer by praying to Brother André, Father Mitri would ask for medical documentation, including reports from two doctors and from people outside the subject's family circle.

In recent years, the office, I believe, has been discontinued. As Governor General, I represented Canada at the installation of Pope Benedict XVI in 2005. On the piazza in front of St. Peter's, where the ceremony took place, I looked around in vain for any sign of the devil's advocate.

PARIS WHEN IT SIZZLED — 1982

MY OFFICE AT *THE FIFTH ESTATE* was always a total and utter mess. I could say I have never believed you need a neat desk to get good work done, but the fact is that I simply don't know how to keep a desk neat, no matter how large it is.

Shortly after arriving at Rideau Hall, I screened a 1962 CBC documentary about Governor General Georges Vanier and his wife, Pauline. As the camera panned over the office—the very office I occupied at that moment—I could see that every surface was neat as a pin. The only things on the Governor General's desk were two big inkpots on a silver tray. I now had those inkpots in front of me, but they were filled with paper clips, pins from the cities I had most recently visited, and some small change, which, for some atavistic reason, I always believe I'm going to need. The Vaniers sat in front of the fireplace and had tea and looked perfect in every way as the vice-regal couple, distant above the kind of fray that I created with piles of scribbled notes, books that might offer good quotes for a speech, and, of course, all the mail that was listed as "to be done" and drafted. Letters, memos, emails always lie on my desk in paleo-lithic layers. I used to delude myself that I would someday become tidy and organized. This has never happened, and if it didn't happen while I was at Rideau Hall, I now resign myself to the fact that it will never happen. There are illusions that you should cherish because you realize that you can maintain them, and there are illusions that are foolish. A clean desk for me is one of the latter.

One day in my *fifth estate* office, I had a little pink slip asking me to call a Mr. Taylor at Caldwell Partners, a headhunting firm. It was dated three days before. Part of our problems at *the fifth estate*, or perhaps it was one of our salvations, was that we had no secretaries and there was only one receptionist for everybody. This was in the days before email, and people either could get hold of each other or they couldn't. Yet we managed to do pretty timely stories. When I called Mr. Taylor, he told me that the Ontario government was looking for candidates to be Agent General in Paris. They wanted to open an office there to encourage business and cultural relations, just as Quebec had done, and the way Ontario had had an office in London, England, for more than 150 years. I was startled, to say the least, but intrigued, because I had always felt that the rest of Canada should have a relationship with France in order for the French to understand that, although we were a complex country, they could have a good business relationship with us.

I talked it over with John. France had always been a big part of both of our lives, and it was where John's books found their largest foreign audiences. We still had many close friends and connections from our times there. We were keen.

I felt that if I went to Paris as Ontario's Agent General, my French education would have counted for something. When I thought about it, I could not think of many Canadian anglophones who knew France as well as I did. I became certain that I was the person who could do this job, could make Ontario better known in France and could deal with what I knew was a tricky relationship between the governments of Quebec and Canada.

About a year previously, I had gone to France to do a documentary on René Lévesque's first visit to Paris as premier of Quebec and his being received at the National Assembly as though he were a head of state. With his typical public diffidence and apparent self-deprecation (two traits he shared with Pierre Elliott Trudeau), Lévesque made Quebeckers feel that they had penetrated the heart of the francophone world. His demeanour indicated that to him it was a matter of course rather than a big triumph.

In 1976 I found myself, as a journalist, close to him on stage at the Paul Sauvé arena when he acknowledged the surprising victory of the Parti Québécois. Thousands of Péquistes were cheering in a state of euphoria. In one of those curious Canadian moments, I, a Canadian nationalist, felt a surge of pride for this person who was a real, whole person, and not anything made up as a media package. I admired him, and I still do. Both Lévesque and Trudeau were magnetic communicators; people who didn't know them or who disagreed with them were still drawn to them. Later, when I was Agent General, Prime Minister Trudeau came to France for an official visit, and I gathered up my little office of five Canadians and we went to stand in front of the Élysée Palace when he arrived. Of course, the French laid out the red carpet in that staggeringly pompous way they have of doing things, with the uniforms, the feathered helmets, the crossed swords. Mr. Trudeau drew up in an ordinary green Peugeot sedan (I later discovered when I was in a ceremonial position myself how difficult it is to order things to be plain and ordinary) and he leapt out of the car in a brown suit and onto the red carpet. He looked at the small group of us standing just inside the gate and he gave us all a look that we agreed said: "You know this is all a pile of French pretension. But I'm only doing it for you because Canada deserves to be received well." Somehow he had telegraphed that message to each and every one of us in the way he looked at us, the human being cutting through the nonsense and getting to the essential.

This complicity, which had nothing to do with words, was something I think all great leaders share. It goes beyond ideology, policy, or even personality. It has to do with the ability to connect and look in people's eyes. It's surprising how many people, especially politicians, cannot look people in the eye and see the other person. I've come to believe that truism about never trusting anybody who doesn't look you in the eye or keeps looking away from you. I've had enough experiences with people in public life to know that this is true.

So many politicians think the hoopla is all for them as a person, not realizing that the welcome is for their country, their people. In January 2005, at the commemoration of the liberation of Auschwitz, Silvio Berlusconi, then prime minister of Italy, plastered in his usual pancake makeup and trying to insinuate himself into a better position in the VIP seating, was the most egregious example of ego outweighing decency to which I have ever been unwilling witness.

But I'm getting ahead of myself—first I had to get the job. The only member of the four-person interview panel that I remember with any clarity was Hugh Segal, then principal secretary to Ontario premier William Davis. I had never met the premier, nor Hugh Segal, but after our conversation I was very taken, not only with Hugh but also with the Conservative government that he represented and obviously understood. It wasn't just that he was jolly and round and smiled wonderfully, but also that his French was so good. I had become so jaded, I think; English Canadians didn't speak French or would say things like "I don't speak it, but I understand it." It seemed to me that that simply wasn't good enough in a bilingual country.

Hugh asked me what I would do if I went to Paris for Ontario, and I said I would immediately get in touch with all kinds of ministries there, such as International Trade, Foreign Affairs, Health, and Education, in order to see what kinds of things we could do with France. Of course, I emphasized culture, because I knew how important culture was to the French.

I admired the way Hugh could be amusing, perceptive, and tough at the same time. My opinion of him has never changed. Twenty-five years later, when he came to Rideau Hall to receive the

Order of Canada, he spoke after dinner about who had influenced him most in his life. The speech he gave, about his struggling family and their generosity to people who had just a little bit less than themselves, brought tears to the eyes of everyone present. Whenever I think of Hugh Segal, I think of his decency, his good judgment, and his bright mind.

After meeting Tom Wells, minister of intergovernmental affairs, and Ed Stewart, the premier's right-hand man, I was offered the job. All the cabinet ministers I met were low-key and, I thought, very interested in the project of opening an office in Paris. We talked about the industrial possibilities for Ontario, particularly in the auto industry. The provincial government wanted to attract Renault to southern Ontario for assembly of their new model, the Renault 19.

That was my first experience of working with politicians, as opposed to observing them, and I found these ones to be intelligent, good at conversation, and perfectly normal. By normal, I mean that they were not obsessed with talking about themselves all the time and with controlling the agenda. They understood what it was they were doing, and I respected them for that. In fact, when I think of the Davis government, which I worked for from 1982 until 1985, I think of a fundamental decency and a grounded quality that made it possible for me, who came from a completely different background, to communicate with them. There was mutual respect, and later, friendship.

I had not yet met the premier, William Davis, himself. I knew very little about him except that he had stopped the construction of the Spadina Expressway. My friends and I had all worked hard in the early seventies to protest against a highway that we believed would rip the heart out of the city. Good politicians are not only smart but know how to do things that communicate that intelligence within public policy. William Davis was able to do this, even with minority governments. He headed the government for sixteen years adeptly, and created a sense that everything was normal.

There are two kinds of politicians: those that want you to feel that every situation is a tsunami and that everyone must flee to the hills, and those who are able to reassure people that the end of the world is not at hand and in the meantime, things will run smoothly under their guidance. I think that Canadians are particularly attracted to the latter and in a self-flagellating manner say, "We're so dull and we're so boring and that's why we elect these people who do not get excited to govern us." In fact, I believe the opposite is true. We are a very complicated people, far from dull and boring, who are stubborn and who wish to make our sense of the common good perfectly clear. Anyone who interferes with this conviction is in danger of never gaining power or of losing it pretty quickly. Perhaps, because this government was the one that I knew best and worked most closely with, I have always been deeply influenced by its calm and its deliberation.

I first met William Davis in his offices in Queen's Park. While he smoked his pipe, we chatted comfortably as though we had known each other for years. What I didn't know then was that he would be the best boss I ever worked for in all my life. He was a superb executive, with the ability to assess the information that he was given and to help decisions happen quickly. If I had a particular problem, he would think about it and then say, "What is your total assessment of the situation?" I would tell him what I thought was best to do, and then he would say something like, "Well, then, go ahead and do it." It sounds so simple, but I have never met another politician who did this. It doesn't have anything to do with so-called management techniques; it has to do with a profound understanding of how human nature works and of how people must accept responsibility for their actions.

I had always observed politicians very closely, both through my work and also because I like to know what is going on in the public life of our country. What I learned by working for the Ontario government was that the premier had melded a number of very bright, decent people into a superb team, people like Robert Welch, Bette Stephenson, Roy McMurtry, and Tom Wells.

I went off to Paris in 1982. The Socialists, under President François Mitterrand, had just been elected the year before. There was a lot of sabre rattling of the variety of "If the Socialists are here, the Communists must be coming." And many people, even sensible ones, evoked the images of Soviet tanks coming down the Champs-Élysées. My main mission was to entice the French auto company Renault to build a plant in Brampton. I took the task seriously, and succeeded in 1984, assuring three thousand auto-working jobs and the production of the Renault 19. Everyone in the government was satisfied with that, and I felt that the bulk of my mission had been accomplished.

At the time, the Canadian ambassador was Michel Dupuy, a seasoned diplomat who understood all the subtleties of our relationship with France. It had always been my opinion, though, that it would have been better for France to have had an anglophone ambassador from Canada who spoke excellent French (and better for England to have had a francophone ambassador in London who spoke excellent English). I knew there were such people in our Foreign Affairs department, and it seemed to me that this would have presented to the French a new kind of image of Canada. Then they might not have condescended to our francophone population as "les petits cousins" with their quaint accents and tuques (nor the British to the "dear Canadians"). They would know that our bilingualism was a two-way street. The element of condescension on the part of the French was something so ingrained that it didn't have to be expressed. It was just *there*.

It seemed to me that the French undercut their real superiority in many areas—their subtlety, their trenchant logic, their taste— with this false, unnecessary superiority.

The Agent General for Quebec was Yves Michaud, who had a

past and a future in the Parti Québécois. I think he and the Quebec government were very startled, to put it mildly, by the Ontario government's decision to open an office and by their choice of me as agent general. We were also not particularly welcomed by the head of the North American division at the Quai d'Orsay—the French Foreign Affairs ministry. When I went there to make my first formal call on the director general for North America and his assistant director (whose tongue flicked like a lizard's throughout the meeting), I could not help but notice the Quebec flag behind his desk, right alongside the French flag. No Canadian flag was present. I always felt I had the advantage of not being a diplomat and of having learned to ask questions, so after the pleasantries were over, I said, "Tell me, Monsieur, why there is no Canadian flag when there is a Quebec flag." He looked so surprised and said in a fluster, "Well, we don't seem to have one here." I burst out laughing.

He was, I felt, extremely condescending. All he asked me about was my family and my education—nothing about Ontario's having one-third of Canada's population, or the one and a half million francophones who lived outside of Quebec, or our industrial successes. I knew that our twenty minutes would be up shortly, and as I had not even been asked to remove my coat or have it put anywhere, I felt that my exit would be pretty speedy.

I gave what became my little standard speech, which was that I assured them of the friendship of all Canadians—all ten million of them—who lived in Ontario and of how we wanted to work together with the French to our mutual economic advantage, and how I wished that we would be able to exchange ideas, both intellectual and cultural, through the means of universities and artistic groups. The director general's eyes withdrew into the back of his head. Finally, I decided it was up to me to leave. I finished a sentence and stood up rather abruptly. "Thank you so much. It's been wonderful to meet you." I was complimented on my accent and my vocabulary, something I became quite accustomed to in Paris. I was never really flattered because I knew the subtext was that other people from Canada spoke French badly. We shook hands and I left.

I wouldn't characterize the meeting as having been impolite, but it certainly was not welcoming. I was accompanied to it by the number two at the Canadian Embassy, and I asked him as we drove away if he thought we had had the appropriate reception. I had wanted to walk because it was such a short distance to both the embassy and our offices, but I was told that we had to arrive and exit in a limousine in order to conform to international standards. He mumbled something to me that sounded like a strangled yes. Within three years, the director general became the French ambassador to London, and his assistant director was killed a decade later in a suspicious plane accident in Africa. Nobody ever told me if a Canadian flag appeared in that office.

I knew my job in Paris would not be easy because the ground was already pretty well trodden between Quebec and France. But I believed that we could develop a more diversified relationship with France. Our budget was tight, but there was enough to bring four Canadians over from Toronto and to hire six local staff. I found modern office space on Faubourg St. Honoré, and it worked extremely well for the five years that I was there. With this little staff, I was hoping to make Ontario—and therefore anglophone Canada—feel real to the French, and there wasn't much money left over after the rent and the salaries were paid. I think the whole budget was close to $1 million. About six months in, I realized that I couldn't be dealing with the French unless I also offered a cultural component, and I was fortunate to find Moira Johnson, who had accompanied her husband, Andy, to Paris, where he was posted to the Organization for Economic Co-operation and Development. Moira knew the Canadian cultural scene inside out, and we started to think of how we could make an impression on the French while not spending much money. This is the kind of challenge both of us liked, because it stretched our ingenuity, and in this case it culminated with a successful Ontario dance festival at the Centre Pompidou that the French actually paid for!

Meanwhile, something fabulously lucky landed in our laps. President Mitterrand was determined to build a number of monuments during his term (it was not for nothing that he spent his winter holidays in the Valley of the Kings, in Egypt). Besides a new national library and a complete refurbishing of the Louvre, he wanted to have a new opera house in the 11th Arrondissement, on the square where the Bastille had once stood.

Of course, everyone was excited about a new Paris Opera. The old one, the Palais Garnier, defined the Avenue de l'Opéra and was one of the crowning achievements of the Haussmann remodelling of Paris. Looking at pictures of Paris before 1863, you see what is virtually a little foothill between the Louvre and where the Opera is now. All of this was flattened to make way for a large boulevard that we today consider to be elegant city planning but which Haussmann conceived of as a place to charge cavalry down to quell revolts. Since 1789, the Paris population had used the narrow layout of medieval streets strategically, whether it was the storming of the Bastille or during the revolution of 1848. The Second Empire under Napoleon II understood that the city itself would have to be remodelled, and it is one of those fortuitous circumstances that the desire for public safety and the remodelling of the streets coincided perfectly.

To me, this was one of the subliminal pleasures of Paris—the layered knowledge of why the city looked the way it did, the pleasing parts inextricably intertwined with the sense of possible repression. I think that this is one of the reasons why Paris appeals to such a wide range of people in the world. This interlacing of beauty and strict order is something that we respond to in an urban setting. We don't know *why* we like it, but we like it.

President Mitterrand believed that the 11th Arrondissement was ripe for redevelopment. For so many years, it was considered a quaint, working-class part of Paris, with its meandering rue St. Antoine, where cabinetmakers worked their magic on beaten-up old pieces of furniture and where fake antiques of the most garish variety could satisfy even the most vulgar of tastes. The expression "le goût de la rue St. Antoine" was a picturesque way of saying "vulgarity." In the past, any major change to the Paris landscape had been tied to manifestations of town planning or a world's fair. The high style of the Eiffel Tower and the Grand Palais was developed—amazingly, it seems today—for the World's Fair of 1889 and 1900 respectively.

There was a great buzz about the international design competition for the Paris Opera. President Mitterrand made it known that he wanted to have absolutely the best architect in the world to work on this site. There was a lot of muttering and press about how the first opera house, the Opera Garnier, had run into terrific difficulties because it was situated over a water source and it took a great deal of engineering to make the site stable and viable. And, of course, many of us wondered, "If we get a new opera house, will the Phantom of the Opera leave the old opera and come to the new one?"

I wasn't paying much attention to the competition when I suddenly heard from a friend in Toronto that a Canadian architect from the Toronto firm of NORR was submitting a design. His name was Carlos Ott; he was originally a Uruguayan and in his thirties. He later came to see me in my office and told me that Mitterrand himself was going to make the final choice, blind. All identifying marks on the plans were to be taken off, and the great man would first narrow the selection down to three, and then choose the winner. Officials from the Ministries of Heritage and Culture would advise and provide background to the president.

Carlos was full of bounce and a lot of fun; he was not one of our well-known architects, and his major public buildings seemed to have been banks and other medium-sized commercial buildings. It was wonderful to see somebody who had the self-confidence to compete. He certainly never questioned whether he could win.

I felt that if we were able to catch the attention of the French with a Toronto design of the new Paris opera house, we would really have arrived.

Eventually, hundreds of submissions were narrowed down to three, and lo and behold, Carlos was one of the finalists. I don't think people in Ontario or the rest of Canada really understood the magnitude of this event. To be chosen, to even be a finalist, was an enormous boost to Carlos as an architect and to Canadian architecture as a whole. To say that it was a shock in Parisian circles when they realized that one of the three finalists (the other two were a Swiss and a Japanese) was a Canadian, and an English Canadian at that, is a huge understatement. They were flabbergasted and dismayed. It was quite fiendishly gratifying. There were a number of queries to the Canadian Embassy about whether Mr. Ott was not in fact from Montreal, rather than Toronto.

To the French, at the beginning of the eighties, Toronto essentially did not exist. Besides the natural French prejudice against the Anglo-Saxon world (as they thought of the English-speaking part of Canada), there was a feeling that we simply had no culture, despite our having a population of ten million and despite Toronto's being the largest city in Canada, with a unique collection of Chinese art at the Royal Ontario Museum, the Canadian Opera Company, and on and on.

I decided that something had to be done to make Toronto real to the president's advisers. We had no money to take people to Toronto, but I asked for a small additional budget for the judges to travel to Toronto for several days so that they could see the context in which Carlos was working—the TD Centre, the Royal Trust Tower, the old and new city halls. Ed Stewart, the premier's right-hand man, responded enthusiastically: "My goodness, what a great idea! Let's show them what Toronto's all about!" There was never any bureaucratic fumbling about with the Davis government; you pitched your good ideas and they caught them. You had the feeling that if you had a good idea, it was going to be listened to, it would be followed through, and if it didn't work out, well, a lot of things don't work out in life.

Because I could not go with the group from Paris (no budget!), they were hosted by people in the Ontario government, as well as by several people I knew in the cultural sector. At the time, we had no home for our ballet or opera companies, but the French could see how the city was growing and they had an idea of its financial wealth, which I think deeply impressed them.

Some people have said that President Mitterrand chose Carlos's plan only because he thought it had been done by Richard Meier. I know, from my sources and research, that this is not true. The similarity between Meier's work and Carlos's plans for the Opera was certainly evident—they are of the same school—but I never had the impression from any of the people I dealt with at the Opera in the next three or four years, as it was being built, that they had not picked the right design.

When Carlos was announced as the winner, there was almost consternation at the Canadian Embassy. It showed that we still had the "colonial cringe," which made it impossible for us to believe that we could really be excellent. I was frustrated in a number of ways: because the Canadian Embassy was so startled, it did not seem to react with the proper amount of pride, or have the ability to take advantage of such a marvellous coup; and because I kept having to tell people that the architect came from Toronto, I felt almost defensive answering the unspoken assumption that he must be from Montreal. When Carlos was announced as the architect in any French press accounts, his name was inevitably followed by "Uruguay-born" and frequently his

Canadian nationality was not mentioned. This was a typical outcome of the timid way in which anglophone Canada presented itself.

In Toronto, the result of this competition was received with equanimity but no sense that this was really a very important thing for us and for all of our high-end cultural and engineering skills. I felt that if the architect had been from Montreal, the Canadian Embassy would have made a huge fuss, instead of which we were constantly being underplayed.

The French did not look at this opera building as just an ordinary commission for a multi-million-dollar contract; they looked upon it as an expression of their national identity and their national pride. I found it interesting that they would hold an international competition for such a nationalistic purpose, until I realized that for the French, once you had created something for their city, for all intents and purposes you became French. That's where the self-confidence of their culture shows itself. They are the centre of the world and the world comes to them.

I THINK the Bill Davis government understood completely what its responsibilities were as elected officials in a world of Anglo-Saxon tradition—that parliamentary democracy was about electing representatives who would then have the confidence of the people and act as their representatives, not as their messenger. The whole essence of democracy lies in our confidence to elect and demand intelligent representatives who are willing to serve the public and be thrown out if they don't.

I can tell you from the inside out that I never felt, with that government, that the public was being used and manipulated. Neither was I, as their employee. I felt I was consulted, supported, directed. My biggest reward was that they thought I had done the right thing.

Another instance of the Davis government's sense of purpose was our landing the Renault plant for Brampton, Ontario. Of course, it's very easy to say that we had to get it for Brampton because it was the riding of William Davis. But there was already an auto plant there and it was logical to expand that plant and to make sure that all those thousands of jobs were kept in southern Ontario and close to its largest cities—Toronto and Hamilton. The minister of trade, Larry Grossman, and the premier himself did a lot of the lobbying in Paris, but I tried to support them by going to see the ministers involved on the French side, and, particularly, with brief but constant meetings with their chiefs of staff. Mr. Davis came to Paris on an official visit and met all the players. Our staff, totalling eight with local employees, was rather stretched organizing it, but everything went well.

The Canadian message was also carried with great verve and confidence by Lucien Bouchard, our ambassador after 1984. From the moment I first met him when he came to pay a courtesy call, I was impressed by his warmth and high intelligence. The latter showed itself immediately as he started to learn English; he was in his forties and spoke only the beautiful French of his native Saguenay. In six months, he was fluent, reading novels and the press in English. Whenever we had lunch together, he insisted on speaking English to me, asking me the meanings of colloquialisms he had heard. Once we met on the street when I was wearing a pink straw hat, and he exclaimed, "Adrienne, you stand down in a crowd!" It was so delightful, I've never forgotten it.

I used to tell him that his future lay in the national political arena, and he would pretend to be surprised. When he became a cabinet minister in the Mulroney government in the late eighties, I saw him from time to time when he came to Toronto. Unexpectedly, Meech Lake and its fallout occurred, and the Bloc Québécois came into being under his leadership. Then the Parti Québécois claimed him as leader and premier. I watched his remarkable career with the conviction that had the cards been played another way, he would have been the first Conservative French-Canadian Prime Minister of Canada. I am equally convinced that his intense authenticity would have endeared him to Canadians across the country.

I spent a lot of time going to heavy-industry places in France— Le Creusot, Marignane—and therefore learned a great deal about where the French had placed their industries and what those industries meant to them. Automobiles were a critically important part of France's industrial development, but so was their aerospace industry, located mainly in the southwest.

The French are, above all, intellectual people. That is to say that they first conceptualize what they want to do and then the practicalities follow. Their concentration on transportation in the eighties was part of a larger plan not only to link all parts of France by the fastest ground transportation possible but also to use that transportation system to develop urban centres beyond Paris. The aerospace industry was located in the Marseilles and Toulouse area. Therefore, it was logical that the new train industry should go there. The observer who thinks of the French as a happy little people fond of wine and cheese and baguettes has no idea of the concentrated, heavyweight self-interest the French bring to everything. I was glad that I had learned that twenty-odd years before my post there; I was up against people who knew exactly what they wished to do and were determined to do it.

I've always been disturbed by how, as Canadians, we don't think very much of ourselves; we always believe that somebody else might have the better idea. It's only in the last ten or so years that we have realized that we had the better idea. The case in point is the nature of our citizenship, and the kind of society that we have created with 215,000 new immigrants every year. Through either complacency or ignorance, we do not understand that we are totally different from any other society, that we need to promote the unexpected society that we have created in order to make it stronger and more real to ourselves.

ADRIENNE CLARKSON PRESENTS

I LEFT *THE FIFTH ESTATE* to become Agent General for Ontario in France, and when I returned to Canada, Avie Bennett, the new owner of McClelland and Stewart, asked me to come to the publishing house as president and publisher. I was honoured by Avie's request because I had loved the *Anne of Green Gables* books by L. M. Montgomery; Jack McClelland's father, the company's founder, was the first Canadian publisher of the *Anne* books. From the age of ten, I identified totally with Anne—an outsider wanting to make friends, and passionately concerned with everything that was going on around her.

I think the idea of things not being easy for a child was what appealed to me most. And then there was the whole atmosphere of Prince Edward Island and of the political situation between the Grits and the Tories. I had no background whatsoever to this kind of political sparring, so these books were my first political science lectures about Canada.

The last book of the series of eight, *Rilla of Ingleside*, was my introduction to Canada's role in the First World War. That story of sacrifice, heroism, and loss was told so beautifully through the eyes of Anne's youngest child and of their housekeeper, Susan, who is like a Greek chorus of the commonsensical Canadian through the whole four terrible years when Jem and Walter, Anne's two oldest sons, join the Canadian Expeditionary Force and fight in France, Walter never to return. Each battle provides chapters of understanding about what Canadians were going through when their men were fighting overseas. The Battle of Ypres, commonly called "Wipers" in Canada, was a particular difficulty of Susan's. She found both the action and the name incomprehensible, and I think in this represented a great deal of what most Canadians thought. It was fitting that the series should end with this acknowledgment of our nationhood told through this small family whose mother had been orphaned, taken in, loved others, and created a family.

For me, as an immigrant, this portrait of Canada is one that is both real and magical. And I think it is particularly valuable for anyone growing up in a city where people don't know each other to suddenly find that there is a place in Canada, Prince Edward Island, where everybody knows everybody and is related to them at least once over. The *Anne* books gave me fictional parents and grandparents who belonged in the place I had come to as a stranger. They helped me to become Canadian. And all of the *Anne* books taught me a lot about what a young Canadian woman could be.

Jack McClelland gave us a sense of ourselves as a people and had a brilliant eye for talent. All his authors—Pierre Berton, Farley Mowat, Margaret Atwood, Al Purdy, Leonard Cohen, just to name a few—adored him, even if at times he tried their patience. (He published the two novels I wrote, in 1968 and 1971.) He brought a sense of complete humanity and personality to a business that was unfortunately ruled by twenty-column ledgers.

I enjoyed my two years at McClelland and Stewart, especially publishing Michael Ondaatje's *In the Skin of a Lion*, Pierre Berton's *The Arctic Grail*, and Margaret Atwood's *Cat's Eye*. The list made me proud, and the editors, such as Ellen Seligman, were completely devoted to Canadian literature and convinced of its excellence even under difficult economic conditions.

But I knew that I wouldn't be able to bring McClelland and Stewart to where it needed to go. I had the knowledge but lacked the talent to bring the company to a healthy and viable state. I was lured back to television by Ivan Fecan, the CBC's brilliant young director of programming, who offered me my own program on culture, carte blanche. It would be an hour-long weekly show, which the CBC had not had for nearly two decades. The chance to really feature our country through its artists was very appealing to me. And indeed, in the eleven years that I did *Adrienne Clarkson Presents*, I found what I believed to be the most enriching aspects of our country and brought them to everyone who wanted to know about them.

When I look at a list of subjects, I remember wonderful moments: going with architect Arthur Erickson to the West Coast to look at the quality of his work—from his private homes to the Vancouver courthouse and his buildings in Seattle and California. He is generally acknowledged to be an innovator and a genius.

I was particularly eager to show the depth and quality of Quebec, Acadian, and generally francophone culture. In theatre and performance, francophones were edgier, more avant-garde, more willing to take risks than their anglophone peers. In music, they had singers like Richard Séguin and Richard Desjardins. In dance, people like Paul-André Fortier and Édouard Lock were pushing the limits of what the human body could do. In a way, my programming was my subtle attempt at bringing the country together, because you can't be part of a place if you don't understand each other and appreciate each other's talents. This bringing-together does not occur in our national broadcasting system because the francophone and the anglophone networks are completely separate, and there is very little mingling. I was so thrilled that our production of "Peau, Chair et Os" (Skin, Flesh and Bone) was prepared by us in bilingual productions under the direction of the brilliant Gilles Maheu. This mixture of dance, text, and poetry was great performance. But the anglophone audience, although appreciative, didn't truly understand the extraordinary quality of this piece. In Quebec, we were given the Prix Gemeaux—the francophone Gemini—for best performance, which stunned both Gilles and me. We had not even intended to go to the ceremony, because we thought it was so unlikely that we would win, but in the end we trotted off together and nobody could have been more surprised and thrilled than we were. We did *not* get a Gemini Award!

I carried this desire to bring the excitement of Quebec culture to my work as Governor General. The examined life is not a series of jobs. It is beliefs, interests, trials, and dreams to carry through everything we do. This Quebec excellence, and my admiration for it, have, I think, permeated my personal relationship with its artists and people. John Ralston Saul has always published in Paris and in Quebec where he has a large following; I remember just after we met in 1976 his coming back from the Salon du Livre book fair in Chicoutimi and telling me of the lively cultural scene there, of the writers who made le royaume du Saguenay their home.

When, early in my mandate, we announced to our staff at Rideau Hall that we wanted to pay an extended visit to the Saguenay, there was some hesitancy and trepidation—the area is ninety-five percent sovereignist, they said; maybe you won't be welcome. Our gut feeling is that the people you touch on an intellectual and personal basis are able to have relationships that never enter the realm of politics. We never asked people, no matter where they came from in Canada, what their politics were, and it never entered our conversations.

In the Saguenay, we had a warm and wonderful welcome; the local press coverage was serious, friendly, and perceptive. How people vote, express themselves politically, is their business, not the Governor General's. When the RCMP worried about our going to the main street in Chicoutimi for lunch, because there had been a labour demonstration, we went anyway. A lot of the strikers were sitting in outdoor pubs at lunchtime and, as we walked down the street, they shouted, "Adrienne, John! Venez ici!" and we shook hands to smiles and welcomes. We were surrounded by goodwill and, as we talked, I thought of something a young salesgirl had said to me in Quebec City. As she took my credit card, she looked from it up to me and said, "C'est bien que vous êtes gouverneure, vraiment bien" (It's a good thing you are Governor General), and when I smiled and asked why she thought so, she said, "Parce que vous êtes bilingue; vous parlez français." As the first anglophone Governor General to be fluently bilingual, I felt gratified. Canadians, and particularly Quebeckers, notice these things.

Imagine how anglophones would feel about a Governor General who could pump out only a stilted phrase or two in English? Would anglophones feel they had anything in common with this person who represents the state? Speaking French is an absolute necessity. And I think that we as a couple represented what could be viewed as consideration, respect, and comprehension in our knowledge of Quebec culture and the French language.

The problems we face as a country we all share in every part of Canada: loss of traditional ways of life in our commodity-based communities—coal, fishing, pulp and paper, family farms. In the Saguenay, the mayors of Alma, Jonquière, and Chicoutimi told me that the equivalent of a busload of young people leaves every week to go to Montreal to look for work. We share more than we ever acknowledge in Canada; I am fortunate to have seen that in six years.

The second residence of the Governor General is the Citadel, on the highest point of Quebec City. We would go there every few months and see and entertain as many people of Quebec City as we could. We held ceremonies there for the Order of Canada, the Caring Canadian, and Bravery. We fully integrated the activities of the vice-regal office into the life of the city. I was proud to receive an honorary doctorate from the Université de Laval, the first Governor General to be so honoured, and John Ralston Saul received one from the Université du Québec à Montréal.

I LOVED ALL THE PROJECTS we did season after season on *Adrienne Clarkson Presents*. But the one documentary into which I put my heart and soul was about James Wilson Morrice, arguably one of Canada's finest painters. He came from a wealthy family in Montreal, and his aspirations to become an artist were listened to, surprisingly, by his father, probably because Sir William Van Horne of the CPR told the elder Morrice that young James had talent. Van Horne was quite the amateur artist himself and perhaps he saw in the young man's dreams something he himself had not had a chance to fully express.

I discovered a great deal of material written about Morrice by people like Somerset Maugham and Arnold Bennett, who used him as a peripheral character in some of their fiction. He played the flute and probably drank seriously, although that has never been mentioned in any of the official biographies. He was always referred to as somebody who had "ill health." He went off to North Africa in the winters, not only for the benefit of its light and the climate but also to preserve his well-being. He went twice with Matisse to Morocco, and it was Matisse who said that Morrice was one of the most sensitive colorists that he had ever encountered.

Even by 1900, Morrice, who was then only about thirty-five years old, was selling all his paintings at the modernist Salon d'Automne in Paris. His output was huge. Every day he went out with small wooden cigar-box-sized panels on which he quickly sketched what he was seeing—in the Luxembourg Gardens, on the Pont Neuf, and when he was by the seaside in Brittany, the sailing and the water bathing at Concarneau.

I felt that Canadians needed to know more about him, and perhaps lingering in my mind was the memory that in 1963, I had been offered a small Morrice for $2,000. I couldn't afford it. It's always wise to remember things like that because they put your life, if not your tastes, into perspective!

The Morrice story was told as a drama documentary, using actors to play the central roles (Nicholas Campbell played Morrice) and inserting scenes showing the original backgrounds and inspirations for the paintings. I loved doing documentaries about painters because there is something about the use of colour and form that I think transmits well on television. The Morrice film won a Columbus Award in the United States, and I thought how pleased Morrice would be to think that an award for a program about him could be named after the discoverer of the New World when he himself had discovered the Old. He said that he never wanted to come back to Canada except in the winter, which he loved. He felt that the spring was too green and the autumn too pretty.

Morrice became one of Lord Beaverbrook's war artists during the First World War and painted a huge canvas of soldiers marching across a field, which was never publicly displayed from the time it was painted in 1917 until the new Canadian War Museum opened in 2005. It has pride of place there, and I am thrilled to be able to see it with all the thousands of other Canadians who visit the museum.

Sometimes we were fortunate enough to be able to follow up on projects after a first film. This was the case with Frank Gehry, the Canadian architect who had become famous all over the world but, by 1995 when we featured him, had never designed a building in Canada. He loved hockey, and we were able to film him playing in Montreal, when he was giving an architectural demonstration to students at McGill. We followed him to the Czech Republic, where he presented to President Václav Havel his plan for a building in

Prague, a multi-storey wavy design, seeming to throb with rhythm and which he called "Ginger and Fred." Two years later, when he was building the Guggenheim Museum in Bilbao, we knew that we wanted to follow the progress of that too, so we did an update on the original documentary, with a visit to Bilbao in his company. The privilege of doing a series about genuine creative geniuses is to be able to have access to their minds by asking them questions, by seeing, however briefly, through their eyes, through their dreams, through their identity.

Television was always exciting for me because my curiosity can never be satisfied. People often ask me if I want to go back into television, and all I can say is that I did television for nearly thirty-five years; it is my motherhouse, as medieval monks used to say. I was very lucky that it suited me, and I will never regret a single part of that career. But I have often said that a life in television is like the life of a dog: one year is worth seven. If you see the rapidity with which people generally "have a career" in television, it should certainly give you a warning that it is not a stable life suited to everyone.

I was lucky because I was able to learn in the finest school there was—among the producers of the CBC in the sixties and seventies. I truly believed in public broadcasting, which gave a grounding to all the work that I did. I wanted to enlighten and entertain other people and myself. I did not go into television in order to be famous and I have often found that that part of the life was hard to bear. To a great extent that is why I separated my private and public lives so strictly. It is why I have never written about myself until now. I despise the idea of celebrity. I think it cheapens one's belief in integrity. Nowadays when I see how fame is chased after and how all people who are well known are somehow thrown into a bag of dirty laundry labelled "Celebrity," I'm very glad I'm not starting out now in TV.

The ultimate absurdity of this idea of fame as being worth something occurred to me when I was Agent General in Paris. One of
my duties was to go to the Cannes Film Festival, to promote the
Ontario Film Development Corporation and the films it was invest-
ing in. I have to say this event of absurd puffery must rank at about
zero in any of my preferred activities on a scale of one to ten. We
had been to a luncheon at the Carleton Hotel and as we came down
a wide staircase, a woman rushed up to me with a pencil and a piece
of paper and said: "Are you somebody? If you are, can I have your
autograph?"

When I was Governor General, I always refused to give autographs, because I preferred to talk to people face to face. I could not
see the value in giving a celebrity movie star kind of quality to an
office that should inspire respect, be warm and communicative—
and autographs are the exact opposite of all of that.

I don't believe fame gets you anywhere, even if they do always
spell your name right. Fame has no meaning. It has no justification.
And I will never be reconciled to it. Nor do I respect people who
use it for their own purposes. It is an all-consuming monster, and
our society is unhappily in its thrall.

BEING CHOSEN

MANY PEOPLE THOUGHT that Prime Minister Jean Chrétien asked me to become Governor General because I was on television and was well known. But I believe that Mr. Chrétien did not associate me with television. I know he saw me as someone who had been Agent General for Ontario in France, and I am sure that that is the way he continues to think of me.

In June of 1999, when Roméo LeBlanc announced that he would be leaving in the fall, I was discreetly approached by the Prime Minister's Office to see whether I would be interested in becoming Governor General: "Would you be willing to let your name be on a shortlist for this position?" (I'd heard almost exactly the same words about a year before in regard to the position of lieutenant-governor of Ontario.) I believe this is tantamount to saying, "You've got the job if you can just keep your mouth shut."

John and I were at our Georgian Bay cottage, and we talked about it that weekend and all through the next week. On the one hand, we had lives that we could describe as fulfilling and fun. My television work, while always challenging in the face of the strangeness and benevolent neglect of the CBC management, was going well. John's writing was successful. Every book was a bestseller, in English and in French, and *The Unconscious Civilization* had won the Governor General's Award in 1996. We had our island in Georgian

Bay, where we were able to spend much of the summer, and we spent time in France, as well as having an engrossing life in the artistic world of Toronto.

We had an inkling of what being Governor General would be like, because in 1997 we had been invited as two of the thirty-five people who went with Roméo LeBlanc and his wife, Diana Fowler LeBlanc, to India and Pakistan on a state visit. We saw how they had to change their clothes four times a day and be rushed around in groups of limousines and how they had to represent Canada everywhere (which they did with great dignity). It gave us some idea of the constraints of the position.

John and I talked a great deal about what we could do in the job—visit the whole country and help Canadians to know each other, and champion bilingualism. I asked myself if, as Governor General, I would be able to bring dignity and openness to an institution that is so important to our Constitution but dangerously misunderstood and at the risk of being out-of-date and irrelevant. Every country is the sum of its history. I felt we could infuse history into my representing the Crown in Canada and being the guarantor of responsible government.

While we were turning these things over in late spring, I had a conversation with Jean Pelletier, the chief of staff to Prime Minister Chrétien, and although we discussed the Governor General's position, he never asked me what I thought *I* would do with it. It was becoming clearer and clearer to me that they would be offering the job to me. Because of my journalism background, I assumed that the RCMP was checking my background and looking into everything that either of us might have done. The job is so important, constitutionally and symbolically, that I know due diligence was carried out. I wondered with amusement how the RCMP would report that I had gone on a student trip to the Soviet Union in 1961; as there was no more Soviet Union, I relaxed. (In fact, just before I left office in 2005, Mr. Pelletier confirmed that meticulous research. With that wily, wise look in his eye, he said, "We knew *everything* about both of you.")

Both Mr. Pelletier and Mr. Chrétien are consummate politicians and tacticians. They know where they want to go and whether they want to take one, two, or three downs to get that ten yards made. I felt confident with them because they were smart and because whatever they did, they would do, as the French say, "en toute connaissance de cause"—fully aware of all the ramifications. Both of them understood the role of the Governor General: that the Governor General is the constitutional apex in our political system. They would not take any risks.

In time, after my second long conversation with Mr. Pelletier, in which we addressed the possibility of my being offered the job, I realized that it was likely going to happen. John and I talked about perceptions as well as realities. We had been together as a couple since 1976, and were not married. I had not wanted to get married, because, if worst came to worst, I didn't want to be divorced again; once was unpleasant enough. But, knowing I was going to be Governor General, we did not want people who might be upset by our not being married to have that as a reason to criticize us. We were deeply amused when the newspaper articles appeared about how I had married my boyfriend in order to become Governor General. I thought it was rather sweet that after twenty-three years he should be considered my "boyfriend."

In any case, we had a lovely wedding in July 1999, which John said was the best wedding he'd ever been to. Both of us have been to large, crowded weddings with families on both sides sometimes behaving badly, usually to each other, and having fights over where a reception was going to be or what colour of flowers would adorn the aisle. We went to the chapel at St. Mary Magdalene Church in Toronto, where we are parishioners, accompanied by dear friends of

forty years—Cathy and Bill Graham and Michael and Dorothy
Peers. Dorothy had come to Toronto when Michael had become
the primate of the Anglican Church in Canada, and she had worked
for me, first at McClelland and Stewart and then at the CBC. It was
primarily a Trinity College group encompassing decades of friendship. Michael married us, assisted by Father Harold Nahabadian.
After a glass of champagne at the rectory, we went to the Bar Italia
on College Street for our wedding breakfast, which was just the
regular brunch there. Then the six of us piled into our cars and
drove north to spend the weekend together on our island. It was the
perfect wedding and the perfect honeymoon.

When I had said to the Peers and the Grahams that they should
drop everything because we were getting married that weekend,
without indicating in any way why we had decided to do it then,
they expressed their delight and accepted it without question. You
know who your best friends are when they can keep a secret, or
don't even ask the questions that could lead to having to keep a
secret.

Shortly after our wedding, Mr. Chrétien's assistant called and
asked if we would go to Lac des Piles, near Shawinigan, for the day
to talk with Mr. and Mrs. Chrétien. We arrived at their very charming cottage, by no means grandiose but surrounded by hideous wire
security fencing and more RCMP officers than you would ever
want to see in one domestic space. A huge thunderstorm began as
we arrived and the rain poured down; my mother had always said
that rain brought good luck and you should always wish for rain for
anything auspicious to happen. Mme Chrétien brought tea and
smiled in that way of hers that combines a kind of warmth without
interference, which I think she has perfected as a political wife. We
chatted together, and then Mr. Chrétien asked me if I would accept
the post of Governor General if it was offered to me. I said yes, I
would. He said, "Well, I'm going to Sarajevo next week and I'll call

you from there because we're still investigating you." I said, "Fine." (What else was I going to say?) And we finished our tea and then took a walk around the property.

The next week was truly extraordinary. I went for a routine medical checkup and the monitors picked up an irregular heart-beat—atrial fibrillation. Straightaway I went to my doctor, who sent me to a cardiologist, who said I had to have an angiogram immedi-ately, just in case there was a blockage of my arteries. A mere three days after having been to Lac des Piles, I was in a catheter lab having an angiogram. It turned out nothing was wrong with my arteries, but indeed I did have an irregular heartbeat. We didn't tell anybody about this, except our very closest friends, and the next day I had a cardioversion, an electric-shock procedure to put my heart back into a steady rhythm. But I was told that if it ever slipped out of rhythm again, I would have to repeat the cardioversion. (Since then, I've had the procedure at least twice a year, and it was during one of these treatments that it was discovered I had a problem that a pacemaker would have to regulate.)

I had no sooner returned home from the hospital early that after-noon when the phone rang, and it was Mr. Chrétien calling from Sarajevo. We exchanged pleasantries, and I told him that John and I had been married the previous weekend. There was a little pause and then he said: "Well, I would like you to be Governor General. That's my wedding gift." I told him I thought it was a nice wedding gift but coyly added that we hadn't done it for that reason. In fact, nobody had ever mentioned to me that this was a necessity for the job. I think they felt that I would simply cope with my situation. This was a modern world and we would see what happened.

I had always envisaged that John and I would live like Jean-Paul Sartre and Simone de Beauvoir and, indeed, in our more than twenty years together, we had travelled separately for work and had friends together but never felt crowded by each other. In fact, when we moved to Rideau Hall, we spent more time together than we probably had in all the twenty-odd years previously!

The last thing Mr. Chrétien said to me in that phone call was, "This is a secret." I said, "I know." It was a legend that a candidate for Governor General some years before had been warned to keep it a secret but subsequently spilled the beans to a stewardess on the way home and to several of his friends. Somebody else was chosen. If you are asked to keep a secret as a prospective Governor General, it's a kind of test. It's like the elf in the Grimms' fairy tale: if you can't keep a secret, then you don't deserve to be Governor General, because as Governor General, you have to keep a lot of secrets. Fortunately it's in my temperament to be able to keep secrets. I have a special storeroom in which I put secrets and I never think of them or use them in any way. John is the same way, and on many occasions people have said, "Didn't John tell you that I told him and asked him to keep it a secret?" A secret is a sacred thing between two people. My vice-regal secrets are in the National Archives, and just before I become a hundred years old, they will be opened to the public. I will be happy to discuss many matters then.

We were next contacted by Mel Cappe, the clerk of the Privy Council, who told us, "We will not be announcing this until the week after Labour Day." That date had been chosen so that Mr. LeBlanc could preside over the international meeting of the Francophonie in Moncton the week before. That meant there were six more weeks to go in which we couldn't tell anybody, not my father, not our closest friends—not anybody. We were so anxious to keep that secret that when we decided that we should read all the academic constitutional material regarding the office and duties of the Governor General, we didn't go to the library and take the books out. Instead, we went day after day for a week to the Metropolitan Toronto Library and read the books at the study tables there. We worried that it might be noticed if we checked out books on

Canadian constitutional matters, so we disguised our pursuit with a pile of books about the American Constitution and South American land problems, and sat behind them reading books like Jacques Monet's *The Crown in Canada*. Luckily, we already owned former Governor General Vincent Massey's autobiography and a collection of his speeches, and *The Biography of Georges Vanier* by Robert Speaight. But there was absolutely no literature on what a Governor General actually *did* once installed at Rideau Hall that wasn't connected simply to the opening and closing of Parliament, the reading of the Speech from the Throne, receiving state visitors, and ceremonies like the Order of Canada.

I stayed away from Ottawa during all that time because speculation was rising about who would become Governor General, and I didn't feel that I should make any kind of appearance that would feed rumours. On reflection, I think I could have had a very useful time at the Parliamentary Library, but of course, then everybody would have guessed, wouldn't they?

I was busy in August for two weeks with the visit of our godchildren from England, and of course I was somewhat preoccupied and worried, so therefore I fell ill. My ears plugged up and I had a sore throat for some six or seven weeks. Perhaps all the illnesses I could possibly get came rushing in because my body knew that there wouldn't be time in the next six years for me to be sick!

Our discretion was rewarded, because I wasn't hounded by rumours through the month of August, when I needed to concentrate on writing my installation address. Mr. Chrétien had told me that I must give a good address, as it would be my first contact with the government and the Canadian people as Governor General. Mr. Chrétien was very knowledgeable about the role of the Governor General, and as prime minister, he had a correct relationship to the office. During all the time he was prime minister, in public and in private meetings he always called me "Madame la Gouverneure" and I called him "Prime Minister." On the other hand, he and John were on a first-name basis.

From then on, there seemed to be a kind of inevitability about events. I spoke once more with Mr. Pelletier on the phone, but most of my communications were through the clerk of the Privy Council, Canada's top civil servant. When the announcement was about to be made, we went up to Ottawa the night before and stayed at the Château Laurier under assumed names. Just before we left, there had been one inquiry from the press, from Graham Fraser, then at *The Globe and Mail.* Because we knew Graham socially, I told John that I would not call him back because I didn't want to lie to him.

When I walked into the press conference, I realized what a surprise I was to everybody, and I knew that the adventure had begun.

They tell you when you go to Rideau Hall that you run everything and there's this curious paradox that you both do run everything and yet run nothing. Structurally, Rideau Hall is like a small agency or ministry—the Governor General is the equivalent of a minister, and the secretary to the Governor General is the equivalent of a deputy minister. But on the other hand, the Governor General does not represent anything politically partisan, and for everything to operate correctly there is no room for a political staff contending with the permanent staff. If renewal was to come, it would have to begin from within, with energy, commitment, and vision.

What struck me after the first couple of weeks at Rideau Hall was that some people had been there for a long time, and that the phrase "It's always been done that way" didn't even need to be said, because the thinking was so entrenched. For instance, John was made to buy a top hat, which he wore twice in six years. On the other hand, there were a number of very bright people with ideas bursting out of them just waiting for direction. We focused on them to carry out what we wanted to do, and felt the others could be swept along as enthusiasm grew.

ALMOST FROM THE BEGINNING of my television career, I have taught myself how to say "Yes" to life and "No" to particular suggestions. I have been asked to run for each one of the three major political parties, and been offered other political positions. I never wanted to be in politics and so I didn't even seriously consider any of these overtures.

But it went rather deeper than that as I became better known, especially during and after my experience as Agent General in Paris. I was asked in the eighties to become the head of the Canada Council. When I replied to the minister that the last time I had looked there was already a head of the Canada Council, the reply was, "Never mind. We'll take care of that."

One afternoon in Paris in 1984, my phone rang, and a man from Prime Minister Brian Mulroney's office asked if I would like to be the head of the Canadian International Development Agency. I was astounded, because I had never had anything to do with international development. As well, the person asked me to make up my mind in two hours. I said that I couldn't possibly make up my mind in two hours or even two weeks. I was then informed that it would have to be within two hours so that the prime minister could make the announcement before taking off for an international trip in which CIDA would play a role. My astonishment was followed by disbelief, and I asked him, "Why did you want me particularly?" He replied: "Because you're a high-profile woman." The unforgettable answer that came back after I demurred was: "Don't think about it anymore. Just accept it. You'll have your own limousine and first-class travel all the way!"

To say that I was appalled is only to note that this was quite early on in my contact with these kinds of people in those kinds of positions. The cynicism, the manipulation, and the contempt for citizens were something I wasn't used to. A number of years later I spoke to the person who had been head of CIDA then and the person who, presumably, would have been thrown from a limousine in the dark if I had decided to take the position. That person told me that she had been told that my acceptance was a ninety percent done deal. Luckily, as she was more experienced than the people manipulating behind the scenes, she had realized that this could not possibly be true.

Each time anything like that happened, it took me completely by surprise, and it made me wonder whether people actually did accept these sorts of positions immediately, without thinking about the ramifications either for the job they were taking or for the country if they were inexperienced and simply being used as a token. I've never had the answer to that, but I'm ready to listen.

The last major thing I had been asked to do before I was asked to be Governor General was to become a senator, in 1994. I had never thought of being a senator, but I immediately answered that I couldn't do it, as I couldn't afford not to have a full-time job in television; if I were a senator, I wouldn't be able to work for the CBC anymore, because it would be a conflict of interest. I did not consider the role to be some kind of retirement package, and it did not interest me to simply have the position because it's considered a feather in one's cap. One prominent journalist said to me, "I understand that you have refused the top job." It was several seconds before I realized that he meant declining being a senator. It is a job that is written into our Constitution, but I had no idea that it would be considered, even by a so-called cynical journalist, "a top job." This shows the kind of ambivalence that journalists have—they would criticize senators and the Senate but also in their heart of hearts think of it as a real prize.

With all these requests, I always thought "Can I do this job?" and the answer was always no. First of all, I simply didn't want to do the job, and that means that it would not have been right for me to even try. I think for any position you have to have a certain excitement and wonderment and a challenge thinking of what you could bring to it that nobody else could. In none of the situations I've just shared could I say that. I think it would be leading a dishonest life. In my brief time at McClelland and Stewart, I enjoyed everything about helping Canadian writing to be appreciated and sold, and the fact that it wasn't ultimately a good fit for me doesn't make me regret having tried. I respect everything about publishing and every person who works in it.

I'm very wary of being used, for all kinds of reasons that have nothing to do with my qualifications or my choices in life. I simply have an abhorrence to being used in any way. The history of women has always been tragic when they allowed themselves to be used. That objectification of women is the greatest hurdle to freedom— economic and spiritual and sexual—that we face. I have never believed that you needed to use your certain advantages as a woman—being attractive, for instance—in any way that would get you ahead. I can say frankly I've never had any respect for people who used their beauty to help them get chosen for certain kinds of work. My father discussed this with me when I was a teenager, and we agreed that certain of my friends were cute or sexy and might get ahead by using that. My father said, "Your appeal is definitely for a high-fidelity, stereophonic receiver." I believed that—and I still do.

Sharon Stone has said that you can only sleep your way to the middle. In my observation, this has certainly been true. All the women I know who have done extraordinary things have done them with a combination of high intelligence, physical and emotional fortitude, and the knowledge of their femininity.

My feminism begins with Virginia Woolf's *A Room of One's Own* and continues through the 1970s with Germaine Greer's *The Female Eunuch* and Mary Jane Sherfey's *The Nature and Evolution of Female*

Sexuality. Those are only two of the guideposts that led me through the late sixties and seventies to a reinforced position of women's struggle and women's worth.

I'm often asked whether I think that being a Chinese woman was particularly helpful in my career. I think the subtext of this question is whether or not I felt I was a token. I never felt like a token, because I don't believe that the people who chose me for my first job in television thought that I was a token either. I had more of a feeling that I was chosen because I was different, and that made me feel very comfortable because I *was* different and unique. I accepted that. I don't mean that to sound arrogant, but to start in Canadian television in the mid-1960s as a young Chinese woman was certainly unusual. I don't think the CBC was looking for anyone like me, but they stumbled across me and we fitted each other.

It strikes me as both weird and offensive to be asked whether I am Chinese *enough.* I don't know that people ask Ukrainian Canadians whether they're Ukrainian enough or Italian Canadians whether they're Italian enough. Perhaps it's simply a kind of racism that comes out only towards those who are not white. I hope this is going to disappear, because it's a dead-end street. In this country, people can be what they wish to be and take on as much of their heritage as they want. We should never feel that we must impose on them something that is not them.

I have had people ask me why I don't speak Chinese. I don't speak Chinese because we never spoke Chinese at home and my father spoke hardly any Chinese. My brother and I were brought up speaking English. My parents wanted us to do extremely well in Canadian society, and that was why the emphasis was on English. Would I have liked to speak Chinese? Yes, of course, but you can't do everything.

We are creating a new country here, and that country will have all kinds of longings, ambitions, desires that are going to be met by all the people from all over the world who come and live here *in their own way*. There is no formula for becoming a Canadian and there is no formula for looking at people in terms only of where they have come from and whether they have kept enough of their background. People choose to do things at different periods in their life, and I found that I was almost forty when I learned what the significance of having a Chinese background was, when I went to China.

I don't think being chosen for jobs, including Governor General, had anything to do with any single attribute of mine that might have been perceived. That is why I approached the job with confidence: I knew that I was a package of interesting facets and that by 1999 in Canada, I could contribute everything that had made me a Canadian to my beloved country.

BEING GOVERNOR GENERAL

EVEN AS AN UNDERGRADUATE, I knew from the writings of Walter Bagehot that the representative of the Crown "encourages, advises, and warns." Rather grimly, MacGregor Dawson adds that "the value of the Office of the Governor General depends entirely upon the willingness of the incumbent to forgo his own wishes, to devote himself with a single mind to the public good and to be content with exercising a moderating influence, quietly and without public acknowledgement or acclaim." It seems that it's a saint that is called for, and I am not one!

The reason that I had some confidence that I could fulfill the role of Governor General was that, besides being able to keep secrets, I knew the country very well, thanks to my years at the CBC. I knew what the duties of a Governor General were: to ensure that there is always a democratically elected government, to uphold traditions, to sign all laws into effect, to recognize and award excellence with public ceremonies, to represent Canada and all of Canada's interests on state visits abroad, as determined by the government of the day, and to receive foreign heads of state. This is the general outline of what I knew and what I felt was the bare minimum of what should be done. Someone once compared the position of Governor General to a highly coloured fire extinguisher—ceremonial but functional. But even in the context of a minority government, I don't think there was any danger of large fires.

The great political philosopher C. B. Macpherson of the University of Toronto observed: "The most important way in which social institutions and social relations [shape] people as political actors, is in the way they shape people's consciousness of themselves." So much of what John and I did when we travelled around the country was to hold up a kind of mirror and ask people to reflect on what they, as citizens, were doing in society, in their lives.

In every town, whether it was Swift Current, Charlottetown, Winnipeg, or Sioux Lookout or Chetwynd, we held meetings for the entire town, some of which we called levees—an old-fashioned term that we hoped to make modern. We would simply announce that we would be available to meet people from 2 until 4 P.M. in the local armouries or the gym of the high school, or a public park if it was summer. We served cookies and tea, coffee and lemonade. People would line up for as much as half an hour to chat with us, to make us feel part of their lives. Sometimes the exchange was only thirty seconds long, but a lot can be said in thirty seconds, and it does not have to be superficial. In Saint John, New Brunswick, a man who was wearing extremely worn but spotlessly clean clothes told us that he was unemployed and living on less than $300 a month. But he said, "Don't worry about me. I worry about the people who have one or two children and have to live like that. I don't know how they do it." We heard that sentiment echoed all over the country. People always believe that even if they have it bad, somebody else has it worse. In Canadians, we found stoicism, stubbornness, and selflessness in equal measure.

In the six years that I was Governor General, I took part in more than six thousand events, travelling about 150,000 kilometres a year. We visited close to four hundred villages, towns, and cities. And even though some contacts were brief, the very act of shaking hands and touching someone and looking into their eyes can bring an instant and genuine rapport. Too often we pass by without really noticing others, even those with whom we work or share some time of day. I'm convinced that by looking people in the eye, whether it's in a subway or a store or at a social event, we can learn a great deal about them if we have an open heart.

It was a privilege to meet so many Canadians, most of them strangers to me, and to find, in grasping their hands and meeting their eyes, a true human connection. I write this at a risk of sounding banal, but I can assure you that my own feelings reflected their warmth. It was as if an electrical circuit had been completed. As individuals, we should never discount the value of this simple connection, the fact that we can enter each other's space, each other's consciousness, in this direct way. I am an introvert by nature, but when you are doing something with a purpose, with a mission even, whether or not you're introverted doesn't come into play.

People would tell me how they worried about the future of their family farm, or that all their children would leave Cape Breton to work in Alberta. From time to time, a parent would bring a mentally challenged child. There was a sense that by including this child there would be validation and recognition. None of this can be brushed off as people just wanting to be a part of a crowd or to be where the action was that day. I never had that feeling in any of the encounters, from Conception Bay to Igloolik. Everyone wanted to connect. And in doing so, I think that they deeply acknowledged other people and acknowledged themselves as citizens of Canada. It was this that made me understand the capacity of the institution of the Governor General to bring Canadians together. This is how a Governor General can help to shape people's consciousness of themselves.

Emphasizing our North was a way of making people aware that our country includes this vast landscape, with its Aboriginal peoples, its rich resources, its snow and ice. Sleeping in igloos, travelling by snowmobile and dogsled, helped me to participate in the valuable aspects of Arctic life. I knew that Canadians did not know enough about it, and that to draw attention to it would at least be a start to helping people have a consciousness of and, perhaps from that, a responsibility for the North.

It is because of my passion for the North that my official portrait is set in a background of snow and ice—winter, in fact. I'm rather pleased that mine is the only official portrait of all the Governors General from 1867 on that has snow as its setting. As Gilles Vigneault sings: "Our country is not a country, it is winter."

The more we realize that our country is winter, the more we can understand ourselves and know what our strengths and weaknesses are. We have to work hard for our food, for our shelter. Nothing is given to us in this harsh land. We know that the parameters of our society are fixed by climate and geography. We know we have to look after each other, because someone might come to our door when it's minus twenty outside and ask us for shelter. We would bring them in because we know that we might someday be in the same position. Nature is a frightening and uncontrollable force in Canada, and we are wise as Canadians to listen to it and to adapt to it.

I also knew, of course, that on a more day-to-day level there would be ceremonies like the Order of Canada and the Governor General's Literary Awards. I felt perfectly comfortable with the prospect of these kinds of ceremonies because in 1992 I had become an officer of the Order of Canada myself. John Ralston Saul had received the Governor General's Literary Award for *The Unconscious Civilization*. I also happened to have hosted the Literary Awards the year that Alice Munro won, when the ceremony was held in Toronto, in the lobby of the O'Keefe Centre. After John got his award in 1996, at the Monument Theatre in Montreal, we took the train to Ottawa so that the laureates could read at the National Library. We both said to somebody from Rideau Hall that we thought the awards should be given there and much more made of them. Whether it was our advice or whether other people also advised the same thing, the next year the awards were brought to Rideau Hall by my predecessor, Roméo LeBlanc.

As to the constitutional role, I knew that "the Crown" is the ultimate expression of the legitimacy of our democracy, and therefore the office of the Governor General is of paramount importance. It is the kind of position that demands dignity, detachment, and neutrality, and an intimate knowledge of Canada and its history. This doesn't mean that a Governor General can't have ideas and opinions. When people asked me if I felt free to express my ideas, I always said an emphatic *yes*. That's because ideas aren't political (although the policies that stem from them may well be). If they were, can you tell me any political party in a society like ours would be for keeping people poor or homeless? Would be against free discussion or healthy regional and national development? All societies should be considering questions and discussing ideas, and the Governor General can provide leadership to show that the discussion can happen in a non-partisan way.

Anyone who spends any time reading our Constitution and talking to the experts knows that the role of the Governor General has deliberately been left rather vague. What could be more Anglo-Saxon? The power all lies in the unspoken, the unexercised. In terms of *formal* constitutional powers, one constitutional expert says: "The Governor General's principal function is to represent the Crown, the institution which embodies executive authority. And in this capacity, the Governor General rarely takes the initiative for himself or follows his own inclinations, but rather speaks and acts in accordance with the counsel given by his constitutional advisors, the Cabinet."

Or, as the historian W. L. Morton put it, "Character is of more than usual importance to someone who, by the nature of his office, must persuade rather than command." I read that before assuming office, and I have to say that I asked myself whether I would have the powers of persuasion. I certainly felt it was tested during my term as Governor General, but I feel free to give only a very minor example: dissuading the government from refurbishing the Governor General's railway cars and making them available to CEOs. The Governor General had used the cars to go everywhere there were rails. Roland Michener was the last Governor General to make continual use of them. For several decades, they had been falling into dusty disrepair. I felt the Governor General's train was not something that could be used in this proposed way. Better to accept that the days of the Governor General's private cars were over, rather than traffic the office and the history to commercial interests.

I had had a pretty good look at our political system in the years that I was at CBC, particularly on *the fifth estate*. I know that politicians are no better or worse than the population that sends them to Ottawa. I was not cynical about the political process, but I am, and was, wary of the actions, and often the motives, of those who gain public office and acquire a taste for what is a remarkable amount of power. A close observation of power would bring you as close to being an anarchist as any experience could. I believe that I was always optimistic yet careful, hopeful yet skeptical, open yet exigent.

And I don't think in the six years I spent in the post that my attitude changed. As a matter of fact, that mental stance stood me in very good stead throughout. It has allowed me to not take criticism personally but to look at the source from which it came; it taught me not to spend a great deal of time wondering why people were doing things. In many ways, being Governor General depends on an existential basis for being—it is often less valuable to question

motives than it is to judge actions. I'm convinced that most people
don't even know what their motives are, and that can be very true
of politicians who behave in a completely reactive manner.

Within the first year that I was Governor General, I was attending an event to honour those who had served since 1953 as
Canadian peacekeepers in Korea, Cyprus, the Golan Heights, and so
many other places. There I saw curious transactions taking place.
There were two ministers present and, as is usual with ministers, a
number of pilot fish and assistants and assistants to assistants. At one
point, I saw somebody giving one minister folded white sheets,
which I assumed to be a speech, and another set of sheets to the
other minister. As Governor General I spoke first, as is the custom
(either first or last has always been the rule). When I had finished, I
saw the same person quickly speak to both ministers and exchange
their documents. They both spoke from these papers, and it was
perfectly clear to me that neither of them had ever set eyes on those
words before. Later, I did a bit of sleuthing and I discovered that the
person who had written both speeches thought that they should be
read in a different order and each should be given by the other
minister.

I suppose I shouldn't have been surprised, because we've all
become so brutalized, expecting words not to be the expression of
the person delivering them. These words are mouthed by people
who frequently have no idea of the concepts behind them and
whose capabilities in language couldn't match them if they were
able to. And the public senses this.

I gave more than six hundred prepared speeches as Governor
General; I probably gave another four hundred as impromptu
remarks. I would think about the two or three ideas I wanted to get
across: say, for Bravery Awards or military funerals, the selflessness,
the instinctive gesture. I would discuss the general line of the speech
with my editorial assistant and suggest the kind of quotations I

wanted to use, and we would exchange ideas about the subject. A draft was prepared, and then I used that draft to dictate the speech. When that second draft came back, I revised and finalized it.

Speeches are oral—the sound of the voice is very important. My speech at the Tomb of the Unknown Soldier is the best example of my method for communicating with a formal speech. I began it with a quote from Herodotus: "In peace, sons bury their fathers; in war, fathers bury their sons." I have a fondness for classical quotations—Thucydides, Herodotus, Homer, and the Bible, especially Isaiah. These are the underpinnings of Western civilization. The Governor General, who represents continuity of our structures, should place that civilization in a Canadian context. For Canadians, I depended on Northrop Frye, Margaret Laurence, Hérmenégilde Chiasson, Jean-Guy Pilon, and many of our poets, among them A. M. Klein, George Bowering, and Leonard Cohen. Writing and making speeches was one of my most meaningful duties, although giving thirty in ten days, as I did on some state visits, could be exhausting! Only Mr. Mann's training and enabling spirit got me through.

There is much misunderstanding about the authority of the Governor General. Even many politicians don't seem to know that the final authority of the state was transferred from the monarch to the Governor General in the Letters Patent of 1947, thereby making Canada's government independent of Great Britain. This means that it is the Governor General who is the guarantor of responsible government and of our parliamentary democracy. I was amazed by how many people would ask me how often I spoke with the Queen and what advice she had to offer for our government. The Queen, of course, knows and respects the Letters Patent. In conversations with her, we never discussed a single political or constitutional matter. As she is a highly intelligent and knowledgeable person, I have no doubt that she kept up with what was going on, but she gave no indication of what she thought in any of my encounters with her, nor did she ever ask what I thought.

All laws have to be signed into effect by the Governor General, not the Queen. It is the Governor General who opens and closes Parliament and reads the Speech from the Throne. When the Queen was coming for her fiftieth Jubilee visit in October 2002, the government asked me to read the Speech from the Throne the week before she was to arrive in Canada. But, the speech was still "from the Throne," which symbolizes the abstract concept of the Crown's authority.

I differentiate between "the Crown" and "the Queen." It is true that the Queen is the Queen of Canada, and that is what legitimizes the Crown as the Crown in Canada. Somehow by the middle of the twentieth century, the royal family became confused with celebrity, and they have had to adjust to what that means. Meanwhile it has led to grave misunderstandings of the political position of the Crown. To treat the Queen like a movie star is to fundamentally misunderstand what the incarnation of legitimacy means. We are fortunate in Canada, as are the other Commonwealth countries, to have inherited a system of parliamentary democracy that dates back to the Magna Carta of the thirteenth century, an ordering of relations between human beings expressed by the British Common Law and the Civil Code—all of which is entrenched in our 1982 Charter of Rights and Freedoms.

In many ways, people prefer to know power as a direct force. Power is an interesting thing because even a modicum of it usually does what Lord Acton said, corrupting absolutely. What is fascinating in the Governor General's case is that the power is far reaching but almost never exercised. The Governor General has a reserve power in rare difficult situations—such as the death of the sitting prime minister—to act on his own initiative, although tradition usually means he doesn't. The most important occasion with far-reaching consequences for this rarely used power was the case of the death of Prime Minister Sir John Thompson in 1894. This left Governor General Lord Aberdeen to ensure there was another prime minister.

In our tradition, the Governor General would ordinarily have spoken to the caucus of the governing party to see who they felt should become their new leader and hence the prime minister. But the party in this case was the Conservatives, and Lord and Lady Aberdeen were English Liberals of the Gladstone variety. I have always thought that it was the most interesting manipulation of the system that we've experienced in Canada. Lord and Lady Aberdeen, who knew exactly what they were doing, made a choice whose results would be disastrous to the ruling Tories. Lord Aberdeen, passing over several talented and much younger cabinet ministers, asked Mackenzie Bowell, who was a senator and over seventy, to become the prime minister. The Aberdeens knew that an election would have to be called within the year and they knew that Mackenzie Bowell would be unlikely to make a mark as prime minister before that election, if ever, and was at any rate scarcely up to the job. The Governor General thus prepared the way for a Liberal victory in 1896, led by the young, charismatic, handsome, and brilliant Wilfrid Laurier.

Not that many people talk about the Aberdeens' blatant manipulations; they prefer to examine how Lord Byng did the right thing but got the wrong political result in the constitutional crisis of 1926, when he refused Mackenzie King's request to dissolve Parliament and called upon Arthur Meighen to form a short-lived government, which was then trounced in the next election. In that case, Byng's reputation was besmirched, and Mackenzie King was able to campaign on a platform of Canadian nationalist sentiment, deriding the British Governor General.

Most constitutional experts, including the late Senator Eugene Forsey, agree that Lord Byng was perfectly correct in refusing to grant the dissolution to King so quickly after the election. He should have realized that King was too clever by half and would find a way to use him politically. Byng also was not able to judge that Meighen did not have the political astuteness to seize the opportunity given to him.

In the case of Lord Aberdeen, no such criticisms ever occurred. No one ever talks about the manipulations of the Aberdeens partly because it resulted in the coming to power of one of Canada's most popular and extraordinary politicians, and the first French-Canadian prime minister to boot. The Aberdeens' actions changed Canadian history in a way that no Governors General, British or Canadian, have since.

It's typically Canadian that this exercise of the reserve power is vague, uncertain, and to some degree debatable. However, the power exists. I think only a very astute and politically conscious Governor General would be able to exercise this authority. And it would be justified only in the most exceptional of circumstances. When all is said and done, the Governor General usually acts upon the advice of the prime minister.

The question arose during Paul Martin's minority government of whether or not I as Governor General would grant dissolution and allow an election to be called if the prime minister requested it. After considering the opinions of the constitutional experts whom I consulted regularly, I decided that, if the government lasted six months, I would allow dissolution. To put the Canadian people through an election before six months would have been irresponsible, and in that case I would have decided in favour of the good of the Canadian people and denied dissolution.

When the controversy was whipped up around the state visit in 2003 to the circumpolar countries of Russia, Finland, and Iceland, I was deeply disturbed, not so much about the personal criticism—that I had taken friends on a frivolous junket—but because nobody, particularly the elected representatives and the ministers, seemed to understand that the Governor General does nothing, especially undertake voyages to other countries, without being asked to do so, in writing, by the prime minister. In the case of all my state visits, to Chile, Argentina, Germany, and the circumpolar one, our office received a letter from Prime Minister Chrétien requesting that I, as Governor General, go on these state visits in order to forward Canada's foreign-policy goals in those countries.

The furor was encouraged by the ignorant and malicious who wished to make it seem as though I had travelled abroad on a whim. The circumpolar state visits had been two and a half years in the planning. One journalist started the controversy by arbitrarily stating—without checking the figure with anybody—that the visits to the three countries cost $1 million. When the Department of Foreign Affairs announced that the budget was $5 million, these baying hounds cried that the budget had been wildly overspent. The actual trip was on budget, and that budget was comparable to Team Canada trips abroad, which cost $6 million, and the visit of the Queen to Canada in 2002, which again cost the Canadian government roughly $6 million.

Our office repeatedly stated that the Governor General travelled only at the request of the government, and we reiterated our pride in people like Michael Ondaatje, Jane Urquhart, Denys Arcand, Atom Egoyan, and the head of the Canadian Beef Association or the head of the Dairy Producers of Quebec joining us on these trips— but the media never printed or commented upon this. Most disappointing of all, no politicians of any of the parties, including the government, stood up in the House of Commons to say that the Governor General never travels except under advice from the government. It was hugely disappointing to me that they could not, or would not, do that. Given the total lack of courage and consistency, we were forced to cancel our subsequent trip to Norway,

Denmark, and Sweden, after time and money had been spent in preparation. I strongly suspect that the sponsorship scandal in Quebec made the government use our "over-budget" state visits as a diversion.

The question is not so much about the expenses, as the trips are budgeted for by Foreign Affairs, and always have been. My predecessors went on state visits, and John and I accompanied Mr. LeBlanc on his visit to India and Pakistan, together with thirty-five other Canadians, a diverse group of artists, representatives of non-governmental organizations and foundations, and a few business-people. This was the makeup of our visits as well, but I think they were a little more high powered, as we were able to personally persuade people like Michael Ondaatje, Denys Arcand, Paul Desmarais Jr., Maurice Strong, and Bob Rae to accompany us. To have these state visits characterized as junkets for my friends was the cheapest kind of calumny. We had taken seven outstanding Aboriginal leaders with us, including Peter Irniq, the commissioner of the Northwest Territories, and Sheila Watt-Cloutier, president of the Circumpolar Conference.

In July 2006, President Putin presented Russia's Order of Friendship to me, the only Canadian ever to be so honoured. Shortly afterwards, he made a point of mentioning it to Prime Minister Harper at the G8 meeting in St. Petersburg when they were discussing the natural gas question, saying how our state visit there had opened the doors for bilateral trade and cultural exchange. I am gratified that the Russians understood what we were trying to do and, three years later, honoured it.

In his official biography, written by Peter Stursberg, Roland Michener reports that the Queen encouraged him to go abroad on visits as Canadian head of state. She said: "I go abroad representing the Commonwealth but I'm always accepted as the Queen of the United Kingdom. I can't represent Canada on these State Visits. I think that you should in your role as Governor General encourage your Government to send you." Mr. Michener, who began his mandate in 1967, made several such visits at the request of the Canadian government, including one to Belgium, the Netherlands, and Luxembourg, travelling on a navy supply ship, accompanied by three destroyers!

Anyone in public life gets used to a great deal of criticism, but criticism compounded by wilful misunderstanding and intentioned malice makes you very discouraged about human nature. I accept responsibility for the fact that some in our office handled the situation ineptly, with a cringing attitude that belittled the office. I was badly advised to speak out myself about the trip on several occasions. Throughout history, the Governor General never speaks on behalf of his or her office; the prime minister speaks for the Governor General in the House of Commons. As this did not happen, I'm afraid that our office was flummoxed as to what we should do next. It also didn't help that we were in a kind of inter-regnum period, when the power structure was shifting. People lose all sense of moral balance and direction if they don't have a clear idea of what is good for the country. I'd like to be generous and believe the politicians were simply ignorant or negligent. Somehow, I don't think so.

Another example of how the role of the Governor General is disregarded and misunderstood involved the swearing-in ceremony for Paul Martin after he had won the Liberal Party leadership in 2003. I was informed that the Prime Minister's Office wanted him to be sworn in at the Hall of Honour at Parliament Hill. I immediately said that the Governor General could not go to Parliament to swear in the prime minister. In the entire history of Canada, and in the mandates of my twenty-five predecessors, this had never been done. The prime minister always goes to Rideau Hall to be sworn in, as does his cabinet. This tradition has been observed since 1867. In any case, the

Governor General goes only to the Senate Chambers in Parliament
and never sets foot in the House of Commons.

The idea of having a big ceremony at the Hall of Honour at
Parliament Hill seemed to me to be imposing a presidential-type
installation on our unpresidential system. I refused three entreaties
from the Prime Minister's Office, including one from Mr. Martin
himself. The decision was entirely mine to say no. I never hesitated.
I believe in modernization, I believe in Canadianization, but I do
not believe in Americanization.

Our political system is very vulnerable, and tinkering with it
out of ignorance or attempting to make radical change in it for
vainglorious reasons would require a whole rethinking of our
structures, our Parliament, our judicial system. Meanwhile, we're
going on very nicely and, while respect is due to our past, we must
continue to work through our present.

The reality is that Canada owes its stability to parliamentary
democracy, the common law and the civil code, and the separation
of head of state from head of government. We have a completely
different tradition from the United States, and it has served us well.
I don't think any prime minister, now or in the future, would want
to be threatened by an elected president such as they have in France.
There would be great rivalry between the two of them, and the
costs of an elected president's office would be enormous.

I believe that there are ways to choose a Governor General that
would involve a choice being considered by parliamentary committee and then ratified by Parliament. This choice would be conveyed
to the Crown, as it is now, for technical approval. Much as our
Supreme Court has begun to be more transparent, I believe that the
health of the office would benefit from Canadians' understanding a
process that would be open and not require constitutional change.
Being Governor General is difficult enough without the public
questioning the legitimacy of the choice. An open process, in our

parliamentary tradition, would give Canadians continued confidence in our institutions. Personally, I would have been comfortable going through such a process because I feel my career, my experience, and my accomplishments would have spoken in my favour. The system isn't broke, but it still could do with fixing.

Since the Constitution effectively gives the prime minister the power to choose the candidate and recommend him or her to the Crown, under this revised approach, the prime minister would consider the recommendation of the committee and take it to the House with a motion to be seconded by the leader of the Opposition. The House would then vote on it and confirm the choice. In order to avoid the politicization of the office, it would have to be clear that the term of the Governor General would be fixed, and not subject to political whim.

I think traditions have meaning and should be respected. The Crown represents everything that is stable in our society, and as the representative of the Crown in Canada, the Governor General has an obligation to make sure that the respected institutions continue to be meaningful. I finally had to say to Mr. Martin, "I have to tell you that this has nothing to do with you or me personally. What it has to do with is our respect for our rules, our system, and our historical tradition. I'm sorry that you feel that I am not co-operating with you personally. There is nothing personal in this, believe me." My job as Governor General is to stand by all that we have always stood for. That is the truest thing that a Governor General can do.

Barely two months later, the projected trip to Norway, Denmark, and Sweden was cancelled. There were no unpleasant consequences for the government because the prime minister was no longer the same one that had asked me to take on the mission. I spoke to both Prime Ministers Chrétien and Martin about this, and in each case the response was: "We always have problems with people looking at our expenses, why shouldn't you?" Because you're the ones who ask me to do things, that's why.

AS I LIVED MY TIME as Governor General I realized how timing, governmental attitudes, and the individual character of the Governor General affect the way the role is both interpreted and enacted. A Governor General must understand that there is a crucial separation between the importance of the role and the person who inhabits it or incarnates it at any given time. Only fools think that the respect due to their office is due to them personally. The Governor General must be apolitical and in a sense above politics. This has been taken to mean that he or she is superior to politics, but that's not what it means. To be "above politics" is to be able to see the whole field in the way that Tolstoy saw the whole field in describing the Battle of Borodino in *War and Peace*. It is the ability to see all the sides of the question and to bring into play the almost visual concept of the way our system works.

I always liked to say, especially to young people who were confused about what the Governor General was, that the role of Governor General is constitutionally conceived and culturally lived. If we are truly to participate in our democracy, the first prerequisite is to help people participate in the process and not see themselves as simply consumers of it, to help them to create for themselves the development of their own talents and capacities.

It's no wonder that it's so difficult in Canada today to understand that the Governor General is the guardian of the Constitution. The Governor General is not a rock star, or Princess Diana, or a superannuated mannequin. The Governor General must have a broad concept of our history as well as of the role the Governor General has played in our history. After all, the fundamental role of the Governor General has been clearly established since 1948 and Lord Elgin's acceptance and encouragement of responsible government.

We took a major step as a country with the Statute of Westminster in 1931, which disconnected the Governor General from the British government but not from the Crown. Technically, it was possible after 1931 for Canada to have a Canadian Governor General, and we were no longer watched over by the Colonial Office, of which British Governors General were emissaries. Australia appointed an Australian in the thirties but then went back to the British. Since Vincent Massey became the first Canadian Governor General in 1952, we have had only Canadians in the office.

As Canadians, we seem to prefer to be confused rather than truly understand how independent we are. Of course much contributes to a confusion about the role of Governor General. When you receive thousands of invitations to do everything from opening a shelter for the homeless to attending a ball in aid of a disease, it is hard for people to keep focused on the activities that are really important for a Governor General: the rewarding and underlining of excellence in all walks of life and the ability to be respected as the person who could ultimately be responsible for guaranteeing that our system is always conducted by its elected members in the tradition of parliamentary democracy.

There is an oscillating misunderstanding between a perception that the Governor General does nothing and that she or he can do anything. I received a lot of requests from people asking me to intervene in everything from the size of anchors on coast guard ships to the restoration of funds for hot meals in a downtown urban area. I never hesitated, with the help of acute and sensitive staff, to formally contact a minister, drawing the problem to his or her attention. Then I would write back to the person to tell them what I had done. I always tried to make sure that there would be no misunderstanding that the Governor General makes or influences policy.

At the same time, it is important that the Governor General understand what policy is, how it is created, and who is creating it.

In our system, as anyone with a basic education knows, policies are put forward by political parties. When one of them becomes the government, the policy emanates from the Privy Council Office.

I also received many letters asking me to exercise mercy, which is on the books as being "within the Governor General's purview," particularly in the Latimer case, when Robert Latimer received a ten-year prison sentence for killing his disabled daughter. My office would explain that the case had proceeded through the legal system and that I could not interfere. Raising false hopes with emotional promises is not in the purview of the Governor General.

It is important that a Governor General not get grandiose ideas about his or her powers. The title of Excellency, the standing for the Governor General, are courtesies to the importance of the office, *not* to the individual who carries out its duties. Having people try to curtsy (in fact, curtsying was banished at the time of Governor General Michener, in 1968) is a meaningless way of respecting the office and what it stands for. Personally, I never allowed anyone to curtsy to me who was over six years old and not wearing a pink dress and a rhinestone tiara. Little girls are different!

It's hard for anyone to realize how important it is that the power of the Governor General remains in reserve. I would compare it to the way Sweden has remained a neutral country. We all know they're neutral, but do we all know the amount of money they spend on their armed forces and how much it costs them to remain neutral? Just because you're neutral doesn't mean that you aren't prepared at any moment to take a life-and-death decision. The preparedness of the armed forces that simply waits for two hundred years in case their country is attacked is something that we should understand is the price of neutrality. And so it is with the Governor General.

To complicate affairs, there is often an unspoken rivalry between the Prime Minister's Office and the office of the Governor General. We have become used to seeing the presidential style just across the border, so it is difficult for a prime minister (and remember that the words *prime minister* do not even appear in our Constitution) to accept that the Governor General is the head of state in Canada, and is treated as such when abroad. Whether it is to a funeral, a commemoration, or an inauguration, the Governor General receives the same treatment as a king or queen or president. I suspect that in many prime ministers' minds there is the feeling that the Governor General is a constitutional necessity, but hardly merits the same treatment as European heads of state and South American presidents.

I understand this human reaction from the politicians, but, on the other hand, the nature of our Constitution and the way in which we are regarded by other countries depends on this acknowledgment that head of state and head of government are separate. Our parliamentary system works, and Canadians should be proud that most prime ministers have understood the necessity of discussing issues of state with the Governor General. John Diefenbaker and Georges Vanier, Pierre Trudeau and Roland Michener, just to name a few, all understood the significance of these conversations, "to encourage, to advise, and to warn." For instance, when Mr. Chrétien decided that Canada would not take part in the Iraq venture in 2003, he told me before he was to announce it in the House, and I encouraged him. The Governor General is commander-in-chief of the Armed Forces—one of the most precious of the vice-regal duties—and he knew it was important that I know his decision before he rose in the House to announce it.

Mr. Chrétien and I had ninety percent of our discussions in French, and frequently he would give me a book that he had read. Mr. Martin was someone with whom I had been a contemporary at the University of Toronto, so my relationship with him was somewhat different. He was always extremely agreeable to me when we would meet, and I felt that his lack of acknowledgment of the traditions was not entirely his fault. I was deeply impressed by Jean and Aline Chrétien's solidarity as a couple (actually, they're probably not a couple but two halves of the same person). They had come from modest beginnings, with goals that ultimately became reality. Their appealing simplicity masked their experience and sophistication. When Mr. Chrétien called me sometimes at lunchtime from 24 Sussex Drive to speak to me before Question Period, I could hear Mozart or Bach playing in the background. The people around Mr. Chrétien were experienced in government and knew all the players in the bureaucracy. I don't think Mr. Martin was well served by the non-elected people who surrounded him, because they could not add to his knowledge of our structure and of the way our system worked.

Mr. Chrétien had held so many cabinet positions in his four decades of political life that he understood problems from all points of view. I cannot help but think that Mr. Martin, whom everyone acknowledged as one of the best finance ministers we have ever had, suffered from this lack of variety and experience. When Mr. Chrétien looked at foreign policy or financial or Aboriginal questions, he could study them from the inside out, having been the minister of those departments.

When the new Martin government was sworn in in July 2004, it was a beautiful sunny day. After the swearing-in in the Ballroom we went out to the garden to have our pictures taken. It was then that I noticed that some of his closest non-elected advisers had come to the ceremony wearing running shoes and T-shirts. I could not believe my eyes. These people had worked so hard to get this government in place, and yet when the time came for the legitimate turnover of power, they could not even bother to dress with respect for the office. I also noted that they neither greeted nor spoke with anybody who was from Rideau Hall, including me. I don't believe in empty formalities, but I can say that I, along with everybody else at Rideau Hall, was shocked and embarrassed.

Having held the office of Governor General for six years, I think I'm in a position to say that the role is an important one. It can enforce our history and our society and give meaning to people's lives without stepping into the political sphere. If I had wanted to be in politics, creating policy and implementing it, and living or dying by my mistakes, I would have gone into politics.

Years ago I observed that people who went into politics didn't have to adapt to the life of twenty-hour days, eating pizza and smoking big cigars. It was the other way around: people who liked doing those things went into politics. If they liked having a gang around them like a locker-room club, they would have done that whether they were in business or at a university or in politics; if they were aloof loners with only one or two confidants, they were probably like that when they were in public school.

We don't admire our politicians because they are nice people, no matter what we say. I think we want them to do the job for us, and we grudgingly admire a certain kind of ruthlessness that is just this side of manslaughter. It was said about the avuncular Prime Minister Harold Macmillan of Great Britain that he proved in his dealings with his cabinet that "greater love hath no man than that he should lay down his friends' lives to save his own."

My personal view is that the world of politics is like this because it is a male world with male values—the worship of triumphalism, contempt for weakness, and distrust of compassion. All of these are male feelings and attributes and, even though women are now part of the political world, I suspect that many of them feel discomfort and a certain hollowness because that world is so masculine. The late Judy LaMarsh's amusing observation that there was no female lavatory on Parliament Hill when she was elected is a funny aside to real life. Sometimes the most trivial things tell us a great deal, and the lack of female lavatories is one of them. Does it mean that women are not supposed to have the same basic needs and that they are not thought of in the same way that men are? I still think our political system is absorbing the shock of having women in it. After all, things don't integrate that quickly, and it has only been eighty years since women were declared persons.

Many students of the psyche tell us that the best-developed personality contains elements of the masculine and feminine, but Jung talks about the soul in each of us, the *anima* in the man and the *animus* in the woman. It is only when you are aware of where your soul is located, and how to properly express it, that you are able to become fully developed.

What I have seen in political life has made me realize that the *anima* in male politicians may be there but is quite often described as a killer *anima*—that is, a monstrous feminine streak that attempts to kill their humanity, strangle it at birth as it were. The same thing can happen to a woman with a killer *animus*. But politics is the place where you see men behaving this way with the most blatant freedom. The system of competition, of winning, of annihilating, encourages this behaviour.

When this is all there is, the direction of a country is lost. We know that people develop disgust or distaste for what they can see is a dehumanizing attempt to use power, which, after all, is given only temporarily to those who are elected.

I find it fascinating that every time there is a contest between politicians, the press reports that never before has anything like this been seen, never has there been anything so savage. I wish more history were read and understood so that the media would recall the ruthless engagements between Sir John A. Macdonald and Sir Richard Cartwright, Sir Wilfrid Laurier and his putative son, Armand Lavergne. Somehow, we think we have invented this every time it happens. In politics, whether people stab each other in the back or in the front, blood runs.

People are fond of saying that politics is a blood sport. I think this is an oversimplification that can mislead and bring out exactly the wrong things in people who are seeking to lead us politically. Politics may be a contact sport but only resorts to being a blood sport when the people involved do not understand that a sport is played by stiff regulations with penalties for violence. It's perfectly evident to anyone who has been around Ottawa for the last few years that Parliament does not lead with informed debate that concludes in coherent public policy. I think Canadians still do believe in the democratic process and our particular way of expressing it; it is up to our politicians to keep safe the trust that we give them by voting for them.

Where this is all going is not too mysterious. During my term I observed power being centralized, not to the government or the cabinet but increasingly to the Prime Minister's Office—a group of people who are supposed to be helping the prime minister to put forward his political policies but who are, in fact, unelected people with a huge amount of power over everything, from who is invited to a state dinner to the appointment of an ambassador to a major allied country. I worried about the Prime Minister's Office having usurped the power that properly belongs to the Privy Council Office. In our system, the Privy Council Office is headed by the clerk, the senior civil servant in Canada, who is supposed to support the prime minister and the cabinet, no matter which party is in power, with impartiality.

The operation of this system still commands a great deal of respect from those who understand the way our government works, and we should always be aware when it isn't working that way. As citizens, we must be assured that it is the elected people who have the most influence, from the prime minister on down. We have elected them to be our representatives, and if we don't like what they do we will get rid of them. It's not easy to get rid of people who are not elected.

Maybe I'm naive, but I still believe, even after all this time, that we elect people to represent us in our Parliament. Most who seek office are sincere, hard working, and want to accomplish something. You don't hear about them often, even when they are doing their best. Some people stand for election simply wanting to use the system. It is only one step from using something to manipulating it. I think most Canadians are tired of manipulation and want to see real proposals acted on by the appropriate people. When disrespect for the Prime Minister's Office reached the level at which some of the people advising Mr. Martin were routinely referred to as thugs, we knew that we were not doing our best as a country. I think we were all embarrassed. And we are all responsible. It never bothers me to hear elected people described as ruthless, wily, or even Machiavellian (I have a high tolerance for the foibles of human nature), but I feel confident that they will not survive their "best by" date.

ONE OF THE MOST PLEASANT DUTIES I had as Governor General was to encourage excellence and to reward it. The Governor General's Academic Medals for top students at a high school, university, and graduate school level, Medals of Bravery, the Order of Canada, and the Media and Visual Arts Awards, among many—all of these recognize excellence among Canadians and remind people that excellence is worth striving for. There is a body of thought that tries to equate elitism with snobbery. If elitism has any point, it should mean striving to be the best and recognizing that the best is attainable. The popular notion of elitism—which makes it seem an accident of birth or associated with snobbish choice—is misleading. In Canada, we can ensure that people have an egalitarian start—good public education, excellent health care, justice before the law, freedom from bigotry and prejudice—so that every person starts on an even footing. But of course people are not all genetically alike and in different situations will react differently.

Many people feel that they have to best another in competition, but that is not the true mark of excellence. People concerned with excellence are always in competition with themselves, with what the sports world calls personal best.

All nations should honour the citizens who contribute to the betterment of their society, whether it's through a talent such as writing or painting or composing, or by helping others. The Governor General's office can remind citizens that there is a call to higher values, to greater achievements, to gold standards of citizenship. Awards can emphasize that there is more to life than economic well-being and the acquisition of goods. The expectation of democracy that a free people make free decisions urges us to pose ennobling questions.

The Order of Canada, our highest civilian honour, conferred for the first time in our Centennial year, 1967, by Governor General Roland Michener, was much contested at the time as being "not Canadian" on the grounds that no distinction should be made between members of the population. Luckily, those who approved excellence and the recognition of it won the day, and now more than three thousand Canadians are companions, officers, or members of this honour, whose motto is "They desire a better country." The writer John Buchan, who was Governor General Lord Tweedsmuir, called to Canada "to [make] her own music," and that was an unquestioned and firmly established part of the viceregal function while I held the office. The Bravery and Caring Canadian awards were particularly meaningful and touching because they demonstrated selflessness and instinctive identification with the other. When I asked the man who had stopped on the highway to pull someone from a burning car why he did it, he said, "I looked down at that guy and I thought, that guy is *me*." Two-thirds of the Bravery recipients are strangers to the people they save. They know how, in the words of Margaret Laurence, "to feel in their deep heart's core, the reality of others." And the Caring Canadians are "unsung heroes," as Roméo LeBlanc said when, as Governor General, he created the award. They give their time to drive people to doctors' appointments, to do tax returns for people in nursing homes, to give free piano lessons to kids in the inner city.

Nothing makes me more irritated than hearing politicians and members of the public saying that the arts (which demands excellence, otherwise it cannot succeed in its mission) is not worth subsidizing or should be downplayed because we need education and health care more. I simply don't buy this "either/or" argument. In a society as affluent as ours, there is no reason why we cannot have education and health *and* a rich social and cultural life. Only in Quebec have I seen that Canadians truly understand that culture is an expression of their highest aspirations as human beings. This is what makes Quebec culture integrated and admirable—the artistic fabric is closely woven into the social fabric. I think there's an unconscious envy of this in the rest of the country. The rest of Canada should just stop envying and start emulating Quebec.

Living in a democracy should mean more than just going to the ballot box every few years to say whom we like or don't like. John Stuart Mill wrote 150 years ago that "the good society is one which permits and encourages every one to act as 'exerter,' 'developer' and 'enjoyer' … of his own capacities." For Canada to be a true democracy, citizens must exercise their abilities, their ideas, their actions in such a way that we are continually aware of the kinds of questions that a truly enlightened society must be posing to itself. The right questions make for wise decisions.

IF GIVING AWARDS to the worthy was a deeply rewarding duty, being commander-in-chief of the Armed Forces was a fulfilling honour. I already had an interest in military matters because I was a child of war, my father had been awarded the Military Medal for his part in the war in Hong Kong, and John's father was in the first wave of the Normandy landings as a captain in the Royal Winnipeg Rifles and later became a career officer with the Princess Patricia's Canadian Light Infantry.

I had known a few of the veterans over the years, but during my time as Governor General, I felt encouraged and supported by the Royal Canadian Legion and by Col. Cliff Chadderton, who gave me not only his own wisdom but also the opinions of many veterans' organizations, and by my contacts with Victoria Cross recipient Ernest "Smokey" Smith and Paul Métivier, a survivor of the First World War. I saw these two for tea every Remembrance Day, and Smokey was the only one who got Scotch, even though the sun wasn't over the yard arm, because he said he didn't drink tea! Both are now deceased; I am grateful for having known them.

I had assumed that all Governors General went to visit our troops in the field, but two weeks after my installation, I learned from Gen. Maurice Baril, then chief of Defence Staff, that this was not the case. I was determined to change this. I wanted to assure the troops that their commander-in-chief took her duties seriously and would go and see them wherever they were deployed. Again, the elements of foreign policy, defence, and the government's policies come into focus here. Even as commander-in-chief, the Governor General acts on the advice of his or her ministers, and, as the link between bureaucratic authority and the military, must be careful to act in the context of government defence and foreign policy.

Where our troops are and why they should be acknowledged should be brought into the mainstream of what we do as a nation— what we do in foreign policy, what we do to encourage trade. The military in a democratic country should be part of society as a whole, not excluded.

John and I took our first trip to the troops by going to Kosovo six weeks after I became Governor General. We calmed our Rideau

Hall staff, who worried about our wanting to sleep there. First of all, the military were used to having high-level visitors fly in and out, staying only for several hours. John and I took it as a matter of course that we would spend time in the camps and sleep where the soldiers slept.

Our visits in that year, and in all subsequent years, followed a pattern. We would have dinner with officers, share other meals with the men, and review the soldiers so that they would know their commander-in-chief was there with them. In the Arabian Gulf over Christmas 2002, aboard our two frigates HMCS *Winnipeg* and HMCS *Montréal*, I gave out two hundred service medals, going to every person on the ship where they were working. When I promoted two officers in Kosovo—one a colonel and the other a young captain—they both nearly burst into tears, giving me a glimpse of how much it meant to soldiers to be promoted while on active duty.

That first Kosovo visit showed me right away how much Canadian soldiers do besides keeping peace: our soldiers had started Boy Scout troops and soccer teams, and had tried in other ways to make life more civilized for the kids growing up in the middle of conflict. We also looked at CIMIC—Civil and Military Co-operation—projects, where, for instance, troops were working with a Montreal non-governmental group putting roofs on houses (it was November) so that people would actually have some shelter through the winter.

Everywhere we went—to camps in Bosnia, to frigates in the Arabian Gulf, and twice to Afghanistan—we saw that what our military did was orderly, clean, and thoughtful. We had lots of opportunity to chat, and it was good to understand what they believed their mission was. They had a sense of purpose, but, being Canadian, were modest about it. Years ago, the writer Arthur Koestler told me that when he thought he was sentenced to death, what kept him going was the thought that what he had done in his life had made life worthwhile. At their best, our troops do know that they are doing something worthwhile. Often, they haven't received the level of recognition and support, both moral and financial, that they deserve, even while they know they are an integral part of the Canadian presence in the world.

In all of my encounters with soldiers—from the memorial service in Edmonton for the four soldiers killed in friendly fire in Afghanistan to the special Governor General's commendation for the battle fought at Medak Pocket in the Balkans—I saw extraordinary dedication to duty. One of the great, outstanding examples of this is Roméo Dallaire. His experiences in Rwanda illustrated the problems of peacekeeping with an inadequate mandate to "make" peace and became a focus for the conscience of our country. That he took the suffering of nearly a million people on to himself is almost biblical in its depth, in its sorrow. To look into the eyes of this man is to understand what compassionate human suffering means. In 2003, when he received an honorary degree from Queen's University, he drew an overflow crowd to the ceremony and to his speech, and the way the students responded to him showed me that Canadians understand what it is to admire someone who shows a noble response to suffering and injustice.

In our egalitarian society, I believe our Armed Forces have evolved to fill a remarkable role in creating young men and women who gain a sense of order and a capacity for leadership. My closest view of young officers was from my aides-de-camp (I had eighteen during my six years), all captains who came from all branches of the services. There were always five aides-de-camp at any given time, and we thought that they enjoyed as much as we did a very high energy concept of how to organize our program; it required a special kind of personality, encompassing intelligence, humour, precision, plus a lot of adrenaline. Of course, being bilingual was a necessity. It was known that we wanted only officers of the highest

quality, as the aide-de-camp is the person in charge of every detail
of the Governor General's visits, from the minute-by-minute
timing, to who travels in which car, to making sure that proper
protocol is observed, that O *Canada* is played—on a piano, with a
CD, or by the school orchestra. These young people spent much of
their time going to small, isolated communities, and homeless shel-
ters, and learned to mix with an astonishing variety of Canadians
because John and I wanted to meet them.

We learned from these young officers: their often shy ambitions,
their attempts for emotional security, and their awakening to the
larger world of their own country which they visited, were eye-
openers for them. I used to occasionally address these captains as
colonel or general and tell them that was what I expected of them.
As I have never been disappointed in any one of them, my expec-
tations, I am sure, will be met.

Our deployment in Afghanistan requires a special explanation. We
spent two New Year's periods in Kabul. I was told that I was the first
head of state to spend the night while visiting, and we were able also
to pay a visit to the king, now called the father of the country, who
is an extraordinary person who had lived for nearly forty years in
exile in Italy until returning in 2001. We also visited with President
Karzai, and each time felt that his bodyguards, who were Americans,
certainly had an important job. Our young Canadian ambassador,
Christopher Alexander, was a source of great pride to me because, at
the age of thirty-four, he had a total grasp of what our role should
be in this country and how the military and the civilians would
interact. We are so fortunate to have people of his calibre going into
our foreign service and being able to bring their skills to very
dangerous situations while they are still young—and single!

In Afghanistan, Brig.-Gen. Andrew Leslie (now lieutenant-
general and commander of our land forces) was No. 2 at ISAF—
the International Security Assistance Force. John went out on a

night patrol with General Leslie and a platoon—another vice-regal first—and learned first-hand what it is that our soldiers do to try to keep the peace. That was New Year's Eve and, while he was out on patrol, I was dancing at the officers' and non-commissioned officers' quarters. I don't think I've ever had a better welcome into the New Year than a big kiss from a young lieutenant from Petawawa. I think they felt quite good about blowing off steam with their commander-in-chief!

The troops knew how important they were to me, and they were kind enough to give me a special "fond farewell" when I left as Governor General in September 2005. That wonderful ceremony, held on Parliament Hill, deeply moved me, and I will never forget it. A number of the generals and colonels with whom I had had close contact during my six years were on parade, and the chief of the Defence Staff, Gen. Rick Hillier, gave a profoundly touching tribute to me. When everyone shouted "Hip, hip, hooray for the commander-in-chief!" I felt so proud that I had completed my duties in a way in which we all—the soldiers and I—knew was meaningful and real, and which will always make me be part of them.

My close relationship with our Armed Forces was destined to continue. On March 17, 2007, when Lady Patricia, Countess Mountbatten of Burma, retired, I became the third colonel-in-chief in the history of the PPCLI, the regiment raised by Hamilton Gault at the outbreak of the First World War in 1914. The regiment was named for Princess Patricia, the daughter of the then–Governor General, the Duke of Connaught.

My familiarity with the regiment is very personal and direct. John's father, Colonel Bill Saul, was a Patricia for his professional post-war army career, and I had seen the Patricias at close quarters often during my tenure—in Kosovo, Afghanistan, Edmonton, and Winnipeg. I am honoured to be the first Canadian colonel-in-chief of any regiment in Canada. I am sure I will not be the last.

RIDEAU HALL

Anyone visiting rideau hall soon realizes that it is a historic building with very little architectural integrity but a certain grandiose rococo charm. The grounds alone are beautiful—thirty-two hectares in the centre of Ottawa, a fifteen-minute walk to downtown.

The house is administered by the National Capital Commission. (The NCC administers as well the other five official residences: 7 Rideau Gate, the guest house of the Canadian government; 24 Sussex Drive, the residence of the prime minister; Harrington Lake, the prime minister's country residence; Stornoway, the residence of the leader of the Opposition; and The Farm at Kingsmere, the residence of the Speaker of the Commons.) The vice-regal couple are considered temporary tenants, but we could certainly ask the landlord for certain things. After the swearing-in, we couldn't move into our private apartment right away because we wanted to install a small kitchen. It was unbelievable to me that all my predecessors could have lived there without ever having a kitchen in the private quarters. Our private quarters consisted of a beautiful, large bedroom overlooking the garden, a sitting room over the delivery entrance, two bathrooms, and a dressing room. Other occupants with families have used the attached Minto Wing, with its four bedrooms. We liked our two large rooms, and wanted a kitchen so that I could retain some of my cooking skills and wouldn't become a babbling idiot staring at menus. This was not a comment on the excellence of the Rideau Hall kitchen, but I couldn't accept the idea of giving up domestic activities. I've always loved cooking; I've always loved organizing dinners.

The private kitchen made the press because it cost $40,000. But, having redone a kitchen in my house in Toronto before we moved to Rideau Hall, and having since completed one at my new house in Toronto, I do think that a well-equipped kitchen is well worth the money spent on it. In any case, the National Capital Commission was in charge of making sure that the cupboards and installations were all of a quality that could be considered durable for future occupants. When there was shock and awe about the price of the kitchen, I realized that I was in a position where no matter what things cost, they would always be followed by exclamation marks. I should have known: when I was chairman of the Canadian Museum of Civilization, the press shrieked about my annual travel costs of $10,000! No one bothered to explain that the sum covered fourteen trips a year between Ottawa and Toronto, as the job, although part-time, required me to be in Ottawa regularly. Despite the uproar, I still feel that although you inhabit a public space for five or six years, it's important that you make it comfortable and durable and neutral enough so that those following you will like it, too.

Rideau Hall has shared the life of Governors General since 1867; every prime minister has come to have his tête-à-tête with the Governor General of the time, and every head of state who has ever visited Canada has been received there and probably dined there. Rideau Hall has dozens of rooms, housing all the offices of the Governor General's staff, and has facilities to entertain up to two hundred people in two different rooms at any given time.

We firmly believed the interior of the house should be elegant, reflecting the historic nature of the building. Still, we were determined that we would live in it as though it were a house and not treat it like a faded grand hotel. One of the first things we did was to insist that we use the front door as the real entrance to the house. There was a so-called Administrative Entrance on the side of the house, which some staff used. I was told that the reason for using this entrance was to avoid running into members of the public at the front door. Well, what we wanted most of all was to do exactly that—run into members of the public, welcome them, find out where they were from! We persisted, and after two months we were finally able to use the front door as the main entrance, and it even had its own coat rack, boot tray, and umbrella stand.

We struggled for a year and a half to have the lights turned off in the hallways at night so that we wouldn't feel as though we were living in a subway. We were concerned also about the installation of industrial-strength ventilators, which could be heard on the main floor. All of the work was done with the best intentions, to ensure that the house operated well, but it certainly didn't create a sense of coziness. There seemed to be an attitude, conscious or not, that the Governor General and spouse were inmates rather than residents. Our suggestions were frequently met with surprise (though ulti-mately acquiescence, if we persisted) and made us wonder if we were insane to want things like lights turned off at night. In any case, the straitjackets never appeared and we continued in our bumptious way.

Living in Ottawa meant that the major pole of cultural and social attraction was Montreal. I had grown up thinking that Montreal was the de facto capital of Canada—the brilliance of its culture, the beauty of its mountain, the intensity and contradictions of its urban life. I still think it is a glorious place, full of the joy and contradic-tions of a bilingual city. I discovered the innovative program for street kids, Chez Pops, there and the great generosity of the Musée d'art contemporain, which loaned Rideau Hall its masterworks of

September 6, 1999, was the day of the press conference when
Prime Minister Jean Chrétien announced my appointment
as Governor-General. Note the beautiful paintings
by Jean-Paul Lemieux on Mr. Chrétien's wall.
(J.M. Carisse, Office of the Prime Minister)

We would ride in the state landau for Canada Day and on the
occasion of a speech from the Throne. In 2005, we had our
sixth Canada Day without rain! *(Rideau Hall)*

Sheik Zayed bin Sultan al Nahyyan is in the right foreground,
to hunt. We are in the tent of the Sheik's hunting grounds in
Abu Dhabi, the United Arab Emirates, at Christmastime 2003
on our way to visit our troops in Afghanistan.

With President Vladimir Putin of the Russian Federation at the press
conference during our state visit there in October 2003. He has just
said that Canada and Russia are neighbours around a lake called the
Arctic Ocean, fully endorsing our two countries' northernness.
(Rideau Hall)

Captain Patrice Germain, of the Royal 22nd Regiment
(the Van Doos), was one of my aides-de-camp from 2003 to 2005.
These young men did everything with us and we felt they were
part of our family. *(Courtesy of Captain Germain)*

Nelson Mandela is the greatest living human being.
I had followed his imprisonment and political career when
I was a journalist. As Governor-General, I was honoured
to spend time with him in Ottawa in 2002. *(Rideau Hall)*

These puppets of us (terrifyingly realistic) were made by
Noreen Young, whom I had known in the past at the CBC.
We have had a lot of fun with them, doing skits and scaring people.
(Rideau Hall)

I had known Leonard Cohen
for almost forty years when
he came to Ottawa to be
inducted as Companion of
the Order of Canada in
2003. His unique presence
graced Rideau Hall for
several days and made John
and me very happy.
(Rideau Hall)

We visited forty-eight places in our North and loved its people. In 2000, in Grise Fjord, Nunavut, the northernmost village in Canada, I enjoyed tea and bannock in an igloo with an Inuit elder Abraham Pijamini. We were beside a large iceberg in the frozen bay, and the tea, made from iceberg water, was delicious.
(Rideau Hall: Sgt. Julien Dupuis)

I loved Iceland when I first went in 1962. The geography is otherworldly, and John and I are enjoying this waterfall during our state visit in 2003. *(Courtesy of the Government of Iceland)*

President Karzai of Afghanistan accompanies me as I inspect the guard of honour in Kabul during our second visit to Canadian troops there in 2004. The bodyguards with their machines guns are an ever-present reminder of imminent danger, even though we are in a walled palace enclave. *(Rideau Hall)*

In December 2003, a member of the Royal Canadian Regiment shows us the latest equipment. Captain Alex Haynes, my aide-de-camp, standing between John and me, is with the Royal Canadian Regiment. *(Rideau Hall)*

In 2003, with my friends, from the left, Cynthia Scott, Bill Glassco, Cathy Graham and Diane de Obaldia. Staying at La Malbaie in Quebec, we went for a picnic at scenic Port-au-Persil. As it poured all day, we ate inside our van and emerged only long enough to capture this moment.

My mother in 1986, two years before she died.

With Kyra and Blaise at a welcome-home party in November 2005.

The Adrienne Clarkson peony, developed and named for me in 2004 by the Canadian Peony Society. It is deep, creamy white with pink flashes. The peony has always been my favourite flower. *(Rideau Hall)*

Paul-Émile Borduas, Jean-Paul Riopelle, Jean-Paul Lemieux, and Jean McEwen. As the second residence of the Governor General is in Quebec, at the Citadelle, high on the cliff overlooking the St. Lawrence and the old town, we spent time there, especially in winter. People in Quebec City love winter, and it made us happy to walk around in snowstorms and be greeted by other pedestrians, smiling and saying, "C'est merveilleux, n'est-ce pas?" There's no question that the Citadelle was a comfortable and magical place to be, but we could never spend much time there.

To inhabit a house of Rideau Hall's scale in a normal way actually shows respect for the building. Like a beauty past her prime, she needed a good deal of love and personal attention. The Reception Room, where we served coffee at the end of events and gathered recipients of all awards for pictures, had a floor that, for some unfathomable reason, had been broadloomed in white. Over the years, this had become stained with coffee, tea, wine, and many unidentifiable sauces and could pass muster only when big buffet tables were laid out on top of it. The red carpeting throughout the foyer and hallway was threadbare. John and I were convinced that there must be good wood floors, probably oak, under both the red and white broadloom. For one thing, this part of the house dated from a time when there was no broadloom. We were told that studies would have to be done—studies!—to lift the carpet in order to see what was underneath. One night after some guests had left, John and I lifted up a small piece of red carpet in the foyer and, lo and behold, the oak floor appeared. All that was needed to return it to its beautiful original state was one sanding and a coat of finish. Later, an anonymous donor generously provided a beautiful Heraz carpet from 1901, and the foyer took on a new allure, especially when Michael Fortune, a master furniture maker, created two pier tables out of Canadian maple wood and Manitoulin marble to complement the nineteenth-century pier glasses on each side of the main door.

Carpets, in fact, seemed to cause a lot of furor. In the 1970s, some of them, like the carpet in the Ballroom, had been made at the Royal Carpet and Tapestry Factory in Madrid. None of us could ever figure out why—perhaps it had to do with Jules Léger's state visit to Spain in the 1980s, or simply that the National Capital Commission was sourcing what it felt was the best possible carpet in Europe. Our Canadian carpet for the State Dining Room, with its pattern of golden maple leaves designed by Anne Bianconi, the NCC house designer, cost $58,000 and was of course criticized as being too expensive. Hot-line shows invited owners of broadloom factory outlets to voice their displeasure. This carpet was huge—fifty by twenty feet, ten times the size of an ordinary twelve-by-nine carpet—and woven in one piece. Compared to what had been spent in the past and what it would cost to buy even ordinary broadloom, I think that we came out extremely well.

One thing that I wouldn't change for all the world, even though it was gently suggested by the plumbers that I might do so, was my large 1920s bathtub with the drain in a large tube on the outside. I knew that this was the tub in which a previous Governor General, John Buchan, had had his fatal stroke. I always felt close to Buchan, who had become Lord Tweedsmuir, because he was a writer, because he began the Governor General's Literary Awards, and because he truly loved Canada and travelled all over the North and the West. When I invited James Buchan, his grandson and also a very fine writer, to stay at Rideau Hall for the 2004 Literary Awards, I showed him the bathtub. Afterwards, he wrote me the most beautiful letter, quoting in Greek the lines of Orestes looking at the place where his father had been slain at Mycenae on his return from Troy.

For us, Rideau Hall was primarily what it said on the sign next to the front gate—the Residence of the Governor General. We felt it should look inhabited, as if every room was entered at least once a day, and that you should be able to read newspapers in easy chairs. When we arrived, there was not one single reading lamp in any of the down-stairs sitting rooms; we soon rectified that with little halogens. Rearranging the furniture meant that we could have sitting areas at the two ends of the Large Drawing Room, which modified its scale yet kept its beautiful proportions. (It was here that I received credences from more than a hundred ambassadors during my mandate—a ritual that is the same in every country that carries on diplomatic relations. Until those credentials are presented, the ambassador cannot do the work for which he has been sent.) The great formal rooms—the Tent Room, the Ballroom, the Reception Room—were meant for stand-ing, but in the Minto Wing, which housed the Large Salon, the State Dining Room, the Small Salon, and the Small Dining Room, we were determined that people should feel at ease, and would prefer to sit down comfortably rather than stand formally.

I learned that all six official residences followed a repainting cycle, and I was delighted to learn that Rideau Hall's turn was coming up soon. I wanted to change the colour of the walls from the timid tinted whites to colours that complemented the strong architectural details in the mouldings. And I felt that rooms that had retained some of their Victorian integrity should be painted in strong colours. Colour ruled in the Victorian era—in Canada, you can verify this simply by visiting Upper Canada Village and looking at the interiors of the houses painted in ochre, dark green, mustard. At the time we moved into Rideau Hall, I was reading Christopher Hibbert's biography of the Duke of Wellington, in which the old duke, in his retirement, writes to a friend that he has been exhaust-ing himself galloping about the countryside "eating in one red dining room after another." It's not for nothing that one of the famous English paint companies produces a colour called Dining Room Red. The period from the Regency through the Victorian loved colour; white was the colour of the lime that poor people washed the insides of their houses with to keep lice down.

The Victorian look at Rideau Hall was further enhanced with the arrival of some period furniture. British Governors General had for years brought over furniture and then taken it away with them at the end of their term. What remained in Rideau Hall was not of great quality. There weren't many remarkable or unusual pieces. Some years before, the Canadiana Fund had begun to collect furnishings from private donors for the Crown Collection, which is the holding place of all furniture objects and works of art that are valuable to the nation's cultural heritage. These are used in all government locations, from the Houses of Parliament to the Speaker's residence called The Farm at Kingsmere. Although Rideau Hall benefited from some of this largesse, it was not until two remarkable collectors, Bill and Wynn Bensen, with their passion for Victorian furniture-makers of eastern and central Canada, appeared on the scene that we began to recreate that authenticity. They acquired, and loaned, remarkable pieces: a Nesbitt table that matched two others, and the Imari dinner set that had belonged to Sir William Van Horne, one of the founders of the Canadian Pacific Railway.

At the government warehouse, where furniture is stored as different occupants rotate in and out of the official residences, I found an extraordinary 1830s curly birch chaise longue that had a plaque on one side explaining that it was a gift from the people of Ontario. When? Why? The mystery remains, but the piece is beautifully ensconced in the Large Salon and fits perfectly underneath one of the large, low windows. I made several trips to that warehouse to discover nineteenth-century chesterfields of the button-tufted variety, with stuffing and springs hanging out of them. As they were historic artefacts, I felt they should be repaired and, if possible, brought back to historic Rideau Hall.

When I first walked into my office, which had been added to the main house in 1911, I realized that it had certainly been built for a man—it was panelled in oak, and no doubt much cigar smoke helped maintain its patina. I decided to hang paintings all over to soften this effect, and painted the walls above the panelling a pumpkin colour. Getting rid of the black leather sofa and chairs also helped me to feel more at home. I put my own living-room furniture from our home in Toronto in it, and, if you can be assuaged by inanimate objects, that sofa and the chairs brought me a great deal of comfort for six years. I have those chairs now in my new house and they are the chairs on which each prime minister I served with, leaders of the Opposition, and every head of state I had a tête-à-tête with sat. It's good to have those memories in my own home.

One nice touch in the office was that all names of the Governors General were carved in oak on separate panels around the top of the room. Mine was already in place the day I entered my office. I noticed, however, that Mr. LeBlanc's plaque was obscured when the door was open, so I took the liberty of moving his over beside mine, where it would be seen at all times, particularly on those occasions when I would have pictures taken with visitors in front of the fireplace.

Across the hall from my office was a pair of rooms connected by two arches and with a double fireplace between them. One was the original office of the Governor General, a fairly small room by Rideau Hall standards, and the other had been the billiard room and was now the Small Dining Room. The original office was so small because the British Governors General had had an office in the East Block on Parliament Hill, where they could watch what was going on in Parliament and hear the gossip. The office is still there but nobody goes to it; as far as I know, it remains unused. All the work of the Governor General is done out of the office at Rideau Hall.

I WENT TO RIDEAU HALL in 1992 to be invested as an officer of the Order of Canada. I invited my father to accompany me, as I felt that, in a way, my receiving this honour was a completion of his life.

Everything was strikingly well organized: we were to assemble at
6 P.M. at Rideau Hall, where we would be given our Orders, and
then a dinner would follow.

At the Holiday Inn, before going to Rideau Hall, we all had our
pictures taken, and I was humbled to meet the diverse group of
people with whom I would be inducted: a midwife who had delivered babies for decades along the west coast of Newfoundland,
another woman who had taught music by Braille in Alberta, and a
man who had skied to the North Pole.

At Rideau Hall, I was struck by a sense of awkward formality,
which made even me, who was used to difficult and demanding
deadlines and situations, edgy and ill at ease. A brief citation about
each of us was read in a neutral voice that sounded like a weather
report. Then we went up, got our medals, shook hands and returned
to our seats. I remembered that when I was in France in the eighties, I read about how François Mitterrand, the president, gave out
every honour himself, with a speech about each person, without
using notes.

For dinner, I was seated at one of the head tables and my father
at another. Almost as soon as coffee and dessert arrived, our host, the
Governor General (who is also chancellor and principal companion
of the Order of Canada), left, telling us that he could not miss the
World Series on television. Twenty minutes after coffee, we were
herded gently towards the exit and the buses to take us back to the
Holiday Inn.

I looked at all the people who were on the bus with me and I
thought, "They all care about what's happened tonight, just as I do."
Although some had appeared to treat the evening's events as mere
ceremony, for most of us, it was a meaningful occasion, because the
Order of Canada stands for something that we, each in our individual ways, had worked hard for without knowing that this would be
the result. No one who is not an unbalanced megalomaniac thinks

that they are doing something in their life with the goal of getting the Order of Canada. I hope that in many ways all of us together were part of a wave that desired a better country, as the motto of the Order exhorted us to do.

At every dinner we seated guests to make them feel that they would have a good time. A database was set up to learn about their eating preferences, their language abilities, their hobbies. We never seated husbands and wives at the same table, as we felt the experience of meeting new people was important. A member of Rideau Hall staff hosted each table, and initially we rehearsed them in how to do introductions and start conversations. The aim was to make everyone (not just honorees) feel special, so that they would remember Rideau Hall with happiness. John and I spent at least a half-hour on the day of each event reviewing table plans and making changes. It was worth it!

When I became Governor General I was determined that Rideau Hall would become a national home—a place where people would come to admire a heritage house filled with beautiful things made by Canadians. Instead of knocking down trees to accommodate a bigger Visitors' Centre just outside the gate (as was intended then), why not have people visit the house itself? They could take a substantial guided tour, which would talk about the role of the Governor General while unveiling the history of Canada's oldest official residence. We prevailed. The Visitors' Centre disappeared off the horizon, and by the time we left, in September 2005, Rideau Hall was receiving nearly 200,000 visitors a year.

If we were going to invite more visitors, then we had to show them something more than how the rooms looked. We reviewed all the paintings on the walls, and saw that exactly five had real artistic merit.

I met with Pierre Théberge, director of the National Gallery of Canada, and asked him if he would let us have a few paintings on

loan. To my delight, he offered us a choice from among the great
Canadian masterpieces. The day that John and I went to the
National Gallery and saw the thirty-odd paintings that Charles Hill,
the curator of Canadian art, had laid out for us was one of the
happiest I can remember. To know that we could fill the national
house with these extraordinary paintings by the likes of Lawren
Harris, Alex Colville, Christopher Pratt, David Milne, Riopelle, and
Borduas was to realize that we could show our heritage in a domestic setting. Very few Canadians get to see great art in people's homes,
and I am happy that they did see it when we were at Rideau Hall.

Once we had organized this deal with the National Gallery, I
asked other public galleries across Canada if we could look at their
paintings and sculptures to see if we could borrow some. That was
how we got a wonderful Bill Reid carving from the Royal British
Columbia Museum, done in honour of Canada's Centennial, in
1967, which now highlights the Long Gallery. The Winnipeg Art
Gallery, the Vancouver Art Gallery, the Art Gallery of Nova Scotia,
the Ottawa Art Gallery, and the Museum of Contemporary Art in
Montreal, among others, lent us magnificent paintings that express
our artistic heritage as far back as the beginning of the nineteenth
century. To flesh out the collection (and there are a lot of walls!), we
rented a number of pieces from the Canada Council Art Bank,
which makes a point of collecting the work of younger artists; the
Bank has been collecting for so long that some major artists are
represented there by their early works.

Many of our more modern objects came from the Art Bank and
we rotated them every two years, selecting works by craft artists too.
The Canadian Museum of Civilization suggested lending us a selection of the Saidye Bronfman award winners in crafts to highlight in
the big cabinet in the main hallway. Whenever I passed it, I felt a little
spark of delight looking at the works of our major artisans over the last
twenty-five years: the glasswork of Daniel Crichton, the outrageously

flamboyant and exquisite china of Leopold Foulem, and others all helped to create levels of enjoyment, I feel, in the house itself.

We hung all the portraits of the spouses of Governors General in the Large Salon and the State Dining Room because the English gents took up all the space in the Tent Room. We could not move any of the paintings in the Tent Room because it had been smoked in for about sixteen years, and if we'd moved the paintings it would have revealed the colour of the original fabric wall covering and how it didn't match anymore.

The portrait of Pauline Vanier was one of my favourites. It was done in the 1920s, when she was a young married woman, by Philip Alexius De László, one of the most famous society portrait artists in Europe at the time. The elegance of her posture as she looks over her shoulder boldly emphasizes her strong, yet feminine, face and body. Her portrait speaks of a time when a few Canadian women had their clothes made for them—sailing to Europe on ocean liners with names like *The Empress of Canada* and returning with trunks full of handmade outfits. It's one of my favourite portraits because it tells me a story more than any of the others.

GARDENS TELL STORIES, TOO. When we arrived at Rideau Hall, we had the gardeners unearth a rock garden on the lower terrace buried under beds of white and red impatiens. It had belonged to Lady Byng, the chatelaine at Rideau Hall when her husband, Lord Byng of Vimy, had been Governor General from 1921 to 1926. I had read her autobiography *Up the Stream of Time* and learned of her passion for gardening and her affinity for native Canadian plants. She had gone into the Gatineau Hills and to Aylmer to look for plants and had various farmers help her learn which plants could grow on her site. She went on motor trips through the West and gathered plants everywhere in order to put them into the garden at Rideau Hall.

Years of neglect and more than several tons of brown earth had covered her work, but I felt particularly gratified that we could follow the old patterns and plant the rockery with newer material, which I think she would have appreciated: *pulsatilla*, Japanese anemone, and even Himalayan blue poppies. We managed to have them for two years in a row, this exquisite plant that is the heartbreak of even the best gardeners. But they are perennial and, who knows, they may flower again!

One of the things that John threw himself into, heart and soul, was the creation of a woodland garden on an unpromising slope that was mainly ferns and oak trees, one of them planted by General de Gaulle in 1960. Over four years, with the enthusiastic help of the Hall's gardeners, he created a completely native Canadian woodland garden with jack-in-the-pulpits, trilliums, trout lilies, every imaginable woodland plant. We weren't fanatical about Canadian plants, however, so we also put in some beautiful Korean and Formosan plants—toad lilies—which last until the killing frost.

Before we moved to Rideau Hall, we were certain that on an estate like Rideau Hall there must have once existed a potager, a vegetable and herb garden. We found it, a quarter of an acre surrounded by a high cedar hedge, but it was a sad sight. The herbs consisted of some mint growing inside large black rubber tires that had been sunk into the ground. There were a few flowers for a cutting garden, but no vegetables.

We broached the idea of planting an organic vegetable garden that could supply our kitchen in the summer, including the cafeteria where the staff ate. Everybody liked the idea, and now Rideau Hall is self-sufficient in vegetables from August until the middle of October. (It was my dream to have a fruit and vegetable stand for our visitors, but that didn't happen.) Then John designed the herb garden using old slate tiles that he found piled in a corner of the property where the NCC used to dump junk and compost. He conceived the idea that the herb garden could be like a checker-board, with tiles and squares of herbs in between, which meant that you could walk to the herbs you wanted across a large area without disturbing the other ones. It has been a great success, and we're going to repeat it in our own garden.

The planting of these gardens and then the reward of seeing them grow in over our period at Rideau Hall made us very happy. The process of restoring the gardens is well described in the beautiful book that was done on Rideau Hall, *Canada's House*, by Margaret MacMillan, Marjorie Harris, and Anne Desjardins. I guess I didn't feel free then to say how much of ourselves we invested in those gardens, how we planned and watched over every detail of them. I knew almost every plant by name and loved collaborating with the gardeners, who supported and carried out all we were trying to do. I am proud that the Canadian Peony Society named a new, white peony the "Adrienne Clarkson." Gardeners love what they do, and we gardeners recognize each other.

ABOUT THREE WEEKS AFTER we moved into Rideau Hall, I was presented with a plan, which was quite far advanced, to build a four-storey administration building in a woody area just below the house. The trouble was that they intended to build on the site of the skating rink created by Lord and Lady Dufferin in 1879, probably the oldest outdoor skating rink in continuous use in the world. Not only is it used by Ottawa residents, it was on that rink that the children of Lord Stanley, including Isabelle, his daughter, played shinny hockey and inspired Lord Stanley to create the Stanley Cup for excellence in hockey. I was horrified that a nondescript four-storey stucco cube could be placed in such a historic spot, and knew we had to find an alternative site.

We asked to be taken around to every outbuilding on the property and finally fixed on an old stable that was being used as a garage. We knew that modern offices could be built within an exist-ing historic structure. The stable was turned into a handsome, func-tioning office building in harmony with the other buildings and was awarded the Ottawa Heritage prize.

Rideau Hall had once been a two-hundred-odd acre gentleman's farm, complete with livestock and orchards, owned by businessman Thomas McKay. We wanted to bring back some of those things, and so we planted espaliered fruit trees and grapevines around the tennis courts that Governor General Michener had installed. I've explained that my husband and I do not indulge in any sport requir-ing the hitting of small circular objects, but we welcomed the fact that lots of people working at Rideau Hall used the courts all the time, and the courts were scrupulously maintained for any succes-sors who might be mad for tennis.

We also planted a nut orchard, after discovering that a number of nuts are native to Ontario—the black walnut, the butternut, some hazelnuts. It will be thirty or forty years before they bear fruit, but it is good to think that they will. We also replanted maples about three metres out from the existing maples that line several of the lanes through the property, just in case the large ones died. One must remember that Napoleon planted plane trees on the highways of Europe to shelter his soldiers marching to battle. The conquests ended long before the plane trees provided shade, but the dream was there. I had no martial ambitions, but shade is always a good thing in an Ottawa summer.

The week before we left office in September 2005, John and I planted two oaks at the top of the woodland garden; they joined the pines of the Micheners and all the varieties all over the grounds that have been planted by all my predecessors and their spouses. I hope they will live for a long time and that they will always look over a Canadian woodland landscape.

THE QUEEN

MANY PEOPLE EXPECT that the Governor General of Canada will have a close relationship and frequent conversations with the Queen. In fact, this is a formal, constitutional, and politically neutral relationship, and is treated as such by both the Governor General and the Queen. Before I was installed, but after the announcement was made, John and I were invited to Balmoral, in Scotland, to meet the Queen and some members of the royal household. It's an extraordinary estate of some twenty thousand hectares along the River Dee, and the Queen seems to be most comfortable there; she drives her own four-wheel drive to tour the property, and tries to have a barbecue if it isn't pouring with rain, which it is ninety-five percent of the time. She exudes intelligence, intensity, and shrewd appraisal, which are dissimulated behind a flashing and often disarming smile. Spending any length of time with her makes one realize that she is the consummate professional who knows exactly what she is doing.

The Queen is a thoughtful host. We had bagpipes after dinner, and every single piece that the piper played was a Canadian composition or was connected with a Canadian regiment. We were determined to begin this thoughtful tradition at Rideau Hall. We did not hear one note of "Scotland the Brave" while we stayed at Balmoral.

The dinner was a small one, with about fourteen people, including members of the royal household, among them the Queen's private secretary, Sir Robin Janvrin, and one of the Queen's ladies-in-waiting, who was Scottish, and some guests, including the assistant headmaster of Eton College. The conversation flowed amiably, with the Queen pointing out rather gleefully that she is a generation younger than her husband, Prince Philip, even though they are third cousins.

I was interested to see that since we were having lamb chops they were (as I had always been told in good etiquette books) picked up between thumb and forefinger to finish them off. And also that the Queen powdered her nose at table. In Canada, we had always been brought up to believe, from the time we were little girls, that we were never supposed to do anything to our makeup at the table, so I am simply passing on the information for those who like to keep up-to-date with royal etiquette.

After dinner, we chatted in the small drawing room, ate chocolates and found that all of the household were people who, without visible effort, could keep conversation going—even if their guests had been from the moon. At a certain point in the evening, one of the Queen's aides-de-camp whispered in my ear that it was time to leave. According to royal etiquette, the guests must leave before the Queen can, so we all bade her good night. She said goodbye to us because we were informed that she never comes to breakfast with visitors.

The next time we met was on the occasion of the celebration of her Golden Jubilee, when all the Governors General of the Commonwealth—about two dozen—were invited to Windsor Castle for the night of April 17, 2002. Windsor Castle, on the outskirts of London, is as large as most small cities in Canada, but it seems to be where the Queen prefers to live when she is in the capital. We all arrived in time for tea with the Queen and Prince Philip and were introduced to each other, and then were free to circulate and discuss the differences between our countries. Naturally, I homed in on the Governors General of Australia and New Zealand, as their countries have the same kinds of population and are industrialized, and generally have the most in common with Canada. The Governor General of Barbados told me that he drives around his country in one day and admired my stamina for being able to travel in Canada.

We then went upstairs where our bags had been taken, and John and I were informed that we were staying in the apartments that the Queen Mother had used whenever she was at Windsor. The apartment was larger than the second floor of Rideau Hall, with the bathroom at one end and the bedroom and sitting room at the other. The long corridor in between had mysteriously locked doors all the way down. I decided that I had better have a bath, even though we had only forty-five minutes to get ready for drinks before dinner. I began to run water into the big mahogany-encased bathtub and went back to the bedroom to make sure that my things were ready to hop into for dinner. I got distracted, and suddenly I remembered that I had left the water running. I raced down the hall and to my horror saw bathwater brimming over the mahogany and flowing onto the broadloomed floor. I turned off the taps, leaned against the wall and thought, "This is not what my parents brought me up to do." I called my aide-de-camp, the super-cool Lt. Jeremy Sales—appropriately, it now seems, of the navy—who came in, stared at the water flowing into the green carpeting and said laconically, "Oh well, I'll inform them immediately." I ran back to the bedroom area to get dressed, and by the time I went back to the bathroom, Jeremy had the maids and footmen mopping up the water. All I could think, as I saw that water being squished up from the carpet, was that I had drowned the honour of Canada.

As soon as we went down to have drinks, and before the Queen arrived, I said to the Master of the Household: "I'm terribly sorry.

The most embarrassing thing has happened. I've let my bathtub run over and I'm terribly concerned that it might come right through this ceiling." Without missing a beat, the true courtier smiled and said, "Well, you know, it's something Prince George of Hanover does *every* time he comes to visit." Smooth or what?

That was a memorable evening, with about a hundred of us dining in the Waterloo Room, which is a vast hall with the table in the centre, twice as wide as an ordinary dining table and with two rows of flowers running down the centre. Portraits of all of Britain's allies at Waterloo surrounded that of the Duke of Wellington. We were all seated according to our seniority, and Canada has pride of place as the senior dominion. There were no speeches of any length, but we were welcomed by the Queen and we acknowledged our presences when she mentioned our countries.

Before my accident with the bathtub, I had been wandering around in the halls of Windsor looking at the beautiful Van Dycks and Rubenses and Rembrandts in the hallway. I had turned down a corridor and realized I had lost my way. I was hoping to find one of the twelve royal corgis who would lead the way out when I ran into an elegant older gent, who was Governor General of Grenada. He said, "Where are you going?" I said, "I don't know where I'm going but I would like to get back to my room." And he said, rather abruptly, "Well, try turning left." I said, "Thank you so much, Governor General. I will see you later."

As we all moved out to have coffee at the end of dinner, he came up to me with his eyes so wide he looked almost hyperthyroidal. "You are the Governor General of Canada!" he said. I said, "Yes, I am." He said, "I must apologize for speaking to you the way I did before dinner. I thought you were just someone's wife." I couldn't miss the opportunity. I said, "Well, I'm that too."

The Queen led a guided tour from the dining room through the restored St. George's Hall, which had been devastated by fire a number of years before, and pointed out all the details that had been restored. Members of the household then informed us that we were going into the library, which I was thrilled to hear because I knew that the Windsor library was actually a part of the palace where Elizabeth I had lived in the sixteenth century.

In the library, a special exhibit had been set up to honour each of our countries, with botanical drawings from the Caribbean countries, beautiful photographs of Canada and its scenery, engravings of mammals from Australia, and so on. I wandered down the narrow part of the library and was told by the Royal Librarian that this indeed was the quarters where Elizabeth I had lived. As I had grown up worshipping her and reading everything about her that I could lay my hands on, I could hardly believe that I was walking where she had actually walked. The woman who told her army before the Spanish Armada that although she was a woman, she "had the heart and stomach of a king," is the woman I most admire in history.

At one end of this area, there was a big glass case with a white linen shirt in it, with the large sleeves and voluminous body typical of the seventeenth century. The Queen looked at it with me and said, "It's believed that this is the shirt in which Charles I was executed." The Royal Librarian added, "There are brown stains on it, you can see." Indeed there were brown stains in the appropriate places. I thought it fascinating that the shirt Charles I was executed in should be on display in the library—perhaps as a cautionary reminder?

We were to have breakfast the next day and a service in the chapel. After that, everyone was going to go back to London, to Westminster Abbey for the memorial service in honour of Princess Margaret. But at seven in the morning we learned that four of our soldiers had been killed and several others wounded in a friendly fire incident in Afghanistan. John and I decided in thirty seconds that the right thing to do was to go to our soldiers. I regretted not being able to go to the memorial service, but I knew Canada would be ably represented by former prime minister John Turner, who had been a friend of the Queen's sister and would perform his duties for Canada with great dignity.

We rushed through our breakfast and said our goodbyes, then hurried back to London to see how we could get to Ramstein, the American air base in Germany, to be there in time to receive the dead and wounded. We had arrived in Britain on a Challenger jet, which is the normal way that the prime minister and the Governor General fly, but the Challenger had returned immediately to Canada. We were trying to figure out what commercial flights would take us to Frankfurt and then on to Ramstein, but nothing would have gotten us there in time to be on the ground when the Armed Forces Hercules with the soldiers arrived. Luckily for us, with the help of the Canadian High Commission's military attaché, we were able to be flown to Ramstein by the Queen's Flight, which is part of the military group that flies the Queen, just as our Department of National Defence Challengers fly the Governor General in Canada.

OF THE FOUR PLACES I have met with the Queen, Buckingham Palace is the one that has the most impersonal feeling. It is a large, ill-lit place, and until you get to the Queen's drawing room there is little to make you feel as though you would want to stay there, with the worn gold trimmings and the dim chandeliers.

But Sandringham, in Norfolk, is a private house (as is Balmoral)—the Queen owns it, and it has very much the feeling of an English country house, albeit a huge one, with an extraordinary two-storey entrance—a great hall, which is also a drawing room. The Queen is a country woman at heart, and even though it was winter, she went riding first thing every morning at Sandringham.

Her exercises are part of her everyday life and not something that she does because she feels she has to keep in shape.

The last time I was with her, in 2005, she was subjected to a ride in teeming rain in an open landau during the celebrations, in Regina, of Saskatchewan's centenary. I worried that she might catch not only a cold but even pneumonia, because even though she had an umbrella it was obvious that everything around her was drenched, including Prince Philip, who sat rigidly, staring straight ahead like a good soldier.

I went to the steps of the carriage to greet her and give her a hand out, and she said, "Don't take my hand in this glove too tightly. It's soaking wet." She said it with an ironic smile, but I could see that she was not soaked the way the rest of us were, because her coat, although not a raincoat, was water repellent and her shoes seemed to be made of some kind of plastic or rubber. While the rest of us were squishing around, she was perfectly comfortable and not at all upset. It is Prince Philip who watches for all the details, and it was he who put the kybosh on the Queen's signing the province's Golden Book on a table in the pouring rain. He made it clear that the table would have to be moved into the front hall of the Legislature, and that was that.

After all these years, he still notices the tiniest things. When we were saying farewell to them in 2002 at the Ottawa airport, "God Save the Queen" was muffled by the idling engines of all the security cars. The Prince frowned at them for the whole time and said to us afterwards: "They shouldn't be doing that during the anthem."

I have the feeling that not very much misses the Queen's attention, either. When she arrived in Regina, one of the first things she said to me was, "Prince Charles so much appreciates the fact that you both came to his wedding in April, as do I." We had glimpsed her for only a brief moment at the wedding reception at Windsor, but she remembered, as she remembers all her twenty-odd visits to Canada and the various events that struck her each time.

STAYING IN THE QUEEN MOTHER'S APARTMENTS at Windsor was perhaps a tribute to the fact that I had given the Queen Mother an honorary Companion of the Order of Canada on the occasion of her hundredth birthday. She was thrilled with this and insisted that we come for lunch at her home, Clarence House. We had been expecting just to lunch with her and a few of the household, but she had gathered together a most interesting party of people, all of whom had some connection with Canada— either their fathers had been Governors General or they had served as aides-de-camp to Governors General. It was all very carefully thought out and there was much laughter. The Queen Mother exuded gaiety and did indeed drink Dubonnet and gin. She looked very well on it. She admired my shoes with their tiny high heels and said she wanted to get some. Where had I bought mine? I had bought them in England and I gave her the name of the store. She pointed her toes out and said: "I love shoes. Don't you?"

She obviously had a taste for art, and in her private drawing room, where I presented her with the Order of Canada, there was a beautiful painting by Augustus John of her in a Norman Hartnell dress. "I told him I wanted it done with all the diamonds." She smiled sweetly. "All the jewellery!" At her table she used the charming, but now considered rather out of date, custom of using mismatched (but beautiful) glasses and different services of china for each course. The whole idea of matching anything did not seem to be in tune with this woman who had lived for a century, had weathered all kinds of storms and still was the pretty, flirtatious person whose vivacity and charm it would be hard to match.

In pride of place in her little drawing room, she had a painting of Prince Charles with a left profile, a full face, and a right profile, using Van Dyck's portrait of Charles I as a model. It occurred to me that it was rather an unfortunate model, but the Queen Mother seemed to love the picture and showed it to all the guests. It was obviously a new acquisition because it was still standing on an easel. I never did have a chance to ask Prince Charles what he thought of it.

The Queen and Prince Philip stayed once with us at Rideau Hall during her 2002 tour to Canada. On the Sunday morning, they went off to a tribute on Parliament Hill, which happened to be again in the pouring rain, and were presented with a curious combination of music and dance, quasi-religious and strangely hybrid. John and I watched part of it on television, because this was the prime minister's event for the Queen, and when they came back, I mentioned to Prince Philip at lunch that I thought the rendering of "Amazing Grace" was quite remarkable. He looked out at me from under his eyebrows and said: "I'm surprised you thought it was 'Amazing Grace.' How could you tell what it was? Is that what it was? Are you sure?"

All our contacts with the Queen and with Prince Philip were cordial and easy. In fact, in all my visits with the Queen, there was not the least feeling of stiffness or officious protocol. For all that people talk about her shyness, I think that she has overcome this over the years and has had enough experience to hide it and perform her duties. To me, she is duty personified.

STATE VISITS

VISITS OF HEADS OF GOVERNMENT, such as prime ministers to each other, are not on the same level as state visits. State visits are exchanged by heads of state—presidents, royals, and Governors General. In my time at Rideau Hall, I received nearly thirty state visits from the presidents and kings of various countries. In my first year alone, I received eleven of them! That was really a trial by fire, but I think there were so many because Mr. Chrétien's government was well established and had many outstanding invitations that had to be honoured. The only thing in which the Governor General had any choice was the date of the visit.

Almost like religious ceremonies, state visits follow a strict and particular order. You wouldn't realize it from looking at some of the photographs in the press, which usually feature two smiling people who could just as well be at a football game. In fact, every single nuance of a visit is taken into consideration by both nations' protocol authorities. The head of state is welcomed with a hundred-person guard of honour, the playing of their national anthem, the inspection of the guard of honour, and a twenty-minute tête-à-tête with their host. Later in the evening a state dinner is given for them.

The state visits usually last two to two and a half days and sometimes include the visiting head of state travelling to some other cities. All the state dinners that I hosted were held in Ottawa except for the one for the president of Iceland in 2000, which we offered in Winnipeg so that as many people of Icelandic origin could attend as possible. When we had the president of Portugal, it gave us an opportunity to invite many Portuguese Canadians who have contributed to our life—by designing and marketing recreational vessels for the Great Lakes, in the intellectual world, and in businesses.

I had state visits ranging from Russia to Mozambique and found all of them fascinating. If the security is not too extensive, the head of state stays as a guest at Rideau Hall together with his or her staff. As there are only seven bedrooms, this doesn't work for larger countries—the Russians, for instance, take a larger number of rooms in a hotel—but we hosted a fair number of the visits at the house, and it was simply like having house guests. We never met them for breakfast, because every single one wanted to have breakfast as a respite, but after the state dinner we always bid them a formal goodnight at the bottom of the stairs leading to their quarters. Usually to the state dinner we would invite the prime minister and his wife, and a formal picture would be taken with a rigid protocol governing the position of the three couples.

We had some unusual times and requests in our six years. One of our heads of state who was seriously overweight finished up his dinner, then went to call upon his own ambassador to have a meeting with some of his fellow nationals. On his return at nearly midnight, the aide-de-camp asked him politely if there was anything else that he would like, and he said: "I want to play squash. *Now.*" Our aides-de-camp were extremely resourceful, and this one managed to get a club opened and to play squash with the president between midnight and 1:30. I was only happy when I was told about it that he had not had a stroke or a heart attack while playing in our country.

Some countries have smoother and more well-behaved staff than others. The worst and funniest example we had was one president's aide-de-camp who turned to my aide-de-camp at the end of the state dinner and said, "I would like you to shine my boots for tomorrow morning." My aide-de-camp simply turned to his equivalent and said very firmly: "No."

The head of state is always lodged in the Oval Suite, which boasts the oldest ceiling certainly in Ottawa if not all of Canada, because it dates from 1853. It features an elaborately sculpted oval medallion of plaster on the ceiling, which the National Capital Commission restored during a period of several months. In the original Thomas McKay house, this was the Drawing Room and later served as a nursery for the children of some of the British Governors General.

Every state visit includes planting a tree, winter or summer. Small trees are continually being planted at Rideau Hall awaiting the symbolic shovel of earth from the next head of state. Many trees scattered on the grounds of Rideau Hall were planted by people in our recent history, like Charles de Gaulle in 1960 and John F. Kennedy in 1962. It is always the last thing done by the head of state before he or she leaves Rideau Hall, and it is usually much appreciated, if sometimes a little puzzling to them. I was always able to choose between four or five different trees for a head of state and enjoy thinking that the thirty that were planted during my term, whether by the Chinese president or the president of Greece, were trees that the gardeners and I had chosen.

When I went abroad to represent Canada, the protocol was identical—the guard of honour, the national anthem, the tête-à-tête— and in the case of Russia, we were lodged in the Kremlin. This is a remarkable memory for me, and also a singular honour for Canada, as not every state visitor is invited to stay at the Kremlin.

I had first met President Vladimir Putin when he came to Canada in 2000, during my first year as Governor General, and I would say that he ranks among the top three heads of state that I have met with whom I felt a personal connection. I was not prepared for the way in which he listened to everything that was being said. We used inter-preters, but I have a strong feeling that he understands English completely and using an interpreter is simply a way of politely buying time. I don't think there are many other heads of state who listened as carefully. Perhaps that comes from his training in the KGB, where you must listen to everything carefully because that is your job.

When he came we played some awful music, which was the Russian Federation's new anthem at the time. I said to him during our tête-à-tête that all of us had always admired, even during the worst Soviet period, the beautiful old Russian anthem. I asked him why on earth he would want to change it. He said, "Do you really think we should go back to the old one?" I said, "Yes, you must, because I think it's one of the three or four finest anthems in the world." When we arrived in Russia for our visit two years later, the first thing he said to me during our tête-à-tête was, "We changed back to our old anthem, and that's because you told me to!"

It is during these intimate conversations in which no other person is usually present that the visiting head of state invites you to visit his or her country. As far as I can remember, except for Russia, we responded to these invitations only when they met the priori-ties set by our own Department of Foreign Affairs and by the prime minister's policies.

At the state dinner, the host head of state makes the opening speech and the visiting one the second, and there are toasts to each other's countries and to each other's people. I always enjoyed these state dinners, because it gave me a chance to probe into the litera-ture of some of the countries, particularly the African ones with which I was not so familiar, in order to find some quotes and some links on a human and artistic level that I knew they would appreci-ate. I would say that almost all of the heads of state that we received made literary allusions showing a depth of knowledge of their culture that was assured and civilized.

Only once in the time that I was at Rideau Hall did we have an altercation with a state visitor, whose bodyguards insisted on carrying concealed pistols inside the house. When we learned about this, my husband, together with our director of security at Rideau Hall and the RCMP, laid down an ultimatum: they simply were not allowed to have the small arms. We were particularly concerned because they guarded the doors of the Oval Suite, which was perfectly natural in international terms, but we were concerned that for some reason they might panic and shoot one of our own staff. They would not co-operate, and so were told they could either surrender the pistols or move out, president and all. The guns were handed over. With the help of the RCMP, we were able to maintain an arms-free house during all of my tenure.

THERE IS MUCH RITUAL in the world, even though we think we're completely modern and spontaneous. You deal with these rituals when you have to attend things like anniversaries and memorial services—especially at an international level. All the protocol involving foreign countries is the responsibility of the chief of protocol, a high-ranking ambassador from our foreign service. But Canada must be the only country in the world to have a separate internal and external protocol. Maybe we feel we must have two of everything? Or that we don't have the same rules at home as we do abroad? After six years, I still don't know the answers, but all I do know is that everything handled by Foreign Affairs with visitors to Canada and our visits abroad was impeccable and polished. My chiefs of protocol were Rick Kohler and later Robert Collette, career diplomats who made everything run smoothly and efficiently.

I was very fortunate that in 2004 I was able to attend the sixtieth anniversary of D-Day and the sixtieth anniversary of the Canadians' Italian campaign, and in 2005 to celebrate the Canadian

liberation of Holland. In addition, I represented Canada at the sixtieth anniversary of the liberation of Auschwitz. It's amazing to me
that I could have been involved with all of these events having to
do with the war when I was a child of war myself. This gave the
deepest layer of meaning to my heartfelt participation in these
events, and I had the feeling, whether I was watching the Russian
army parade across Red Square or walking with the veterans on
Juno Beach or standing in minus-twenty temperatures with the
survivors of Auschwitz, that this was so much a part of my time, so
much a part of what had created me, so much a necessity for me to
understand because the period was exactly the period of my life.

President George W. Bush was in France for the D-Day ceremonies. We all went to the beaches on which our respective countries had landed, and Queen Elizabeth very graciously came to our
Juno Beach, which meant so much to our veterans. I think we all
feel that the Queen is a part of the Second World War, having been
Princess Elizabeth and having shown hope and courage to the
people who were then fighting by staying with her parents in
London during all the fighting. Prince Philip himself is a veteran.

We were all invited to lunch by President Jacques Chirac at the
city hall of Caen. I had learned that I would be sitting with Albert,
king of the Belgians, to my right and President Bush to my left. I
knew what kind of conversation I could have with King Albert
because we both had bilingual countries and I knew that he had
views on this and also on the whole question of the Francophonie.
I had never met George Bush before and was uncertain what our
conversational ground might be. Then it came to me, the morning
of the celebrations: my daughter the architect had gone to Yale and
Mr. Bush was a graduate of Yale!

When our foie gras was served (the French are so traditional
about their banquets), I spent the first course talking to King Albert
about bilingualism, gardening, and immigration. The second course

was duck, and I turned to the president and said, "We have a great thing in common." His eyebrows shot up and he looked at me with intense surprise. He said, "Really?" I said, "Yes, you went to Yale and my daughter graduated from Yale." He said, with visible relief, "Oh, yes, Yale is a great school, a great, great school." And I said, "Yes, I think Yale is a great school."

There was a long pause while we both acknowledged and attempted to do justice to our lunch and to our regard for Yale. Then I asked him, "How do you manage to stay fit when you have to eat meals like this all the time?" He replied that he used much of the time he must spend on Air Force One by running on his treadmill and lifting weights. I commended him on this because, I said, I thought he must be quite exhausted a lot of the time, but it was wonderful to make time for exercise. He said that he always made time for exercise: "I do one hour of exercise every day. I never miss. And the other thing I always do every day is to read Scripture." I thought for a moment and then asked him, "How do you read Scripture? Do you begin at the beginning of the Bible, read it right through and then start again? What is your method?" He explained, "I follow a reading program which is set by a pastor whom I know. And I read what's supposed to be read every day." He paused, put down his knife and fork and looked straight up at the intricate French ceiling. "I know it keeps me in touch with Him up there." I said, "You're very lucky that you feel this so directly." He said, "Yes, I do, I really do. Keeping in touch, that's what important."

As is custom, the prime ministers and heads of government sat together at the end of the table, and it was on leaving that I was introduced to Prime Minister Tony Blair. He stared briefly at me, with wide eyes, and said: "I've met your chief justice too. Do only women run Canada?" I replied, "No, not exactly. Prime Minister Martin is standing just behind you." We were then whisked out to buses—one bus for heads of state, one bus for heads of government—but I insisted we bring Mr. and Mrs. Martin with us on our bus because I thought it would be good for them to meet President Chirac or any of the others who might be on the bus. Chancellor Schroder, President Chirac, and President Putin huddled together in the seats next to us, speaking German to each other, and obviously "doing business."

We arrived at the massive grandstand on the beach at Arromanches where the ceremony was going to take place live on television. We all tripped out of the bus and took our seats in the first row, according to our seniority of holding office in our own countries. I was pleased to see I was seated beside the president of Greece, who had paid us an interesting visit four years previously and whom I had enjoyed for his humour, intellect, and exquisite command of French. Then the Queen and Prince Philip arrived, to great applause, and it was obvious that everyone there recognized that she was a part of this history and not simply representing Britain.

Then it dawned on all of us that the president of the United States had not yet arrived, and many in the first rows were visibly disturbed because according to protocol the Queen should have arrived last. We then sat for ten minutes until the cortege of eighteen cars drove up and deposited the president and Mrs. Bush in front of the stand. They walked slowly towards their seats, waving, and people started to stand. Nobody had stood for anybody else, as we were all there in commemoration and it was not that kind of occasion. Nobody had stood for the Queen and yet people were standing for George Bush. The president of Greece turned to me and said, "I'm not going to stand for him because he's neither a queen nor a lady." And he sat with his arms firmly crossed over his chest. We later learned by accident from one of the French military who was organizing all the movements of the VIPs that the president's cortege had deliberately taken a long route in order to arrive last. This had not been in the scenario.

As Canadians, many of us were disturbed and even offended that our role in the success of D-Day was not mentioned by the president of France in his speech. It made me angry that our sacrifice and our willingness to save others went completely unacknowledged. When I see my wonderful country disappear in the indifference of people who do not understand the kind of society that we have created and the kind of selflessness that we have shown on so many occasions, it just makes me mad.

At D-Day, in Holland, and at Auschwitz, I discovered that Queen Beatrix of the Netherlands felt the same kind of emotion as I did, as she too was a child of war and had spent her earliest years in Canada, living in the house called Stornoway, in Ottawa—now the home of the leader of the Official Opposition. Her sister, Princess Margriet, was born in Ottawa, in a section of the Civic Hospital that was later declared to be Dutch soil to guarantee her citizenship. In 1947, by the oddest coincidence, John Ralston Saul was born in that very same room, and he once jokingly asked Queen Beatrix whether he could be recognized as a Dutch citizen because of it. Nothing has come of it yet!

We went to Auschwitz from Kraków, Poland, at the invitation of the president of Poland, Aleksander Kwasniewski. Poland was coming to terms with its own history of anti-Semitism and of the Holocaust, and although technically the concentration camps were German, most of us felt that Poland, by acknowledging what had happened there, was helping the healing process, if such a thing were even possible in the face of such evil.

We travelled in small buses to the camp, and John and I sat with Queen Beatrix, the president of Poland, and President Putin. This was the third time that I had met President Putin, so we were able to have quite an involved conversation. He was extremely interested in how Canada was organizing our multi-ethnic society, and I tried out on him my new idea of an institute for Canadian citizenship. He listened intensely, as is his habit, and encouraged me to proceed.

Queen Beatrix, who is a woman of great intelligence (she studied civil law at the University of Leyden), and is a sculptor and knowledgeable art patron herself, was obviously deeply moved by this event. Her country, after all, is the country of Anne Frank. We all stood in the cold and realized that we had no right to feel that we were cold when we were swathed in layers of sweaters and wool coats and hats; the inmates of Auschwitz had suffered the same weather wearing no more than the dreaded striped cotton pyjamas.

The moment when I carried the blue candle for Canada up to the memorial was so emotional for me that I was afraid that I would not be able to walk there and back without tripping. Somehow in moments like that, when you feel that you simply cannot be up to the task, you are given the strength to do it. The snow came falling down, and all the heads of state put candles in a row. We were seated at right angles to the survivors and their relatives. And there was a sense of the deepest emotion and, I think, almost a release: attention of the most sensitive order was being paid, and the emotions that ran through all of us bound us together.

In the Netherlands in May 2005 we, as Canadians, were welcomed with deep and demonstrative affection. I was so proud of the veterans who had earned us this regard. We went to events in Wageningen and Groningen; rain or shine, the enthusiasm was overwhelming and the turnout of the Dutch was extraordinary. On the last day, May 8, thousands of people in Apeldoorn stood for three hours in the rain for the final great parade.

I wish everyone in Canada could feel that relationship between the Canadians and the Dutch. I think it would do us Canadians a great deal of good to realize that we are loved and respected in the deepest way, not just because we aren't Americans but because we are positively Canadians. Too often, I think, we don't understand that we have the kind of qualities that are most admired in the world—tolerance, generosity, self-effacement—but are so rarely found elsewhere. All of these attributes can sometimes have their negative sides, but I think it's good for those of us who have felt it to talk about it and to say, "Yes, we are important." Canadians were important because we helped others and because we prevailed and therefore helped them to prevail.

We crossed the Rhine in a small flat boat with two sappers, veterans who had never returned to Holland before and who had been lent by Canada to the British to help with the "Bridge Too Far" at Arnhem. Just to be in the presence of these two men was an honour because everything they had done they took so much for granted and very matter-of-factly.

ONE OF THE MOST REMARKABLE ENCOUNTERS I had as Governor General abroad was in Abu Dhabi with Sheik Zayed bin Sultan al Nahyan, the United Arab Emirates president who had transformed the nomadic Bedouin, living marginally on the coast-line of the great desert hunting and pearl fishing, into a nation booming with oil and oil dollars. I was excited about meeting him, because Wilfred Thesiger wrote about him in *Arabian Sands*. Thesiger, for everybody who loves deserts, is the writer who best evokes what fascinates people about the desert, and his recounting of his time there, fifty years ago, captured my imagination when I was in university and dreamed of the desert and its shifting sands. The sea, the prairies, and the desert, whether hot as in Arabia or cold as in our North, have a continuing fascination for me.

Zayed and Thesiger became close friends, and Thesiger describes the sheik this way: "He was a powerfully built man of about 30 with a brown beard. He had a strong, intelligent face, with steady, observant eyes, and his manner was quiet but masterful. I had been looking forward to meeting him for he had a great reputation among the

Bedu. They liked him for his easy informal ways and his friendliness, and they respected his force of character, his shrewdness, and his physical strength. They said, admiringly, 'Zayed is a Bedu. He knows about camels, can ride like one of us, can shoot and knows how to fight.'"

On our way to visit Canada's frigates in the Arabian Gulf at Christmastime 2002, John and I could not believe that we would actually be meeting this mythical figure. As I walked into the *majilis*, the huge greeting room, I felt I was stepping straight into the *1,001 Nights*, with the courtiers all lined up against the tented walls and the sheik at the end of the room on a simple chair. A similar chair had been prepared for me. Between us was a small table and on it a large silver dish like a lidded soup tureen. I brought the president our warmest greetings from Canada and indicated to him how much I had been looking forward to meeting him because of what I had read about him, his people, his modernization of their way of life, and because of my love of the desert. We chatted about a number of things outstanding between our countries that Canada was particularly anxious to resolve. I knew that he'd been having severe health problems and had gone to the United States several times for treatment. He was well over ninety, but the life and intelligence in his eyes was electrifying.

He spoke quite rapidly, but a trusted adviser who spoke fluent English translated between us, so I absolutely lost the sense that we were speaking different languages. I think I felt happier about being a Governor General that day than almost any other: it would have been impossible for me to have met the sheik in person, and had such a conversation with him, had I been a woman without a state function. Being Governor General of Canada made me an honorary man, and therefore we were able to speak frankly and directly to each other. It was the realization of a kind of dream I've always had that there would be no sexual differences between people who were of like minds.

I knew that the Bedouin are poetic people. We had a friend, Bill Polk, who was the first American translator of the great Bedouin epic poem, and I mentioned this to the sheik. He was pleased that I knew about this, and when I followed up by saying that I knew that he wrote some poetry himself, his face broke into a beatific smile, he raised his right arm and said something. One of the courtiers brought out a leather-bound book, and the sheik bowed his head as several poems were read and translated to me. They were classical Arabic poems about the beauty of a flower or a woman, or the gracefulness of a tree. The sheik nodded and smiled and clearly enjoyed hearing his own words.

We were surrounded by three or four hundred people, including most of his many sons, some of whom were government ministers. My wonderful senior aide-de-camp, Captain Jean-François Godbout, and I exchanged looks that said, "We will never forget *this*." As the lid of the tureen was lifted, the sheik gestured to me that we should dig our spoons in together. It was a kind of dessert made with honey, which is known as *loucoum*, and it was so sweet I thought I wouldn't be able to manage it, but the sheik wanted me to eat, so I ate.

I then mentioned to him that I knew he had taken Wilfred Thesiger hunting with falcons for a month, and he asked me if I was interested in falconry. I told him I had been interested since I first read that falconry had been brought to Europe by returning Crusaders. The idea of making a bird of prey hunt on behalf of a human being has always fascinated me. It was the theme of my second novel, *Hunger Trace*. He asked if I would like to see a falcon, and I said yes, and in two minutes his favourite falcon, on the arm of a falconer, came into the room with a beautiful emerald green leather mask, studded with jewellery. Of course, the falcons have to be blindfolded because otherwise they would fly, looking for prey. I said tentatively, "Oh, how I would love to see a real falcon hunt."

He asked when we would be returning from the Gulf, and invited us to go falconing with him.

That was the most extraordinary day: tents in the desert, dozens of falcons let out to chase the bustards that had been released for them. The falcon has its mask ripped off, climbs rapidly into the air, spots the bustard and seizes it, either in the air or on the ground. It then waits for the falconer to reward it with food: the bird of prey has been trained to hunt but not to eat. The Bedouin no longer need to hunt to fill their stomachs, nor do they have much time to devote to training falcons. But I was enormously grateful to share the experience.

I spent the evening before the hunt with the sheik's most important wife, Sheika Fatima, in her palace. We sat on sumptuous silk sofas around the edge of a large room while fruit juices and piles of sweetmeats and candies were brought out to us. Sheika Fatima and I, after chatting for a bit, realized that we were both born in 1939. She wore her gold and black mask, making her look like a particularly distinguished bird; I never saw her on subsequent visits without it. She dabbed me with the rose water that she and her friends made together. And then we ate a delicious dinner with food from every Arabic country—Morocco, Tunisia, Lebanon, Turkey, and of course the Emirates.

She told me that she had married Sheik Zayed when she was fourteen and he was forty. I asked her whether she had seen Sheik Zayed before she married him; she said that she had not, but that she knew of him and that he had seen her and chosen her. She had her first child when she was fifteen. I had gone to my first formal dance when I was fifteen. In all, she had ten children, nine of whom were sons and all of whom were very close to her. In fact, she wore a little portable earphone and, during dinner, various of her sons telephoned her from different places—two of them were hunting in Morocco, one was on business in London, and several were in the Middle East. She was obviously a mother who liked to keep her eye on all things.

The harem is not what we conceive of in the *1,001 Nights* way, being all the master's wives and concubines. It is a general term for the world of women, where nieces, aunts, daughters, and daughters-in-law were all included, often living with the sheika and certainly assured of their physical and mental well-being in this cloistered atmosphere. Sheika Fatima had also lived in the desert with Zayed at El Ain before oil was discovered, before their life changed so dramatically in ways none of them, I'm sure, could ever have imagined. She had made the transition with great calm and seemed to me a person who would be wonderful to know better. She told me that she was very proud of me, being at my high station as a woman, and she said that she promised me that the next time I met her there would be a female ambassador from the U.A.E. to a foreign country. She realized fully, she said, that women's rights were to be encouraged and supported. The next time I saw her, there was indeed a female ambassador.

When I said farewell to Sheik Zayed after the falcon hunting, I wished that I could have continued our conversation—to talk about his perilous youth when he and his brother were challenged in their authority in the desert. I felt that perhaps another time we could do that. But by the next Christmas, he was too ill to receive visitors, and he died the following November, just before we went back into Afghanistan. We paid a visit to his grave at the new mosque in Abu Dhabi. And one day I will return to it, to remember a magnetic figure of myth and humanity who did in one lifetime what most people can only dream of.

A FRENCH FRIEND remarked to me recently that in no other country but Canada does the holder of the highest office in the land return to private life so completely. Suddenly, there are no trappings of office such as limousines and large staff. For me, the return to a self-motivated life with the opportunity to set my own agenda, write a book, restore a Victorian house, create a new garden, and see family and close friends frequently are pleasures I savour. I love hailing a cab and using the subway and bus again. I enjoy going to buy underwear at a department store without the watchful eye of one or two security people. I like to think that I dealt with the restraints of my office cheerfully, but now I feel some sense of privacy again, a privacy that brings contentment within. I enjoy it when people recognize me and talk to me; their sense that they know me is a meaningful reward for having been Governor General.

LIKE STATE VISITS, there are things that happened that would not have happened if I hadn't been Governor General, and that make me proud. Two public schools, one in Ottawa and the other in Richmond Hill, bear my name. I was able to shape and inaugurate the Polar Medal to honour annually a Canadian who has enriched our knowledge of, and relationship to, the North. An award for community service was named for me at Massey College, University of Toronto, where I have been a fellow for a number of years. And there's the peony that was cloned and named for me by the Canadian Peony Society.

After I had my pacemaker put in, I went out to southern Alberta, near Lethbridge, to be inducted as a chieftain in the Blood Tribe. The name they gave me was Grandmother of Many Nations, which was very touching. It also was prescient, because of the founding of the Institute for Canadian Citizenship, which is a legacy project I have established to help new citizens become integrated into mainstream Canadian life, beginning with the way in which they are welcomed at citizenship ceremonies. We must make an effort to give access to everyone we have brought here. Canada can help them; Canada will change them. As an immigrant myself, I cannot imagine what my life would have been like if I had not come to Canada; the genetic material would have been the same, but I wouldn't have been me. As a

Canadian I benefited from freedom, education, wilderness, and the affection of people who benefited from the same things.

I hope one of the lasting legacies will be the Clarkson Cup for Excellence in Women's Hockey. The inaugural presentation was in July 2006 to the Canadian Women's Olympic Hockey Team because they were undoubtedly the best. In years to come, women's hockey will grow, and I want the cup to honour that. Like Lord Stanley, I am giving the cup personally to women's hockey. This gift will be administered by a small group of trustees in a not-for-profit way. I plan that any proceeds will go to encourage young girls to play hockey.

These are concrete specifics. More fundamentally, I feel I was able to draw the attention to all Canadians towards the North and to the role of the Inuit and the First Nations. I tried to formalize the relationship of Canadians with the military, and draw the smaller communities and the disadvantaged into the normal conversation. As for the mysteries of our Constitution and the role of the Governor General, both constitutional and informal, I tried to take a step—sometimes a big step—in modernizing and Canadianizing, while maintaining the historical importance in the myriad details and in the general approach.

I hope that all the things I tried to do rang as true for francophones as well as anglophones, for new Canadians as well as people born here, for Aboriginals as well as all of us immigrants, for Canadians living in the thousands of small communities with no road access as well as the millions of us who live in big cities. I tried to help everyone make sense of this incredible complexity called Canada.

Being Governor General was one-tenth of my life lived so far, and that was buoyed up by everything that made me Canadian from the age of three. My answered prayer for an interesting life almost made my heart stop for even longer than seven seconds. Now it ticks on, preparing me for whatever is to come.

WHAT ENDURES

HEART-MYSTERIES THERE, AND YET WHEN ALL IS SAID
IT WAS THE DREAM ITSELF ENCHANTED ME; ...
THOSE MASTERFUL IMAGES BECAUSE COMPLETE
GREW IN PURE MIND, BUT OUT OF WHAT BEGAN?
... NOW THAT MY LADDER'S GONE,
I MUST LIE DOWN WHERE ALL THE LADDERS START
IN THE FOUL RAG-AND-BONE SHOP OF THE HEART.

W. B. Yeats
"The Circus Animals' Desertion"

WHAT ENDURES

WHEN MY MOTHER caught the largest pike that anyone had ever seen on McGregor Lake, it was a triumphant acknowledgment of what living at a cottage in the wilderness meant to us. She had gone out early in the morning with my father, and though he normally did most of the casting, on this occasion she "had a feeling" she might catch Big Mo. This legendary smallmouth bass lurked in the back bay of the Saint-Denis island, and it was rumoured that he must weigh six pounds. Many fishermen had got him on their lines, but nobody had ever managed to land him. It was always some kind of ultimate goal, particularly for my parents. Neville and I fished also, but when my father was in the boat he tended to make us row or run the engine low for him, and each time he cast he would make a low incantation, hoping to land Big Mo, or at least his little brother.

This held true when my parents set out on a very ordinary day, and not far from the cottage she got a bite from a gigantic pike. It wasn't Big Mo; it was even bigger. After fifteen minutes, observed by a number of encouraging cottagers, she landed him successfully. By the time she got him back to our place, the word had spread, and many people came to look at him in the laundry tub. He was pretty ferocious looking with all those teeth, and my mother was terribly proud. She had always been good at landing bass, and now here was this champion pike. Everyone asked us if we were going to stuff it. My mother answered, "No, we are going to eat it," and that was that. We painstakingly filleted it, took out all five million bones, and steamed it with soy sauce, black beans, onions, and ginger. We kept the head for many years, dried, in a corner of the porch.

This love of fishing was one of the most attractive things to my parents when we had a cottage. Having been ill off and on when I was ten and eleven, I was prescribed cottage life for the summer so that I could have lots of fresh air. We had driven north of Ottawa into Quebec to McGregor Lake, where my father's old professor Roger Saint-Denis had an island. We had stayed at a lodge there a number of times. We had learned that several cottages were for rent that summer, and so we were able to book a dilapidated but beautifully situated cottage belonging to the Slattery family, who were the butchers in the Byward Market. We became friends with all the Slatterys and their in-laws, and they seemed never to tire of hearing my parents' stories about Hong Kong, racing, and the war. I really believe that there probably was not another Chinese family within a radius of five hundred miles that had a cottage in the wilderness, living the way we did in the summer.

The lake was half uninhabited, because it was the summer place of the Oblate Fathers. They had a residence and a large hill with the Stations of the Cross going up to the statue of the Virgin Mary. The sense of space was one that everybody on the lake treasured, and the priests never minded when we used a beach or point that belonged to them. We built a cottage there the next year, my father doing a lot of the work himself with carpenters from nearby Perkins Mills.

The friends we had on the lake—the local dry cleaner, the person who had the Buick dealership, several civil servants, a retired major—were an eclectic bunch, and my father was particularly fond of them. My mother felt that most of them drank too much. My memories are of endless days of swimming, going out in our boat, and seeing all the kids, who were, conveniently, all about our age. We had two bonfires at different spots on the lake, and we sat around them and sang and made up stories.

This love of the wilderness came naturally to my father, who had grown up in the country in Australia. And for my mother, it was a beautiful place where she could nurture her privacy. The cottage we built, nobody ever commented about in our hearing. My mother painted it chartreuse and the trim on the windows salmon pink. She thought that the dark brown, dark green, and white of the other cottages lacked flair. She also insisted on having the kitchen at the front of the cottage so that she could see the water and what was going on while she was cooking. Once each summer we had a big party at the cottage, and my mother cooked her summer specialty— southern-fried chicken and coleslaw—which was much anticipated by the neighbouring cottagers, as well as by our friends in Ottawa, who came up for the day.

The boy who cried himself to sleep under a porch and the girl who was dropped on the side of the road found a natural and unexpected haven on that quiet Quebec lake where fish were to be caught. Their feelings of loss and residual fear were assuaged by their sense of belonging in that place—the place where they believed that their children were protected, and seemed happy.

ON SATURDAY AFTERNOONS, if I didn't go to the movies at the Imperial or the Capitol Theatre on Bank Street, I lay on the couch and caught *The Metropolitan Opera*, listening to a voice telling me wonderful stories. I loved the authoritative way with which he would say, "I'm Milton Cross," and then tell us what musical story he was going to give us. I loved *Rigoletto* and *La Bohème* and *Madame Butterfly*. I listened to the music without any intervening value judgments being given to me by adults or friends. I was taking piano lessons, but I never spoke of music to Miss Jamieson, she of the patch over one eye and the swollen left arm that intrigued me more than playing chords. That wasn't music; that was piano lessons, which, like ballet, would prepare me to live a civilized life in this new world where we found ourselves, and where someone might just ask me to play "The Happy Farmer."

My mother encouraged me to see an Italian film version of the opera *La Traviata* at the Elgin. But she didn't encourage me to the extent of going with me; I went by myself. I was stunned by the story, and when I came home my mother seemed to know it (she had seen Garbo in *Camille* several times) and said crisply: "It's good as a story. But no woman should live her life that way."

On my next birthday, I was given Milton Cross's *Complete Stories of the Great Operas.* My mother said, "As long as you are going to listen to that, you might as well put this with your story-books." My mother referred to all my reading as "storybooks," with the unspoken implication that they were dreamy, unreal, and certainly unnecessary.

During the war, when we barely had moved into our little flat in Ottawa, a dancer named Mia Slavenska—how I relished those five syllables—who used to be with the Ballet Russe de Monte Carlo, came to town to perform. My mother and a friend of my father's from work went to see her. They brought home a program, which I pored over. I could not have been more than five years old, and the sight of the white tutus, the tights, and the ribbons was enough to keep me happy for hours.

My father would read a story to me every night. I remember the Arthur Rackham drawings, and the tale of the Pied Piper of Hamelin, who lured all the children away to an unknown place. I thought he looked both appealing and scary. Often, my father would put away the fairy-tale book and tell me a story about us.

He would tell me that when I was grown up, the two of us would go to the opera together. He described (probably from a picture that he had seen) the rows of balconies covered in gold and thick red curtains and the place where hundreds of people played in an orchestra.

Everyone went to the opera, he said, because they all knew each other and could enjoy something together and have fun. My father loved clothes and would describe them vividly. The men would wear beautiful white tie (it seems to me I have always known what that term meant), with starched piqué waistcoats and satin lapels and shoes that were patent leather, like my good ones, with black bows across them. Between the acts, we could go into the lobby, which would be marble and carved wood and painted in gold and silver with scenes of plump ladies (my father indicated that pink and fat were a European taste), wearing very little, with tiny cupids flying above them.

There would be ice creams, like the Eskimo pies we bought at Dawson's Drugstore, only in miniature. We would sit in a box on the right-hand side of the orchestra, at the front of the box. I would sit on the outside so that people could see me, and he would sit on the inside in case he had to leave the box and get me some more of those ice creams. I would wear a long red velvet gown and have a very tiny diamond necklace and teardrop earrings from Birks. On the left shoulder of my gown I would have a diamond clip with a large pearl in the middle of it. I would wear my hair long and knotted up in the back and pulled straight back from the forehead, like Evita Peron. This, my father promised me, was what my future held; this was where he would bring me, in my velvet dress and, of course, a beautiful white stole made of fox fur that covered my shoulders and came down to the ground on both sides. And, of course, I would wear white kid gloves that came halfway up my arms.

"And where will I put the stole while I'm watching the opera?" I would ask. And he would answer, "We will drape it over the back of your chair, one end in front and one end in the back so that, when you lean back against it, you'll look as though you're framed by it."

My father didn't like music and never expressed an opinion on opera. But he made me feel that I was entitled to go, that I could arrive there from our tiny apartment, to wear the red dress, to eat the ice cream. And I have. Which is what he intended. Which is what he dreamed for me.

ACKNOWLEDGMENTS

WRITING THIS BOOK was made even more enjoyable because of the people who supported, in stunned disbelief, my desire to wait no longer.

I owe a great debt to Micheline Steals for her brilliant technological skills. Without her, I could not have done this book.

Many thanks to all the people at Penguin, especially David Davidar and Diane Turbide, who guided the process. To Pascal Assathiany and everyone at Boreal for their support.

To Émile and Nicole Martel for their extraordinary talent and affectionate constancy. To the meticulous Shaun Oakey. And to Alyson Atkinson, who arrived just in time.

To Michael Levine for his encouragement, wisdom, and enthusiasm during all these decades.

To my dear friends who share the desire for an examined life: Cathy Graham, Mary Pratt, Cynthia Scott, and Diane de Obaldia—witnesses of my time riding tigers. And to Bill Glassco and Bernard Paul, who left partway through our journey.

And gratitude to all the others who make me laugh, enjoy life, and continue my search: for knowing what a garden is, where to put in skylights, caring about the authentic recipe for Key lime pie, admiring Perseid showers and the Pantheon, sharing an encyclopedic knowledge of vitamins, and making room for Mozart and Leonard Cohen. They know I love them.

And, finally, to John Ralston Saul, whose mind and heart have engaged mine since the day we met thirty years ago.